Picture Pedagogy

Online resources to accompany this book are available at: www.bloomsbury.com/full-title-9781350144637. Please type the URL into your web browser and follow the instructions to access the Companion Website. If you experience any problems, please contact Bloomsbury at: companionwebsites@bloomsbury.com

ALSO AVAILABLE FROM BLOOMSBURY

Reflective Teaching in Schools, Andrew Pollard with Pete Dudley, Steve Higgins, Kristine Black-Hawkins, Gabrielle Cliff Hodges, Mary James, Sue Swaffield, Mandy Swann, Mark Winterbottom, Mary Anne Wolpert and Holly Linklater

Transforming Schools: Creativity, Critical Reflection, Communication, Collaboration by Miranda Jefferson and Michael Anderson

Readings for Reflective Teaching in Schools, Andrew Pollard

Why Teaching Matters? Paul Farber and Dini Metro-Roland

Picture Pedagogy

Visual Culture Concepts to Enhance the Curriculum

Paul Duncum

BLOOMSBURY ACADEMIC

LONDON • NEW YORK • OXFORD • NEW DELHI • SYDNEY

BLOOMSBURY ACADEMIC
Bloomsbury Publishing Plc
50 Bedford Square, London, WC1B 3DP, UK
1385 Broadway, New York, NY 10018, USA

BLOOMSBURY, BLOOMSBURY ACADEMIC and the Diana logo are trademarks of
Bloomsbury Publishing Plc

First published in Great Britain 2020

Copyright © Paul Duncum, 2020
Paul Duncum has asserted his right under the Copyright, Designs and Patents Act, 1988,
to be identified as Author of this work.

Cover design: Tjaša Krivec
Cover Image (© A Commonplace Life - Everyday Beauty / Getty Images) and (© markos86 / Getty images)

All rights reserved. No part of this publication may be reproduced or transmitted in any form or by any
means, electronic or mechanical, including photocopying, recording, or any information storage or
retrieval system, without prior permission in writing from the publishers.

Bloomsbury Publishing Plc does not have any control over, or responsibility for, any third-party websites
referred to or in this book. All internet addresses given in this book were correct at the time of going
to press. The author and publisher regret any inconvenience caused if addresses have changed
or sites have ceased to exist, but can accept no responsibility for any such changes.

A catalogue record for this book is available from the British Library.

Library of Congress Cataloging-in-Publication Data

ISBN: HB: 978-1-3501-4463-7
        PB: 978-1-3501-4464-4
        ePDF: 978-1-3501-4461-3
        ePUB: 978-1-3501-4462-0

Typeset by RefineCatch Limited, Bungay, Suffolk
Printed and bound in Great Britain

To find out more about our authors and books visit www.bloomsbury.com
and sign up for our newsletters.

Contents

Figures

Where the original was in colour, they are reproduced in colour. This includes all the figures reproduced in black and white in the text, plus other images not reproduced here. Explanation of letters in brackets at caption end can be found in the Copyright Key on page xvi.

Copyright Key

(a) In the public domain in its country of origin and other countries and areas where the copyright term is the author's life plus 100 years or less.

(b) Author's own work.

(c) Purchased from Direct Deposit

(d) This work is in the public domain in Russia according to article 1281 of Book IV of the Civil

  e. Code of the Russian Federation No. 230-FZ of December 18, 2006 and article 6 of Law No.

  f. .231-FZ of the Russian Federation of December 18, 2006 (the Implementation Act for Book IV of the Civil Code of the Russian Federation)

(f) Automatically confirmed by WikiCommons using the Flickr API.

(g) Creative Commons Attribution 2.0 Generic

(h) GNU Free Documentation License

(i) Creative Commons Attribution 4.0 International

(j) Creative Commons Attribution-Share Alike 3.0 Unported

(k) Sheilalau, the photographer, grants anyone the right to use this work for any purpose, without any conditions.

(l) In the public domain according to German copyright law because it is part of a statute, ordinance, official decree or judgment (official work) issued by a German authority or court.

(m) Creative Commons CC0 1.0 Universal Public Domain Dedication.

(n) *Visual Arts Research* Journal

Using this book

Picture Pedagogy explores key concepts and curriculum examples from across a wide range of subjects to empower readers to support students to develop a critical consciousness about images, whether teaching art, media, language or social studies. This book brings the language of visual culture, classroom strategies and K-12 case studies together, drawing on the history of fine art and contemporary, popular visual culture. The book contains a number of images and activities which are highlighted throughout.

Within each chapter

 Questions Quiz-like questions at the end of each chapter to re-enforce learning and promote engagement with key concepts.

 Activities A wide variety of suggested in-class activities at the end of each chapter. These activities can be carried out individually or in groups.

Online

This icon shows where related material can be found online on the book's dedicated website *https://www.bloomsbury.com/cw/picture-pedagogy/,* which offers additional and free resources to support this book:

Descriptions of teaching practice Lessons and whole semester-long programs that have been carried out by teachers in their classrooms, and were taught as part of standard school subjects that include art, civics, history, language, library studies, media, science, and social studies. These draw from teaching in a diverse range of schools, being drawn from every level from kindergarten to senior high and from diverse countries, the USA to Slovenia, Australia to Spain

Additional images This icon indicates that the image mentioned can be viewed on the companion website.

Home > Academic & Professional > Education > Teacher Education > Picture Pedagogy > Companion Website

Picture Pedagogy

Welcome to the Bloomsbury Companion Website for *Picture Pedagogy*.

Please click on the links in the navigation to access the additonal materials that you require.

Sign up for the latest news and offers

Buy the book

PICTURE PEDAGOGY
Paul Duncum
11 June 2020, Hardback
£63.00
Pre-order now

Introduction

Pictures are a powerful from of pedagogy. They are everywhere a part of everyday life and they are seductive; they offer values and beliefs in such highly pleasurable forms that it is often difficult to resist their power to persuade. To live successfully in a visually saturated society we need ways to understand the kinds of pictures – mostly photographic, often moving and largely popular – that appear on TV, in the movies, in magazines and newspapers and on all our electronic devices. Yet visual communication is largely neglected in K-12 education. This book demonstrates how, as viewers, we can assert our own power through the aid of interpretive concepts. Key strategies are offered for everyone, adults and school children alike, to develop a critical consciousness about pictures. For educators, the book also shows how to develop units of study across the curriculum, specifically how to integrate language, social studies, art and media. Each chapter includes sample projects and questions to ask students.

Picture power

Pictures call out to us, demanding our attention. They attract through their colour, their movement and their content. They draw us in by their ability to offer pleasure, often reinforcing our ideas, sometimes challenging our ideas. By representing human relationships as if natural, in the way of things, pictures suggest how we should think about family, friends, the nation, as well as other countries and other people. Advertisements often attempt to tell us how to think and feel – buy this car, this toy and this shampoo – to save money, because you deserve it, to attract others, to feel good about yourself, to succeed. By contrast, drama and comedies show human relationships as if they are simply givens, as natural, and not to be contested. We may balk at being told how to think and feel, but is it more difficult to object when values and beliefs are offered as if they are in the order of things. To imply that a set of beliefs is natural is to imply that any objection would be unnatural.

To imply that heterosexuality, or class division or national pride are each natural is a powerful way of making a case. It takes courage to argue against what many conceive as natural.

Pictures offer views about all kinds of issues – age-old issues like family responsibilities to emerging issues like global warming. Popular images largely reinforce existing social norms about marriage, children and older people and what it means to be successful, a failure, a good person and a bad person. They teach us about the value of education, of working hard, the value of balancing work with leisure and so on. In short, they ground us all in a sense of ourselves and they ground a society in a sense of itself. Popular images usually offer familiar ideas, though sometimes they also challenge us to think seriously. They operate in a highly competitive market place so mostly they confirm what most people already believe. They also appeal through familiar forms; from prior experience we know what to expect from a situation comedy, a horror movie, an internet cartoon meme. Their formulas do not tax us, and we find it pleasurable to be able to predict what is about to follow.

People power

People also have power over images. Images are not all powerful because audiences can choose to accept the beliefs and values they assume, reject them, or some combination of acceptance and rejection. No matter how powerful images are, we also always possess the power of interpretation. The power of images is always a two-way or shared experience. Pictures exercise power over us and we exercise power over them. Pictures offer views about the world in powerful ways but we can always respond by effectively saying: I agree with this assumption but that idea is going too far, or while I accept the general premise this example does not follow and so on.

This book considers how pictures operate as powerful forms of pedagogy and it also shows how we can better negotiate by providing key concepts. This is illustrated below by briefly introducing some of the interpretive concepts developed in depth in subsequent chapters.

Chapter 1 outlines the nature of visual culture, why it has become so significant a social phenomenon and why it is now critical for developing curriculum in a range of subjects for twenty-first-century students.

Chapter 2 examines the concept of representation, considering how things are represented, what is represented and what is often absent. For example, many photographs and paintings physically position the viewer by means of framing and angles-of-view.

Chapter 3 introduces the concept of rhetoric. Rhetoric refers to the making of persuasive arguments. Rhetoric effectively combines the concepts of aesthetic pleasure and ideology, but it does more; in making pervasive arguments through aesthetic means, it also stresses the vital importance of both the perceived credibility of the image-maker and the importance of emotion. Consequently, the chapter will explore the many emotional appeals made by images in making the kind of arguments pictures make about normative beliefs and values. The chapter will also make the case that much of the fine art of art museums can be regarded as drawing upon the same pleasures as popular culture.

Chapter 4 considers specific ways that pictures seduce viewers. With pictures, values and beliefs, or ideology, usually come wrapped in aesthetic pleasure. A long list of aesthetic pleasures is offered before focusing on such forms of seduction as the bright and busy, the exotic, violence, horror, sentimentality and humour.

Chapter 5 complements Chapter 4 by examining the problems raised by many of the aesthetic pleasures of popular culture. While some issues are merely a matter of taste, other problems are moral; they work against an audience's best interests, demean others, or even undermine the fabric of society.

Chapter 6 introduces the concept of the gaze. Where previous chapters stress the power of pictures, this chapter considers the power of people to interpret according to their subject position, that is, who they are in terms of gender, sexual orientation, class, age and so on. For example, there are male gazes, female gazes, heterosexual and homosexual gazes. The concept of the gaze incorporates many diverse ways of looking and also the physical, social and institutional contexts under which we look. There is also a range of pleasures derived from gazing that greatly complicate any simple interpretation of images based on looking at the image alone. By factoring in who is looking and under what conditions means that the meaning of an image is always created through very particular interactions.

Chapter 7 focuses on the concept of intertextuality. Pictures are not islands, existing in isolation to things around them. Rather, every picture exists in relation to many other pictures, both contemporary and from the past, as well as written texts of different kinds, be they novels, song lyrics, poems, dictionary definitions or scientific dissertations.

Chapter 8 introduces strategies for examining pictures that are based largely on the previous chapters. A conventional lock-step approach is critiqued that was originally intended for fine art alone. An approach is introduced – called the Visual Culture Appraisal Compass – that includes eight kinds of questions that address all kinds of pictures and focuses as much on their context and who is viewing as the pictures themselves. Teachers may wish to go straight to this chapter and then go back to previous chapters to understand what it is based upon.

Chapter 9 describes how to develop an intertextual curriculum based on rhizomic structures. Unlike a modernist curriculum, which is tree-like, a postmodern curriculum has the rhizomic structure of grass, where all kinds of images and written texts interconnect through related ideas. Using both high and low technology examples, units of study are developed from popular media such as situation comedies.

Chapter 10 describes how to develop a curriculum involving the making of movies, one of the most dominant contemporary cultural forms. It draws upon the example of the movie-in-minutes genre on the internet, by which youth recreate a movie blockbuster with live actors and invent low technological solutions. Student creative projects are described as exemplars for classroom practice and practical advice is offered.

Additional to the exemplars of in-class practice provided in Chapters 9 and 10, an accompanying website to this book contains over thirty brief descriptions of teaching practice. These are not mere suggestions for practice but lessons and whole semester-long programmes that have been carried out by teachers in their classrooms. They are derived from a diverse range of schools, being drawn from every level from kindergarten to senior high. They are drawn from diverse countries, the United States to Slovenia, Australia to Spain, and were taught as part of standard school subjects that include art, civics, history, language, library studies, media, science and social studies.

1

What is Visual Culture?

Defining visual culture

Consider Figure 1.1, an illustration from the original children's book on which the famous 1939 film *The Wizard of Oz* is based. Both the illustration and the movie are the kind of mass produced, popular pictures that many people think of when they read the term visual culture. In being popular, it is not considered very serious and perhaps it is even a little silly. But visual culture refers to a whole lot more. It refers to all kinds of pictures as produced, circulated and viewed in the context of often conflicting, deeply held beliefs and values. Visual culture is highly inclusive. It includes the fine arts of painting, drawing and sculpture and vernacular images like folk art and selfies. Of course, it also includes the popular mass media, including movies, movie posters, television, billboard advertising, magazine illustrations, video games, internet visual memes and so on. This is how visual culture is defined in this book. However, there are broader and different definitions, and it is useful to consider these other definitions to clarify how the term visual culture is employed here.

What is *visual* in visual culture?

To understand the breadth of visual culture, picture a pie chart that includes all the pictures produced and viewed in the entire world during the time you have been reading this chapter, in other words,

Figure 1.1 W. W. Denslow. Book illustration. Dorothy meets the Cowardly Lion, from *The Wonderful Wizard of Oz* (1900).

in the last minute or so. This would be millions of pictures. Imagine dividing the pie chart into different categories of pictures, as with Figure 1.2.

This would be an entirely speculative exercise regarding percentages but it would help to focus on what this book is concerned with and why. Approximately half the pie chart might consist of just one kind of image. Another section might be, let us say, 8 per cent, and another might be also 8 per cent. This leaves around 35 per cent. Two further categories might be considered to be 17 per cent each, which leaves a final category that is only 1 per cent.

While it is impossible to say whether these percentages are in any way accurate – there is surely no way of knowing – these speculative percentages allow a number of arguments to be made, including the relative social importance of the different categories and the extent to which they are of importance to readers of this book. Only some of these categories are relevant in this book because, ordinarily, only some categories are concerned with people's beliefs and values.

Surveillance

As suggested by Figure 1.2, the first category, of approximately 50 per cent, consists of all the surveillance imagery. Cameras on surveillance satellites operate twenty-four hours a day. Think of how many hover over the Middle East, North Korea and other world trouble spots. And consider that today every heritage site, from China's Forbidden City to Turkey's Blue Mosque, is subject to

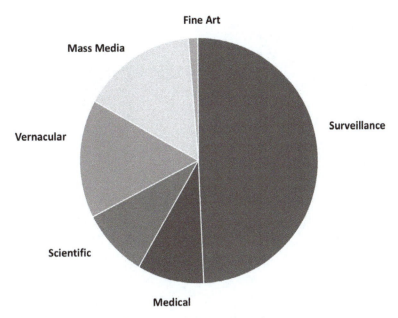

Figure 1.2 All the pictures created in the world at any one time.

surveillance cameras. Even walking down the aisles of a supermarket one is subject to visual surveillance. Even if one is tempted to steal something, we all know that we are being watched, and most of us have learned to internalize good civic behaviour. Most visual surveillance of streets, shopping malls and parking lots is designed to catch theft, vandalism or terrorism, although mostly what they catch is just adolescents behaving badly. In the 1970s, the French philosopher and historian Foucault (1977) described his then society as a society of surveillance. How much more relevant is this today than it was in the 1970s? However, these surveillance pictures are part of a discourse of criminality and terrorism, and in most cases they merely provide data to governmental authorities. Being concerned with mere raw data and not people's beliefs and values, they are usually of no interest here.

Scientific and medical pictures

The second and third categories, with around 8 per cent each are, respectively, scientific and medical pictures. Scientific imagery includes all the pictures beamed back to Earth from the surface of Mars, all the ways the Earth's crust and weather are pictured, all the images that demonstrate how dinosaurs are imagined to have behaved, and so on. Medical images include X-rays, sonograms, nuclear imaging of organs and MRI imaging of the brain. Again, both scientific and medical images provide raw data, and, as such, do not involve values and beliefs, and, therefore, are ordinarily of no interest here.

Vernacular pictures

This leaves three more categories. The first of these categories are vernacular pictures – images created by ordinary untrained people for their own pleasure. This includes folk art, such as

Figure 1.3 Anonymous, *Chinese Paper Cut* (no date)

handcrafted goods like scrapbooking, embroidery and quilt making. For example, for centuries, paper cutting has been an inexpensive way to decorate homes in both Europe and Asia (Figure 1.3).

While once enjoyed by many people as part of ordinary life, today such older forms of vernacular imagery are pursued by only a minority of people as a hobby. Only a few years ago, certainly in the developed world, vernacular pictures would have been a rather small category, but today the category of vernacular pictures also includes all the digital pictures we snap and upload to social networking sites, as well as all the pictures drawn from massive image banks and reused for people's own purposes. These pictures are often invested with deep personal meaning, and consequently they do interest us here.

Mass media pictures

The next category, the second last, are the professionally produced pictures of the mass media, which include television, movies, video games, magazine and newspaper photographs and all forms of mass advertising. More than any other, mass media pictures are the ones that tell us stories, both fictional and non-fictional, which ground contemporary societies in a sense of themselves. Oral societies of long ago passed down social norms from one generation to another through story telling; today, the role of inculcating normative beliefs and values falls increasingly to mass media. Increasingly, mass media provides us with reference points for living.

Both vernacular images and mass media images are popular; one bubbles up from below and the other comes, as it were, from above. These are the images, vernacular and mass media, that most people are most aware of on an everyday basis.

Mass media pictures have become ubiquitous, so much a part of daily experience that they are to us almost like the water in which fish live. In the 1960s, the French theorist, Debord (1995), characterized his then contemporary society as a society of spectacle. For Debord, society was meditated not, as it had been for centuries, primarily through words but through pictures. Pictures, not words, had become the primary communication mode by which values and beliefs were conveyed and circulated. Once again, how much more relevant is this today, in the age of internet interactivity and numerous twenty-four-hour television channels, than it was in France more than five decades ago?

Web 1.1
Introducing
Media
Literacy

Fine art pictures

Just one final category is left, and perhaps it is even less than one per cent. This category includes all the pictures produced in all the art schools around the world as well as all the pictures viewed in all the world's art museums and commercial art galleries. Today, the fine arts are a tiny percentage of the images produced and viewed at any one time. This is not to say that they are unimportant – as indicated below, their social importance is out of all proportion to their number – but it is to suggest their social marginality. The fine arts play only a minor role, if any, in most people's everyday lives (if in this book there is an over-representation of fine art reproductions in relation to all other kinds of pictures that is only because, being old, they are copyright free).

We need to create an education relevant for today's youth, and education cannot be restricted to the fine arts. As educators, we must address the kind of pictures that help our students form their ways of regarding themselves and their world. Yet the sheer number of pictures can be intimidating; far too many pictures appear of so many different kinds. Where is an educator to start?

Excluding many pictures from consideration

Although pictures are proliferating even as you read this chapter, their sheer amount need not be daunting to educators. While the field of Visual Culture Studies is highly inclusive of all the kinds of pictures mentioned above, educators in the humanities and social sciences – of art, language, social studies and media – to whom this book is addressed, need only be concerned with images that primarily refer to beliefs and values. By contrast, many of the images mentioned above refer only to data or raw information and are usually part of discourses unrelated to beliefs and values. Surveillance pictures are usually part of a discourse about crime and terrorism. In the same way, scientific pictures are ordinarily part of scientific description and analysis and decipherable only to scientists in their highly specialized fields. Medical images are likewise ordinarily concerned with the diagnosis and prognosis of medical conditions, and they are similarly unreadable to anyone but specialists in medicine. As indicated by Figure 1.4, most of the pictures produced today are not ordinarily concerned with social beliefs and values.

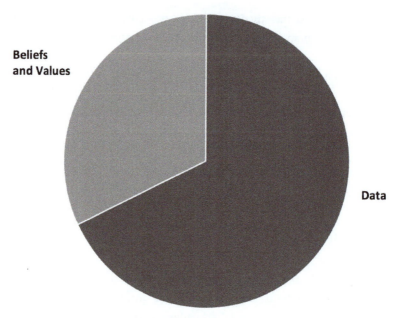

Figure 1.4 Beliefs and values versus data.

However, sometimes pictures that are ordinarily concerned with surveillance, scientific and/or medical data are infused with social beliefs and values. When such pictures enter the domains of the vernacular, the mass media or the fine arts, they invariably signify beliefs and values. But only then do they need to concern us. These exceptions are discussed later in the chapter.

What is *culture* in visual culture?

The visual part of visual culture contains many kinds of pictures. But what is culture? In English, *culture* has been called one of the two or three most complicated words in the language so it is important to understand how it is used here as well as how it is not used. Simply put, in this book, culture refers to artefacts, namely pictures, as mediators of social conflict. Culture is understood as pictures that embody multiple ways of life in perpetual struggle with one another.

Culture as fine art

By contrast, culture can mean high culture, an especially refined sensibility as well as the fine art works that are thought to sustain such refinement. This is a view of culture that first arose in reaction to the Industrial Revolution of the late eighteenth century and nineteenth century. It was critically important to the modernist enshrinement of fine art as an especially refined, quasi-spiritual realm. According to this view, paintings by the great European Masters like Giotto, Leonardo Da Vinci and Rembrandt, and sculptures by Michelangelo and Bellini are the pinnacle of human achievement. These are the cultural artefacts of a very selective tradition belonging to social elites. This is a hierarchal view of culture, where high culture is contrasted with low culture, and in which high culture is prized and low culture is denigrated and dismissed.

Culture as things that signify

On the other hand, culture can also refer to any kind of artefact that signifies meaning of some kind. This is a semiotic definition. Semiotics is the study of signs, of artefacts in terms of what they signify. Unlike the high culture definition, a semiotic definition embraces all kinds of things, including all kinds of popular artefacts. A table, for example, depending on the kind of table it is, could signify functionality or social status. Our clothes can indicate our occupation or our social standing. The car we drive can indicate our economic status and sometimes even our personality. The most ordinary things can be used to signify ideas about us. We can use them to show the world who we are or what we aspire to. Ordinary, everyday things are thereby invested with meaning.

Web 1.2
Semiotics

Semiotics can also be applied to fine art, but instead of assuming that fine art has inherent worth, a semiotic approach considers fine art in the same light in which it considers everyday popular culture. Semiotics treats fine art as if it is ordinary. Consider the portrait by United States artist Gilbert Stuart – a typical example of high culture (Figure 1.5). A semiotic conception of culture might consider it, for example, alongside a photograph of a contemporary fashion model (Figure 1.6). A semiotic approach would not automatically assume that one was a timeless

Figure 1.5 Gilbert Stuart, *Ann Barry* (1828).

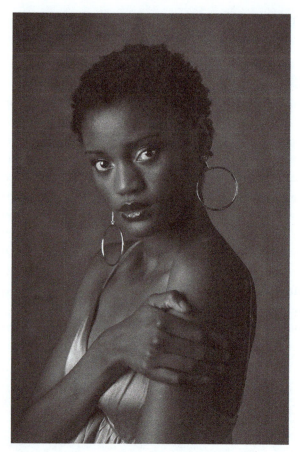

Figure 1.6 *Contemporary Fashion Model* (no date).

masterpiece and the other less worthy; it might, for example compare the two pictures in terms of what they tell us about celebrity, or facial perfection, or womanhood. This is to treat both images as pictures rather than to celebrate one as art.

However, although a high culture, fine art view of culture is very different from a semiotic view, they are similar in that they focus on objects. Each shares a common focus on actual artefacts – an important point discussed below.

Culture as a way of life

Culture can also mean the way of life lived by a particular group of people; with regard to nationality; for example, the Australian way of life or the American way of life. This is the anthropological definition. Unlike the high culture view, but like the semiotic view, the anthropological view of culture does not create a hierarchy, seeing some cultures as superior to others. It rejects a hierarchy of culture in favour of pluralism, seeing all cultures as having their own inherent value.

Culture as multiple ways of life

An anthropological conception of culture is problematic for the purposes of studying pictures in contemporary, complex societies. First, while an anthropological understanding is appropriate when studying a simple society, such as a small indigenous tribe that only has one way of life, modern cultures are all complex enough to include not one way of life but many. In studying the role of pictures in modern societies, we need a view of culture that acknowledges multiple ways of life. Different ways of life are often based, for example, on geography, generations, ethnicity, gender or sexual orientation. This is true even within one nation. Even whether one lives in the countryside or a big city helps determine one's own, particular way of life.

Culture as ways of conflict

Even while acknowledging different ways of life, we need also to recognize that often they do not operate harmoniously. Typically, they do not work together like the organs of a healthy human body, where each organ complements and supports all the other organs. Instead, ways of life are often in conflict; there are almost always tensions as one group tries to assert its influence and power or one group attempts to suppress another. Almost always, there is competition among groups. This is a socially critical approach to culture, one that views society as made up of groups that are continually contesting the influence, and even the legitimacy, of other groups. Instead of thinking in terms of just multiple ways of life, a socially critical approach views culture as multiple ways of conflict and struggle.

Culture as pictures as sites of conflict

However, the anthropological definition and the socially critical view of culture are alike in suffering from a further problem. A way of life, ways of life, or even ways of conflict, are each insufficiently focused for the purpose of studying pictures. Each is too general for the study of visual culture. What is not a way of life, ways of life or ways of conflict? To study pictures, our interest in culture needs to be narrowed in order to be manageable.

The definition of culture used here is a combination of the semiotic definition and the socially critical definition. Succinctly put, visual culture refers to any kind of picture that mediates beliefs and values in a society understood to be in perpetual conflict and struggle. Almost always there are groups vying for power and influence, and so in this book culture is understood as social conflicts mediated through pictures. Or alternatively, visual images are sites of social struggle.

Visual culture today

Today, visual culture is highly dynamic. Consider Figure 1.2 again. Each category is represented as if clearly different from one another. However, these categories are not always hard and fast, and the lines in the pie chart separating the categories should be imagined as dotted or blurred. Sometimes pictures ordinarily concerned with raw data cross over from their specialized fields and become popular. Sometimes too, fine artists appropriate them.

Blurring the lines between data, beliefs and values

A shocking example of where routine surveillance pictures entered popular awareness and aroused strong emotional reactions was that of CCTV footage taken in a shopping mall in England in 1993. The cameras recorded the abduction of a two-year-old boy by a pair of eleven-year-old boys. The low-level quality video shows the pair approaching the toddler, taking his hand, and leading him away.

Shortly after the abduction, the two older boys tortured and murdered the toddler. The police, initially getting nowhere with their investigations, released the video in the hope that someone would be able to identify the culprits. Eventually, the boys were identified through the video and were arrested. With the media playing the surveillance video over and over, the public was forced to confront the horrifying spectacle of children no longer acting like children. Fuelled by the media, the abduction, the torture and the murder caused a public outcry that raised questions about the very idea of childhood. A moral panic set in with the public demanding to know what was happening to their society. Later, during the trial, further questions were raised about the judicial system. Why were the boys tried as adults? And why did the media indulge in sensationalist and often incorrect rumourmongering? In this case, routine surveillance footage became a lightning rod for some of England's social ills.

Today, many people are using their mobile phone cameras to record the actions of the police in an effort to curtail police brutality at demonstrations and police arrests. Protestors in the Middle East and South America have used their mobile phones extensively for this purpose. Recently in the US videos made by bystanders of police arrests and the killings of black suspects have gone viral on the internet and brought a renewed emphasis on race relations in that country.

In short, routine surveillance imagery that normally stays within the discourse of criminality sometimes becomes a focal point for deep social issues, helping to stir public opinion on the nature of crime, but also such issues as childhood, the judicial system, the media, police tactics and race. In addition, surveillance footage has now become a staple means of developing the narrative of both police and spy dramas on television and in the movies.

Medical and scientific images also regularly enter the public domain. Images used by palaeontologists to study the behaviour of dinosaurs fascinate everyone as the *Jurassic Park* and *Jurassic World* movies indicate. And popular television documentaries commonly feature medical imagery on health and medical breakthroughs, as do police and medical dramas.

Some images provide no more than informational data to discourses of crime, science and medicine, but they take on added meaning when they are invested with social beliefs and values. At that point, they become potentially of interest to educators in the arts, humanities and social sciences. Sometimes they are of particular interest because they expose especially striking social conflicts.

Blurring the lines between popular pictures and fine art

The divisions between vernacular images, mass-produced images and fine art are also not hard and fast; in fact, they have become increasingly blurred. Amateur videos of silly family behaviour or the family pet – especially cats – are the raw material for some television programmes. Some videos go viral, becoming so popular that they are shown on television and their producers become famous. Videos are created by fans of a television series to fill in back stories or develop the profile of minor television characters that are then used by professionals in developing further episodes. With this kind of convergence, it is not entirely possible to say who exactly is inventing the storylines, the professionals or the amateurs.

Web 1.3
Combining Art and Popular Culture

Furthermore, fine art no longer exists as an entirely separate category; its boundaries have also become blurred. During the period known as high modernism – the 1930s–1960s – there existed a clear division between the fine art of high culture and low, popular culture. The division was part of high culture's veneration of fine art and its abhorrence of popular culture. Modernist cultural theory held that fine art was an antidote to social ills while social ills were perpetuated by popular culture. One of the major features of our own time, and one of the main reasons our times are characterized as postmodern, is that this once clear divide has broken down. Long gone are the days of high modernism when fine art connoisseurs regarded the popular arts as cheap and nasty and would never admit to indulging in them.

Today, the minority of people who regularly visit art museums, even those who attend openings, go home to watch television, download movies onto their computer or play video games. The once clear division between fine art and popular culture has become fluid. A remnant of the division still exists – there remain separate institutions and social practices – but the division is now far less rigid than it once was. For the purposes of this book, the division has imploded; fine art and popular art have collapsed into one another. This is celebrated by postmodern theory. Postmodern theory is an attempt to understand this different world, where popular media not only saturates everyday living but also where different cultural categories are understood as socially levelled. Instead of understanding different categories of culture as hierarchical, fine art images are seen as different from popular culture rather than superior. Different categories of culture are understood to represent a difference of kind rather than a difference of value.

Many recent artists have drawn their inspiration from popular culture. One of the first was the American Pop Artist Andy Warhol, with his many silk screens of popular celebrities such as Hollywood stars like Marilyn Munroe and popular music idols like Elvis Presley. The influence of popular culture on fine artists should not be surprising. Fine artists have long drawn upon the visual world around them, and what surrounds them today is a proliferation of popular pictures.

Additionally, fine art institutions enter the realm of popular discourse whenever an art museum promotes a blockbuster show with the use of popular media; and many art museums, once exclusively focused on fine art, now also display collections of everyday popular imagery. In Copenhagen, Denmark, the Danish Museum of Art and Visual Culture includes a standing exhibition called 'Everyday Life in the 20th Century'. It includes living rooms from every decade from 1900 to 1980. The rooms include furniture, curtains, magazines, radios and television sets.

Different categories have different social roles

However much the different categories cross over and blur, they tend to play different social roles. The mass media typically reproduces mainstream values and beliefs while fine art oftentimes challenges them by offering alternatives or even by offering opposing viewpoints.

Reproducing social beliefs and values

Most mass media pictures tend to recycle existing beliefs and values. Subject to the demands of the marketplace and/or government legislation, the mass media mostly reproduces mainstream beliefs and values, and it thereby tends not to challenge the status quo, but to support it. As described in greater detail in subsequent chapters, popular media promotes a wide range of values and beliefs about a wide range of topics but the range tends to be limited to what most people already value and believe. Whether the genre is comedic, dramatic, romantic or action based, popular media tends to offer up widely held, pre-existing views. It does not challenge values and beliefs as much as confirm those already widely accepted. This is true whether the issue is crime, marriage, death, gender relations, sexual orientation, the environment or any other issue.

In most countries, very few media companies own the mass media. The same companies own numerous television stations, film studios and many magazines and newspapers. Media companies are vertically integrated megaliths. Since the production of multi-million-dollar movies and television programmes is a risky business – many cultural goods fail – producing challenging material increases risk. One result is that media companies tend to give the public what they think they want. Another result is cross promotion. Many pictures refer to each other in a self-referential loop. A movie refers to a television programme that includes product placement for a product that elsewhere is advertised using one of the celebrity actors who starred in the movie and who also appears in a magazine interview about the movie. These intertextual connections are a routine way of trying to safeguard against marketplace failure. Back in the 1980s, yet another French philosopher, Baudrillard (1988), used the metaphor of a funhouse mirror maze to describe the media landscape of pictures that seem to reflect each other indefinitely. He went so far as to suggest that pictures no longer referred to reality but only to other pictures. For Baudrillard, life had become so saturated with pictures we were no longer capable of distinguishing between pictures and real life, artifice and reality, real life having become nothing but imagery; and this was before the internet.

Another reason why popular mass media typically reproduces the status quo is that the mass media industry is part of a network of other manufacturing and service industries. Television companies, for example, rely upon advertisers for revenue, and advertisers rely on television companies to promote products. They are linked by common cause and common governmental regulations; they are each reliant for success on both sales and government approval.

Mass media pictures are part of the dominant culture. They are dominant partly in the sense that they are by far the most common pictures experienced in everyday life, and partly because in a consumer society they are closely tied to the dominant form of economic arrangement, namely consumer capitalism. Consider that the principal idea promoted by commercial television is entirely in line with a consumerist economy. While most people regard television advertising as annoying interludes between programmes, from an economic perspective, the purpose of programmes is to attract eyeballs to advertising. From the viewpoint of the advertisers, as well as the owners of commercial television networks, the programmes are the breaks, not advertising. Commercial television exists to show advertising. Consuming product X will make you look more attractive; product Y will bring you romance; product Z is not only healthy but tastes good too. Karl Marx was a poor predictor of the future when it came to envisaging the collapse of capitalism, but he believed that all social institutions were directly determined by the economy. As indicated below this too is inaccurate, but he would not have been surprised to find that the principal message of today's dominant cultural form, television, is to consume. And as discussed in Chapter 10, this is equally true of social networking sites like Facebook and picture sharing sites like YouTube.

Critiquing social beliefs and values

By contrast, the fine arts of museums and galleries tend to challenge mainstream beliefs and values, sometimes implicitly, sometimes explicitly. This is their primary social significance and why their significance is out of all proportion to their amount; they act to argue with, counter, resist, and offer alternatives to mainstream viewpoints. Fine art performs a vital social role in standing at some distance from dominant beliefs and values. It stands apart in two very different ways. Fine art museums house and promote two remarkably different kinds of art: what many people consider the best art from the past and new art that frequently confronts established, current ways of thinking.

The fine arts of the past are a form of residual culture, of what is left over from bygone years. Being created in a different time with different beliefs and values, they implicitly challenge contemporary society. Created prior to mass consumption, in a slower time, their very existence implies the value of other kinds of social and economic arrangements. They are valued for their craftsmanship, their painstaking skill, which alone stands in marked contrast to the products of our throwaway society. By contrast to our polluted and ugly urban landscapes, fine art is also valued for its celebration of beauty. It provides a calm, reflective space to contemplate, so different from our normal rushing about in depersonalized, large cities. Fine art seems to speak of better, more leisurely, more personal, times. Landscape paintings offer a world of natural beauty; portraits, a world of elegance, tradition and wealth; genre paintings of peasants, a nostalgic world of quaint customs from long ago: religious icons, a world of certain, untroubled faith; and narrative paintings, of stories whose full significance may be lost on us today, but nevertheless charm with the golden glow of the past.

By contrast, the other kind of museum art is often shockingly new. New art addresses what is still emerging, what is still barely born, and for this reason it is often difficult to decipher. While dominant popular culture employs codes that most people understand, emergent culture not only deals with new and challenging ideas, but also it employs codes that are not yet widely shared. It takes effort to understand.

Challenging conceptions of art

Some new art challenges our conceptions of what art is, while other new art challenges wider social issues. The French artist Marcel Duchamp's so-called Readymades from the 1910s were at the time highly controversial. They are the classic example of art that challenged the nature of what until then had been considered the very nature of art. In the first decades of the twentieth century, no one in the West questioned the idea that art was a one-off, hand-made artefact that was the unique expression of an individual artist in a pleasing aesthetic form. But Duchamp's *Bicycle Wheel* (1913), an ordinary mass-produced bicycle wheel inserted upside down into an ordinary mass-produced stool, was neither an emotional expression by the artist's own hand nor, by the conventions of the day, aesthetically pleasing. The same was true of his other Readymades, especially his *Fountain* from 2017, an ordinary, mass-produced urinal turned upside down. Today's abject art – art that uses bodily fluids such as urine and menstrual blood – explicitly challenges all traditional conceptions of fine art as either beautiful, sublime or picturesque.

Challenging society

Other new art challenges mainstream social beliefs and values. Contemporary Chinese artist Wang Guangyi writes: 'An artist may not be able to solve any problems, but it is his basic professional duty to raise questions by means of his art and to endow his work with signs of intellectual reflection.' For example, in her series *Burned Bosphorus* (2007), contemporary Turkish artist Kezban Arca Batibeki drew attention to the destruction of beautiful, waterfront buildings along the Bosphorus River in Istanbul in order to construct characterless buildings in the name of urban development.

Some art, called activist art, more directly challenges authority. For example, consider Colombian artist Fernando Botero's response to the torture of prisoners at Abu Ghraib in 2003 by US military personnel that followed the invasion of Iraq. When photographs surfaced of degrading treatment and torture of prisoners, Botero produced a series of drawings and paintings that protested US military atrocities. While the photographs showed prisoners forced into deeply compromising positions, but not their faces, Botero showed the prisoners' anguished faces and blood and thereby made their suffering more personal.

Pictures in society

In sum, dominant, popular culture mostly describes social realities in an uncritical, even celebratory way, and thereby reinforces them, while the fine arts offer alternatives and even opposition. The fine arts are often either prescriptive or proscriptive, arguing either for what society should be like or what it should not be like. The German artist Kate Kollwitz's lithographic prints of mothers with dead children rage against the inhumanity of war and poverty. They argue that such suffering should not be. By contrast, revolutionary Chinese woodcut artists of the 1930s and 1940s represented a world as it should be. Employed as part of the Communists' rallying of the peasants, the artists depicted peasants defying traditional landowners and demanding justice. Where popular pictures typically reproduce existing social realities, fine art often produces new, emerging values and beliefs.

Irrespective of the social significance of fine art as a counter to dominant culture, today it is not contemporary fine artists, or the fine art of the past, that mostly influences people. This is achieved by popular pictures, and in a historically unprecedented way.

Why is visual culture important?

Everyday experience is now substantially filtered through popular visual images. We learn about the world and are entertained by cultural forms that are primarily visual and popular. While visual forms of communication have always been important for both knowledge and entertainment, never before in human history have they approached their current significance in forming and informing minds.

The literacy transformation

Popular pictures are creating a transformation in human consciousness that is as significant as the transformation that took place when most members of a society first learned to read and write. The transformation in literacy levels during the nineteenth century meant that, for the first time in human history, most people were able to gain their knowledge of the world as well as their entertainment from the written word. Prior to widespread literacy, societies were based on the spoken word. In these oral-based societies, people were restricted to learning about the world from their own personal experience and face to face with other people. Unless they travelled – and most did not travel far – what people learned from other people was limited to what was known in their own local geographic area. Their horizons were limited to local ideas, beliefs and values.

Once people were literate, they could learn about many other parts of the world and be introduced to a much broader range of perspectives. Newspapers informed them and novels entertained them. They were no longer restricted to hearing the same stories as passed down generation after generation.

The visual transformation

What began to happen towards the end of the twentieth century, and has since increased exponentially, is just as socially significant. Today, our most important cultural forms are no longer just word based; they are based on still and moving pictures. In the age of text-based literacy, the novel was the dominant cultural form, but the novel was long ago displaced by movies, then by television, as our most prevalent cultural forms. Today we carry these forms around in our pockets. Of course, people still read novels, and all pictures also rely for their meaning on words and/or other communication modes, but our most common cultural forms today are primarily spectral.

Three powerful forces, acting in close concert, are driving this visual revolution. New technologies are enabling the revolution, emerging social needs are increasingly being fulfilled by it, and consumer economies are dependent upon it.

Enabling technology

With the introduction of the internet, and especially since the introduction of web 2.0, governments, commercial enterprises and ordinary people are alike in sending pictures back and forth to each other with ever-greater frequency. For many of us, almost no event, however everyday, is deemed unworthy of a picture being snapped and then immediately uploaded to a social networking site; and any of us wanting to find a picture have only to search on one of any number of the massive image banks that seem to have trawled and catalogued the entire history of picture making. With a few mere clicks of a button, almost every public picture ever made is now readily searchable.

Both the availability and interactivity of pictures have been enabled by two major pieces of technological infrastructure. First, starting in the late 1990s, many information satellites were sent up into low orbiting space, many more than had existed before. The United States, China, the European Union and India sent them up. They sent up their own satellites as well as others on behalf of countries without space programmes. Secondly, and more importantly, fibre optic cables replaced the copper wire cables that had for a century lain across the bottom of the world's oceans. Copper cables had enabled international phone calls, faxes and, by the 1980s, text-based computer messages, but little else. But a single thread of fibre optic the width of a human hair can carry the full data load of an entire metres-wide copper cable. The introduction of fibre optics enabled bandwidth to be expanded over a hundred thousand times. The greatly increased number of information satellites coordinated with the new fibre optic cables has enabled a proliferation of imagery unprecedented in human history. Today, anyone with a laptop, tablet, or mobile phone can in an instant send high-resolution pictures from anywhere to anywhere. Yet technological innovation, while a critical part of the visual transformation, is far from the whole story.

Gratifying social needs

Many technologies fail in the market place; only where there is a recognized social need for a technology does it succeed. The new technologies are enabling the proliferation of pictures, but their proliferation at this particular time in history appears to fulfil basic human needs.

Once upon a time, most people revered traditional beliefs and values. They lived in traditional societies. People grew up accepting their parents' views on what was right and wrong, their attitudes, their values and beliefs. People believed in the rightful authority of governments. They identified with their class position and venerated religious authorities. Authorities were respected. Beliefs and values were passed on from generation to generation and widely shared.

Contrast this with the society in which most of us live today. Today we live in post-traditional societies. Many people are unsure of traditional sources of authority, many have become deeply sceptical, and many have even rejected them. Parents, governments, religion and class affiliations have lost something of their previously unquestioned legitimacy. Lacking faith in traditional sources of authority, we tend to develop our own sense of right and wrong, our own systems of beliefs and values, picking and choosing from other less traditional sources for our reference points for living. We still need social norms to guide our behaviour; we still need guidance, for example, on what it means to be a citizen of a nation, to be a good son or daughter, a parent, a male or a female, straight, gay or transgender. In a search for what to believe, what attitudes and values to adopt towards other people, we increasingly turn to popular media. With older kinds of authority in question a hole has been created that popular media, fuelled by monetary interests, is only too happy to fill. Older sources of authority remain important but not to the extent they once were, and everywhere now popular media infiltrates daily life. Whether it is the issues of the day or all the big issues of life – be they birth, marriage, children, death – we increasingly turn for guidance to the social norms embedded in the stories told by the mass media. Stories that were once passed down through families and friends, that both grounded a society in a sense of itself and offered individuals a meaningful view of themselves, are today told through situation comedies, television dramas, action movies, video games and the like.

Responding to the demands of a consumer economy

Technology is enabling the proliferation of popular imagery and, unmoored from traditional authorities, we rely upon such imagery as never before. But a consumer economy also increasingly relies upon the proliferation of pictures. A capitalist economy is dependent for its survival on its capacity to expand continually, and it can expand in only so many ways. It can penetrate previously uncommodified realms of life, or it can speed up the capitalist circuit of production, distribution and use. To speed up this circuit, ephemeral goods like digital pictures are a godsend.

Today's consumer capitalism contrasts with an earlier phase of capitalism, characterized not by the consumption of goods but by their production. During the nineteenth century and well into the twentieth century, developed capitalist economies like those in Europe and the United States were based on the production of goods like clothes, furniture, white goods, steam engines and automobiles. While these countries still manufacture such goods, their economies increasingly rely upon the provision of services like tourism, health care and finance. Theirs is a service economy with the production of many goods outsourced to developing countries like Vietnam, Bangladesh, India and China. In a service economy, services are constantly in need of renewal, which considerably speeds up the capitalist circuit of production, distribution and consumption. For this reason, a service-based economy is often called fast capitalism.

Even the capitalist circuit of goods is faster than ever before. During the time of productive capitalism, goods were usually produced to last as long as possible; for example, when a couple got married, their furniture was intended to last their lifetime. In the US during the 1950s, goods began to be produced with built-in obsolescence; that is, they were built only to last a limited amount of time and so ensure a faster turnover of goods. But now the economies of developed countries are demanding much faster turnover. Consider the lifetime of a television set. Most people expect television sets to last between six and ten years, but the lifetime of a television programme is often just one day. Digital pictures are a blessing for fast, consumer capitalism because interest in them lasts such a short time. If television sets are like flower vases, digital pictures are like flowers.

The cultural transformation of the economy

The above synergy of technology, social needs and the economy is causing a transformation that is both cultural and aesthetic. Now more than at any time in human history, technology and the economy are bound up with the production of cultural goods. Contrary to Marx, the economy no longer determines the beliefs and values held by a society; the production of cultural goods now helps drive the economy. Consider some statistics. Citizens of the US watch television for about five hours per day, and half also play video games, of whom forty-two per cent play upwards of three hours a week. Consider too how much time the average person spends flipping through their news feed each day and sharing pictures. The value of the global media market is estimated to be over 2 trillion US dollars.

The aesthetic transformation

The cultural transformation of the economy is equally an aesthetic transformation. The economy is now dependent upon aesthetics as never before. So many popular pictures compete for our attention in a highly competitive market place they need to be appealing, to lure, to seduce. Even utilitarian goods need to appeal to our emotions and our senses because there are now always so many goods to choose from. There was a time not so long ago when, for example, there might have been only three kinds of radios or bicycles, each at a different price. People were forced to choose solely on what they could afford. Today, the price may still help determine our choice, but also now we have at least half a dozen items in every price range to choose from. How are we to choose? Safety? Safety was once a concern but consumer watchdogs have largely eliminated the worry over unsafe goods. An emotional association with the brand? Often. But we are likely also to choose a particular item on the basis of which one looks the best, which feels best in the hand, perhaps even its smell; in short, its sensory qualities. It is the affective, aesthetic qualities of emotion and sensation that increasingly determine what we purchase. For manufactures, aesthetic qualities are no longer an afterthought, the icing on the cake, but lie at the very heart of design and manufacture.

Reflect on current movies, television programmes and video games. Think of how many of them rely so much on style over substance. Consider too how we are now habituated to seeing picture after picture, quickly discarding a picture as we but glance at another. We skip from one picture to another, skipping through television channels, surfing the internet, scrolling on our mobile phones. Just as the economy increasingly relies upon the production of cultural goods, to succeed, cultural goods increasingly rely on the aesthetic qualities that combine emotional and sensory appeal.

In summary, technologies are enabling the proliferation of imagery, today's typically ephemeral pictures dovetail with the needs of consumer capitalism, and increasingly we use pictures not only to be informed about our world but also how we think, feel and believe about the world. This is a powerful synergy. The visual revolution has deep roots that are not going to be changed any time soon. Contemporary culture is largely a visual culture. It mostly consists of popular images, and they are here to stay.

Pictures and reality

To underline further the importance of today's visual culture, consider that pictures are now entirely intertwined with social realities. Pictures are derived from pre-existing worldviews, and in constructing beliefs and values in visual form, pictures feed these beliefs and values back to us, either reinforcing or challenging our beliefs and values. Pictures and society exist in a symbiotic relationship, with each influencing the other. Pictures do not simply reveal reality or express it, as if pictures had some kind of separate existence from social life; rather, they are part of the very fabric of social life. In a word, pictures are *constitutive* of social life. They are an integral part of reality, with all its complexity, all its struggles. Pictures are now so ubiquitous that they help constitute reality.

Now, more than at any time in human history, it is through pictures that the struggle for beliefs and values are fought out. And now, more than at any previous time, pictures need to be addressed in education. The next chapters highlight key concepts that specifically address today's picture saturated society, and how they can be employed in the classroom.

Questions

1 What is the main difference between movies, television programmes and video games and how we typically use surveillance, scientific and medical pictures?
2 What do the terms *society of spectacle* and *society of surveillance* mean?
3 What does semiotics mean?
4 How is culture defined in this book?
5 What is the significance of the synergy between technology, social needs and a consumerist economy?
6 What are the main differences between modernism and postmodernism described in this chapter?

Activities

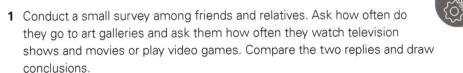

1 Conduct a small survey among friends and relatives. Ask how often do they go to art galleries and ask them how often they watch television shows and movies or play video games. Compare the two replies and draw conclusions.
2 Keep a journal to add up the hours you use popular media during a typical week.
3 Ask older people what life was like before the internet.
4 Consider your favourite television programme or movie. Go onto the internet and look up who produces it, and who owns the company that produces it. Find out what else the parent company owns. Make a chart of their financial connections.
5 Go into a department store and examine a range of products that interest you. Taking price into consideration, consider from the range of products which particular product you would buy and consider why you would choose it.

See Chapter 8 for specific questions on the nature of fine art and popular visual culture: What is the medium? Who made it? Who is the picture intended for? In general terms, why was the picture made? Also consider the fine art theories of evaluation.

2

Representation

How pictures represent

Whether it is realistic paintings from centuries ago or today's digital photography, pictures rely upon a similar range of representational elements. This is true irrespective of whether the subject is a landscape or a portrait, a still life or a historical drama, and many of the elements apply equally to still pictures as they do to moving images. These are the elements of realistic-style pictures. A range of choices exists among each element so that whatever a painter or photographer has chosen is important for us as viewers in deriving meaning from their pictures. The elements of still pictures discussed below include framing, angles-of-view, key, lens, lighting, anchorage and body language. They are followed by elements that apply specifically to moving pictures.

The elements of realistic style pictures
Framing

Framing refers to how close or how far away the subject of a picture appears to us as viewers. Is the subject close-by, at a great distance, or somewhere in between? With framing there is always a trade-off between context, detail and impact. All other things being equal, the further away a subject appears, the greater the context and less the impact; conversely, the closer viewers are, the more detail there is available, and the greater the impact.

With a *distance frame* the subject is so large it must be placed a long way away from the viewer to be seen as a whole; for example, landscapes and cityscapes. Movies and television dramas often start with a shot using a distance frame. When a cityscape is followed by detectives walking down a corridor, viewers know that the detectives are in a large city, not a county town. For this reason, such distance frames are often called an *establishing frame.*

With the rest of the frames it is useful to illustrate with a picture of a person. A *loose full-frame* includes all of a person with enough space around them to include some context, but it has less impact than a *tight full-frame* that has little or no context. A *three-quarter-frame* of the person usually cuts a person off just above the knees so that as viewers we are invited to focus on the upper part of their body. Coming closer, a *half-frame* usually cuts a person off around their stomach. Even closer, a *head-and-shoulder-frame* focuses primarily on the person's face but not as intimately as a *close-up* of their face. With a *close-up,* we are offered almost no context; instead, we are invited into quite an intimate relationship with the subject. In real life this would be to invade a person's private space. An even more intimate relationship is achieved with an *extreme close-up,* such as an eye or a mouth.

None of these descriptions should be regarded as hard and fast. Many pictures use frames that shade between these descriptions and some pictures combine them. Consider a picture of a butterfly balancing on the tip of a person's finger. While the finger would be in *extreme close-up* the butterfly could be shown with a *loose full-frame.* However, these descriptions do provide a basic language with which to examine how much of a subject is shown, how much detail, how much content and, all else considered, the degree of impact.

Angles-of-view

Angles-of-view refers to how high or low we, as viewers, are positioned in relation to the subject of a picture. Looking down on a subject places us in a powerful position. Looking up at a subject positions us as if the subject is the more powerful. A *high angle* is sometimes called a *bird's-eye view* and a low angle is sometimes called an *ant's-eye view.*

Imagine a photograph taken by an adult of young children playing on the ground. The adult would normally be positioned looking down on the children. The photograph would then represent the normal spatial relationship between children and adults as well as encoding the normal power relationship that typically exists between children and adults. A *high angle,* especially when combined with loose full-framing, can have the effect of objectifying the subject; that is, turning the subject into an object to be observed in a cold or calculating way. A *high angle* when combined with a distance frame provides a great deal of context. It could be called a *fly-over view.* Today, with the use of drones, it has become common to view subjects from directly overhead, making these an *overhead view.*

A *neutral angle* positions us as viewers directly across from the subject, neither above nor below the subject. This creates a democratic relationship where power is shared between viewers and the subject matter. When a neutral angle is used in combination with a three-quarter or half frame of a person, viewers are invited into a conversational relationship with the subject of the picture.

Lighting

The placement of light sources can have a significant impact on meaning. Again, it is helpful to illustrate with one subject, in this case, the human face. *Frontal light* tends to flatten the features of a face. Police mug shots use this lighting, where the effect is to bleach out personality. *Sidelight* creates a dramatic contrast with one side of the face lit and the other side dark. A light at forty-five degrees or thereabouts best models a subject's face in three dimensions. *Backlighting* can serve two purposes. Against a dark background backlighting outlines a figure, creating a silhouette. Backlighting can also provide a kind of halo. During the European Middle Ages, religious figures were portrayed with halos to indicate their special, spiritual nature. The halos were often made with gold leaf, and spatially they acted to separate out the venerated person from everything else. Renaissance artist Leonardo da Vinci was more interested in realism than his predecessors and he abandoned this tradition, but in his famous *The Last Supper* (1498) he continued to use back lighting by placing Jesus in front of a window (Figure 2.1).

Today, backlighting is often used in advertisements for shampoo, where it continues to play the role of making someone appear special. Many pictures include multiple light sources. Frequently, a secondary light source supplements the main source where a *fill-in light* illuminates what the main light does not reveal.

Key

Key refers to the level of tonal contrast, to differences between light and dark. *High key* refers to a high level of tonal contrast while *low key* refers to a low level of contrast, to subtle gradations of tone. High key is dramatic. In European painting, *chiaroscuro* was used where subjects emerged into the light from a dark background. In combination with side lighting, high key lighting was

Figure 2.1 Leonardo Da Vinci, *The Last Supper* (1498).

especially used by Baroque artists of the 1600s to help evoke powerful emotions. Low key is more peaceful or restrained. Many traditional Chinese ink on silk paintings of misty, ethereal landscapes employ a low key.

Lens

Camera lenses exist on a spectrum from wide-angle to telephoto with a standard lens in the middle. Each creates particular characteristics. A standard lens approximates the way we normally see things. Centuries before the invention of photography, artists in the West used a device called the *camera obscura*, often with a lens, to achieve a rendering of a scene that approximated normal vision, and artists used the rendering as an aid with which to paint and draw realistically.

A *wide angle* distorts reality, making subjects in the foreground prominent and pushing further into the background whatever is behind the main subjects. The effect is often striking. A wide angle also allows more of a subject to be included than a standard lens. The default on mobile phone cameras is usually a wide angle. This is important for tourists where, for example, in a narrow street it is impossible to capture a scene by simply stepping backwards. Selfies taken without a selfie stick are usually taken with a slightly *wide-angle* lens because most human arms are not long enough to obtain a different result.

Web 2.1
Realistic-
Style
Elements

A *telephoto* lens allows a distant subject to be brought close, though it also tends to flatten the image. The paparazzi use a telephoto lens when photographing celebrities from a distance, and the quality of the photographs tends to reproduce the public's relationship to celebrities. The celebrities appear to be brought intimately close to us as viewers, yet there is a subtle unrealistic quality to the image due to its concertinaing of space. We may feel we know the celebrities, yet, as ordinary viewers, celebrities always remain distant from us; they continue to exist in a space we do not inhabit.

Anchorage

Anchorage refers to grounding the meaning of a picture by means of one or more communication modes. In the case of still pictures, meaning is usually anchored with written words. In art galleries, an artwork is invariably accompanied by the title of the work and other information that can be helpful in understanding it: the artist's name, the media used, the date of the work and the dates of the artist's birth and, if relevant, death. For a more complete understanding, viewers need to consult the art museum's bookstore or a library. Pictures in newspapers, magazines and mobile phones are always anchored with words. Imagine the collection of photographs of ice cream cakes in Figure 2.2 without the accompanying words. Would the cake that looks like a football be interpreted as a football or the doll as a doll? Would any of the photographs be interpreted as cakes made of ice cream?

Anchoring the meaning of moving images is discussed below.

Body language

Body language includes facial expression, gaze, gesture, body position and body contact. Just as each feature of body language is often critical in interpreting whatever is happening in real life,

Figure 2.2 Paul Duncum. *Advertisement for Streets Ice Cream Cakes* (1972).

each can be critical in understanding a picture. Many pictures rely heavily on one or more features of body language for their meaning.

Facial expression tells us a great deal about a person's mood or emotions or even what they might be thinking, and the most important features of the face are the eyes. Many pictures cannot be understood without consideration of either a person's general expression or their *gaze*. Consider Edward Manet's infamous painting *Olympia* (1864). It represents a naked woman lying on a couch. She engages the view with a *mutual gaze*. We look at her and she looks out at us, returning our gaze, and her general facial expression is confronting (Figure 2.3). Both her gaze and expression contributed to the scandal that erupted in France when the painting was first exhibited. Previous images of this kind had represented the woman as demure, as submissive (compare Figure 2.3 with 2.10). By contrast, Manet's version presents the woman as powerful. Asserting her identity as an independently minded woman shocked a society in which women were expected to adopt a deferential role.

By contrast, consider the photograph by Julia Margaret Cameron of a model posing as the infamous Italian murderer of the 1500s, Beatrice Cenci (Figure 2.4). Notorious for killing her abusive father and hanged for the crime, Cenci has been the subject of many paintings, sculptures and several films. Here she is posed looking down and away from us. Could she be looking at

Figure 2.3 Edward Manet, *Olympia* (detail).

Figure 2.4 Julia Margaret Cameron, *May Prinsep as Beatrice Cenci*. Albumen Print (1866).

Figure 2.5 Jacques-Louis David, *Napoleon in His Study* (detail) (1812).

something outside the picture, or is she staring at nothing in particular and contemplating her fate? Is she regretful?

Compare her gaze with the gaze used by Napoleon Bonaparte in a painting by French artist Jacques-Louis David (Figure 2.5). Is his gaze fixed on you or does he also gaze beyond you into the distance? How can his gaze be described? Calmly self-possessed? Assured? Intense? Mysterious? Is it a gaze onto which a viewer might project their confident hopes for a better future? It is the same gaze used by many formal portraits of leaders. The Manet, Cameron and David pictures make little sense without consideration of the gaze.

Gestures are equally critical in understanding some pictures. European paintings from the Renaissance to the nineteenth century relied upon handbooks of hand gestures and body positions that were originally developed for actors and as a language for the deaf and mute. Artists used the handbooks to convey moods and ideas because their audiences were familiar with them from the theatre stage. The subtlety of these gestures is mostly lost on modern audiences, but one example relies on another source. In Raffaello Sanzio (Raphael)'s mural *The School of Athens* (1503), the ancient Greek philosophers Plato and Aristotle are represented with gestures that echo the principal emphasis of their quite different respective philosophies. Where Plato stressed ideals that he thought existed above the earth, Aristotle was interested in categorizing real, material things. One was heaven bound; the other, orientated to the earth. Raphael painted Plato with one arm raised and his hand pointing upwards, his other arm holds a book upright, and one of his feet moves forwards, so that the whole stress of Plato's body is vertical. By contrast, Aristotle is represented with one hand spread out and moving downward, the other hand holds a book across his body, and

Figure 2.6 Raffaello Sanzio (Raphael), *The School of Athens* (detail) (1503).

his feet are spread out. All of Aristotle's gestures are horizontal. The painting cannot be fully appreciated without considering how these bodily gestures literally embody two quite different philosophies.

Body position and *body contact* can also be critical in understanding a picture. French artist Jean-François Millet's 1857 painting *The Gleaners*, again literally embodies the artist's intent—in this case an expression of his socialist sympathies (Figure 2.7). He represents three peasant women bent over, picking up the left-overs from the harvest, emphasizing their daily, backbreaking labour.

Consider Peter Paul Rubens's drawing after a lost painting by Leonardo Da Vinci (Figure 2.8). It is impossible to talk about it without mentioning bodily contact. The chaos of bumping, hitting, slipping and smashing of bodies is integral to the drawing.

In the early 1990s American photographer Sally Mann photographed her own children, often naked, and sometimes standing so close to one another they touch. There is a tender intimacy between them. The children's faces do not suggest they are siblings; this is conveyed by their gentle, body contact.

Figure 2.7 Jean-François Millet, *The Gleaners* (1857).

Figure 2.8 Peter Paul Rubens, *The Battle of the Standard During the Battle of Anghiari* (pre-1550–1603).

Adding the elements of moving pictures

Web 2.2
Elements of
Moving
Pictures
Moving pictures employ all the above elements and also some of their own. Movies, television programmes and video games involve a wide range of camera movements, viewpoints and transitions, as well as forms of anchorage in addition to written words.

Camera movements

When movies began in the late nineteenth century, the camera typically stood on a tripod and simply recorded what was in front of it. The camera did not move, and actors simply went in and out of frame. The effect was similar to a stage play. But moving pictures soon began using moving cameras; they panned, zoomed, tilted and so on. A *pan* occurs when the camera moves from one side to the other. It is used to follow a subject, locate things in space, or to achieve a panoramic view. A *zoom* is achieved by changing the focal length of the lens. *Zoom in* frames a subject tighter; a *zoom out* provides more context. A *tilt* involves moving the view of the camera up or down without changing the camera's vertical position. It is often used to show how tall or deep something is, or to reveal a subject a bit at a time. A *pedestal* shot involves moving the height of the camera up and down without tilting; this is sometimes called an *elevator* shot. A *crane* shot gets its name from mounting a camera on a crane that either swoops in or sweeps out. It is often used at the beginning of a movie to sweep in to a subject and/or to conclude a movie by the grand gesture of sweeping out. Very large swoops were once achieved by mounting the camera on a helicopter; today the same effect is achieved by the use of drones. Small swoops can be achieved by holding a small camera high in the air and swooping it down in an arc, or starting low and swinging the camera high in an arc. A *dolly* shot is achieved by mounting the camera on train tracks to ensure a smooth movement in or out from a subject. It can also be achieved by using a wheelchair or even a skateboard. A *tracking* shot is like a dolly shot except that it involves following a subject from one side. The effect is that viewers travel with the actors, empathizing with them.

The above camera movements are usually designed to achieve a smooth motion where the edges of the frame appear stable. By contrast, *handheld shooting*, as the name implies, refers to a camera held not on a tripod or another stable base but held in the hand. The effect is unstable edges. Handheld is often used for subjective shots (see below) or for documentaries to suggest the realism of everyday life. It is also commonly used to create tension.

Today, many movies are shot with a *steadicam* camera, which is typically carried on the cameraperson's shoulder; they provide much more flexibility than when cameras were too heavy to be carried. Used in combination with digital image stabilization, steadicam cameras provide smooth shots over even an irregular surface. They are often used to move around a subject in a circle, something that would have been near impossible before their invention. Steadicam cameras also allow exceptionally long shots that morph from one camera movement to another without a transition; for example, following people down a corridor, through doors, down a flight of stairs, out into a carpark, and all the time weaving between people.

Transitions

With continuity editing the aim is to transition from one shot to another without the audience being aware. The most common transition is a *cut* where the action continues within the same time and space; for example, where one shot shows someone looking, and then there is a cut to whatever they are looking at. Other cuts include a *straight cut* where one cut abruptly ends a scene and another scene abruptly begins. An *L cut* involves an overlap of the audio from one visual cut to another. *Parallel cutting* involves cutting back and forth between linked scenes such as often happens in a chase sequence between pursuer and pursued. Other kinds of transitions tend to draw attention to themselves; they are usually used to convey a mood, suggest a passage of time, or to separate parts of a story. A *fade-in* or *fade-out* occurs when the picture appears from or turns black or white. A *morph* involves a dissolve combined with a visual effect where one object is reshaped to become another; for example, where a young man is made to morph into a much older one. A *wipe* involves replacing one scene by a second scene that travels from one side to the other, or in the case of an *iris wipe*, one of the earliest in film history, the wipe shape is circular. Today's computer editing programmes contain numerous wipes from different directions and with many different special effects.

Viewpoints

The camera can take either an objective or a subjective point-of-view and thus provide the audience with one or the other. An *objective* point-of-view involves viewing a scene as an observer of the scene, as an invisible third party. A *subjective* point-of-view involves the camera recording what a character can see so that the audience sees through the character's eyes.

Anchorage

As mentioned above in relation to still pictures, the meaning of pictures is always reliant on some form of anchorage. With still images, meaning is usually anchored with written words but in the case of moving images, meaning is also usually anchored with spoken words, sound effects, and music. Mostly, these other modes of communication are used to complement the pictures; someone looks angry and their words and tone are angry; a peaceful landscape is represented and the music is smooth and uplifting. But sometimes they create a conflict with the picture. In the Stanley Kubrick film *A Clockwork Orange* (1971) a very violent scene is accompanied by the soaring beauties of nineteenth-century European opera. The horror of the violence is heightened by the jarring conflict between the music and the picture. Consider a picture of young children laughing accompanied by happy, cheerful music. The relationship here is complementary. Now consider the same picture with dark, foreboding music, and immediately there is the suggestion of something bad about to happen and we are apprehensive for the children. With the happy music, we are content simply to enjoy the moment; with the foreboding music, we create a narrative.

In all the above examples, anchorage relies upon a communication mode other than pictures, but *pictures* can be used as anchorage. Consider a movie in which we watch people fighting intercut with pictures of people watching the fight. If the people watching are laughing good-humouredly, we are invited to view the fight as just roughhousing. But if the intercut pictures are of people looking seriously worried, we are invited to consider the fight as dangerous. The pictures act as a form of pedagogy; they teach us how to look at other pictures. The same is true in the example above where a distance frame contextualized detectives walking down a corridor. With moving pictures, pictures are constantly helping us interpret other pictures.

The formal aspects of realistic pictures are the *how* of representation. The chapter now turns to *what* is represented.

What is represented

Pictures represent just about everything that exists: people, animals, inanimate objects, landscapes, and so on. And just about any idea that we have about different kinds of people, animals, plants, landscapes, and so on, has been pictured, not only recently but also in the past. Many contemporary visual representations have a very long history, being just as prevalent in the history of fine art as in today's popular culture.

Genre

Genre is used here to refer to a category of visual culture that is recognized through socially agreed conventions. Paintings have long been categorized according to genre, the most common being historical, landscape, portraiture, still-life and everyday life. To complicate the issue a little, paintings of everyday life are sometimes also referred to as genre pictures. Movies and television genres include action, adventure, animation, comedy, crime, drama, fantasy, historical, horror, magical realism, musicals, mystery, romance, saga, science fiction, thriller, western and war. Video game genres include action, action adventure, role-play, shoot-em-ups, simulation, sand play, strategy and sports.

Among these forms, each has sub-genres and crossover or hybrid genres. For example, among movies and television programmes the science fiction-fantasy hybrid is common, being effectively a sub-category of either science fiction or fantasy. Many other hybrids exist, common examples being romantic comedies, western thrillers, and historical mystery.

Conventions

Genres are recognizable because of their conventions. Conventions are typical ways of representing. For example, horror movie conventions include slobbering monsters; torture chambers; horrible deaths; abject things like rotting flesh and decapitated bodies; socially inexcusable practices like sadism, cannibalism and necrophilia; and weird, inhuman creatures like werewolves, vampires and zombies. The subcategory of supernatural horror often includes haunted houses, ghosts and agents of the devil. Many of these conventions are derived from images of hell painted in Europe during

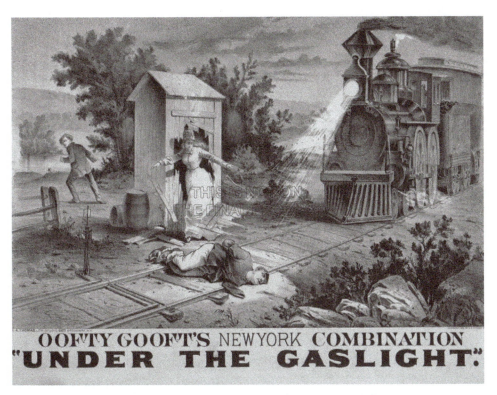

Figure 2.9 H. W. Thomas, *Under the Gaslight*, lithographic poster (1879).

the Middle Ages and based partly on the *Book of Revelation* in the Bible and Dante's twelfth-century story *Inferno*. Horror movies have a vast vocabulary to draw upon with a long history.

Action movies are known for their action heroes who possess extraordinary physical prowess though often a limited emotional range. They are invariably pitted against evil antagonists. Action movies are known for their spectacular explosions; hectic, extended car chases; runaway trains; planes out of control; bombs ticking down; and last-minute rescues. The climax of early action films was often being rescued from an oncoming train, which in turn was often based on nineteenth-century pulp novels and stage plays (Figure 2.9).

Early Hollywood westerns were also based on nineteenth-century popular novels and stage plays. Westerns are easily identifiable despite being a very flexible genre with numerous variants of protagonists, antagonists, locations and other conventions. They are typically set in the western frontier of the US sometime between the 1860s and 1900. Heroes could be sheriffs, army officers, ranchers or a quick draw gunslinger, though villains could also be ranchers and gunslingers as well as cattle rustlers. Locations vary: isolated homesteads, the desert or small frontier towns in which most of the action takes place in the saloon, the main street, and the sheriff's office. Other typical conventions include horses, stagecoaches, long-horned cattle, cowboy hats, spurs and saddles.

Soap operas are a major television genre, with many countries producing their own indigenous kinds, but despite national differences, 'soaps' typically employ the same conventions. They include multiple, convoluted plots involving romance, secret relationships, extra-marital affairs, real love, chance meetings, coincidences, mysterious strangers, unexpected calamities, crime and last-minute rescues.

Stereotypes

Web 2.3
Gender
Stereotyping

Stereotypes are ideas or expressions lacking in originality or inventiveness, and there is often a fine line between conventions and stereotypes. Stereotypes are standard and fixed conceptions, held in common by a large number of people. Being already shared, they are frequently used because they are easily recognized. This is important today when there are so many competing pictures: our attention needs to be grabbed.

Web 2.4
Gender and
Sexuality

The difference between conventions and stereotypes is that stereotypes typically have a negative connotation because they help to reduce complex realities to a single characteristic. When applied to people, or whole groups of people, they can be damaging because people are never as simple as their stereotype. Although there is often a grain of truth to a stereotype, stereotypes are always a cartoon cut-out.

At the same time, many subjects are represented by a variety of often contradictory stereotypes. Media pictures frequently represent schoolteachers as kind, ideal human beings, experts, inspirational and even a sexual fantasy for their students, although also old fashioned, scary and incompetent. Old people are often stereotyped as happy and active, wise and experienced, but also as grumpy, bitter, sick, fragile and lonely. In reality, schoolteachers are often experts and they can be old fashioned, but also they are always more than these stereotypes. Old people may at times be grumpy and bitter, but they too are more than any single characteristic.

Men are often stereotyped as strong, but also aggressive, insensitive, crude and illogical. Women are often stereotyped as nurturing and sensible, but also weak, overly emotional and dependent upon men. Some stereotypes can also be just benign, neither positive nor negative. US media often stereotype Mexicans as uneducated, labourers, criminals and eating beans and rice. African Americans are stereotyped as good at sports, low income, uneducated, drug addicts and violent.

Web 2.5
Geographic
Stereotypes

Jews are stereotyped as intellectual, stingy with money and have overprotective mothers who make them feel guilty. Asians are stereotyped as smart, short, serious, studious, good with technology, nerds and eat rice. Again, whether the stereotypes are negative, positive or benign, and whatever truth they contain, people are always more than their stereotype.

Another important fact about stereotypes is that pictures do not merely illustrate them as if a stereotype resided in words and a picture merely acted as support. Pictures construct stereotypes as much as words. Recall the elements of realistic imagery described above. Teachers that are represented as kind, happy, ideal human beings with glowing skin and broad smiles tend to be pictured in the conversational relationship of a half frame with a neutral viewpoint. Conversely, pictures of teachers as scary tend to use a low angle that makes them seem powerful. Pictures of old people as happy and active tend to use a neutral angle, while old people as sick and fragile are usually represented with a high angle that emphasizes their fragility, and pictures of old people as lonely are often constructed with very loose full frames that isolate them from their surroundings.

Sometimes playing with stereotypes or consciously embracing them can be fun. One group of Chinese students studying in the US that I taught produced a PowerPoint presentation they called 'Seven Types of Chinese Students You Should Know'. The idea that they studied hard was represented with a picture of a serious looking student declaring, 'Finally class is over. Now I can go home and study'. Students were applying the stereotypes as a joke on themselves.

However, when stereotypes are consistently applied to others they can lead to great harm. As considered at greater length in Chapters 4 and 5, when discussing the pleasures and problems of exoticism, stereotypes can be demeaning, even catastrophic. When the assumption is made that one's own society represents an innocent norm and contrasted to another as deficient, especially if it is viewed as also morally inferior, the exotic society becomes a place into which to project the moral deficiencies of one's own culture. This is clearly illustrated by centuries of European representations of the Middle East. Whether it is the paintings of the eighteenth century, the photography of the nineteenth century, or the movies of the twentieth and twenty-first centuries, the Middle East has been consistently understood through visual stereotypes. Costumed and bejewelled men pass the time lying on luxurious sofas, smoking, reading or doing nothing at all but lounging. Women also lounge on sofas surrounded by plush cushions, attended by black servants or slaves. By contrast to the images of sloth, numerous paintings represent violent conflicts between men and between men and wild animals. Common stereotypes are despotic rule as the natural order, violence linked to sex, bloodletting and sensuous excess. Numerous paintings depict slave or marriage markets in which naked slave girls are sold at auction. Despite evidence that harem women were clothed head to foot, and even wore veils, they are usually represented as fully naked and posing provocatively. Jean Ingres's, *Grande Odalisque* (1814) is a good example (Figure 2.10).

Figure 2.10 Jean Ingres, *Grande Odalisque* (1814).

There are many other examples. In many countries Barbie dolls are beloved by young girls and for decades Barbie appeared as white only, but in the 1980s she gained a number of non-white friends from different parts of the world. They appeared with different skin colours, traditional costumes and exotic, stereotypical accessories. China Barbie wore a traditional Chinese robe with a chrysanthemum print and she sported a traditional oriental hairstyle. Turkish Barbie was represented as a bejewelled belly dancer. However, since most nationalities rarely wear traditional clothes or hairstyles, what at first appears to be a pluralist inspired acknowledgement of multiculturalism can also be considered to relegate non-Western cultures to an inferior position by virtue of not being part of the modern world.

Stereotypes facilitate quick and easy recognition. They can be benign, they can even be fun, but they are always less complex than the reality they purport to represent. Like mirages in the desert, stereotypes conceive their subject as if looking from a distance but always stereotypes evaporate on closer inspection. Most importantly, stereotypes can be harmful. When wedded to foreign policy, as with the involvement of the US in the Middle East, stereotypes can have terrible consequences.

What is not represented

Web 2.6
Missing
Representa-
tions

Sometimes what is not represented can be as important as what is represented. Such subjects are like the elephant in the room: the subject no one wants to talk about. Deliberate censorship is the most obvious example, although more subtle examples can be equally influential on our understanding of the world.

Authorities censor for a variety of reasons: alleged immorality, especially related to sex, scandals that embarrass governments and the representation of leaders deemed to be demeaning. A number of examples are described below. They are drawn from different countries and times, though they are merely representative.

Political erasure

In has been a common practice for authorities to erase the memory of people who have fallen from favour by eradicating their visual representation. The ancient Egyptians practised it with four pharaohs including Pharaoh Akhenaten. In the twelfth century BCE, Akhenaten turned tradition on its head by ordering the worship of just one god, thereby rejecting Egypt's many traditional gods and completely disrupting the lives of the priesthood. Following Akhenaten's death, the priests declared him a heretic and his statues and reliefs were destroyed. He was so successfully erased, it was only during the nineteenth century that his existence come to light. The ancient Romans even had a name for the practice: *damnatio memoriae*, the damnation of memory. For the Romans, it was an especially harsh form of punishment because they believed immortality could only be achieved through being remembered in this life, not in a future one. Three Roman emperors were officially erased, the most notable being the third-century CE Emperor Geta. For years Geta

Figure 2.11a Anonymous, *Stalin, Colleagues, and the Erasure of Commissar Nikolai Yezhov* (1940).

Figure 2.11b Anonymous, *Stalin, Colleagues, and the Erasure of Commissar Nikolai Yezhov* (1940).

co-ruled with his brother Caracalla. But Caracalla had Geta murdered, and Geta's stone relief images were subsequently hacked off and his name replaced.

The Soviet Union continued the practice in both paintings and photographs. One example involved the high-ranking official Nikolai Yezhov: when Stalin had him executed, he also had him expunged from photographic memory (Figure 2.11).

Political erasures continue into recent times. Two millennia after the erasure from the historical record of Akhenaten, Mubarak, the President of Egypt for thirty years, was deposed in 2011, and shortly after, he and his wife were removed from all Egyptian monuments. When the US invaded Iraq in 2003, statues of the dictator Saddam Hussein were hauled down and smashed to pieces. In 2013, the high-ranking North Korean politician Jan Sung-take was purged from the Worker's Party of Korea and executed. When documentary footage was broadcast on North Korean television, it was edited to remove all frames in which the former politician had appeared.

In many countries, leaders past and present are often lampooned, especially in cartoons, but in many other countries this is not possible. In some Muslim countries, it is illegal to depict Muhammad in anything other than a respectful, dignified way, and in some instances those who have lampooned Muhammad have been threatened with death. In Thailand, it is illegal to represent the king in anything but a deferential way and those that have broken this law have been gaoled. In 2013, Chinese authorities banned the 1960s silk screens of Mao Zedong by US pop artist Andy Warhol. Authorities claimed that the bright red splotch on Mao's face resembled cosmetics, which they considered disrespectful to the Chairman.

Legislative erasure

Official censorship is also common with sex and illegal acts. In 1934, the US government imposed the Hollywood Production Code, which held for thirty years. According to the code, criminals were always to be shown in a negative light, and films were no longer to show adultery as justified, illicit sex as attractive, homosexuality, white slavery, reference to venereal disease, suggestive dancing or nudity. Even male actors had to keep their shirts on, and underwear was now banned even on a line with other laundry. Western standards regarding sexual imagery have changed a lot since the 1930s, though in many other parts of the world restrictions remain, especially in Muslim majority countries.

Social erasure

Popular celebrities can also fall from grace. Their visual representations disappear along with their reputations. In response to the MeToo Movement, a number of popular media celebrities have been found guilty of sexual misconduct, and consequently, their contracts cancelled and they have disappeared from public view. Similarly, sport celebrities who transgress social norms are commonly dropped by their sponsors and so no longer appear in promotional material.

Not all examples of non-representation are deliberate. Other examples are more a matter of habitual, widely shared social ways of not seeing. For example, for centuries European paintings represented the upper classes with dignity while peasants were typically represented as eating and drinking to excess. Visually reinforcing their class position, the upper classes typically appeared in the upper half of paintings and poor peasants were nearly always depicted in the bottom half. Paintings reproduced the widely shared belief among the elite classes regarding their own legitimacy and the illegitimacy of the lower classes. Only during the nineteenth century, with the rise of socialism, were peasants and the new urban working class represented with dignity by European artists; Millet's *The Gleaners*, mentioned earlier, is an example.

Consider too that in the long history of Chinese art, the representation of the suffering of poor peasants is barely present. For many centuries, Chinese elites preferred pictures of serene landscapes that celebrated the harmonies to be found in the natural world. Rugged mountain peaks, dramatic waterfalls, peaceful valleys and so on, were preferred as symbols of a spiritual connection to nature (Figure 3.9).

It has only been in the past few decades that Blacks, Hispanics, Asians, gays and even independent women, have regularly appeared on US television without being caricatured. These categories of people either simply did not appear or they were commonly represented as criminals or the butt of jokes. Fortunately, this is no longer the case.

Often censorship reflects widely held cultural sensibilities. In Western countries, it is common to hold back from representing extreme violence in the news, both on television and in print. This is particularly true of the US. Although Hollywood churns out numerous movies that contain gratuitous violence, US news outlets shy away from representing the worst of actual war. This applies not only to violence perpetrated *by* Western countries but also to violence perpetrated *on* Western forces. For example, when the terrorist group ISIS released footage of the execution of a US journalist, US newspapers refused to show the terrorist holding a knife moments before the execution, and the picture was released without the knife.

To show or not to represent real atrocities is an ongoing debate. Should the public see graphic violence in order to be better informed about the gravity of situations? Does sanitizing pictures of violence diminish an understanding of the danger inherent in terrorism? Alternatively, if such pictures were shown would the public soon become desensitized and not care? The pictures would no doubt initially shock, but would the public's response become a cry for peace, a trigger to seek revenge, or would people be bemused? Could the eventual outcome merely contribute to dehumanization and the objectification of people during war? These questions apply especially to children, the most vulnerable members of a society. Do they need special protection? As things stand, not as a matter of government decree, but as a general cultural sensitivity, representations of extreme violence are rarely shown in the West, especially in the US.

Artistic erasure

As mentioned in Chapter 1, artists often operate against the grain of society, and for this reason their work is often censored. Sometimes, artists face imprisonment. During the 1930s, the Nazis regarded avant-garde art as degenerate, exhibited it in such a way as to ridicule it, and jailed many of the artists. More recently, in 2010, Zimbabwean artist Owen Maseko was arrested and gaoled for exhibiting paintings and installations that depicted a five-year span in which the Zimbabwean army unleashed an orgy of violence against one particular tribe. As many as 20,000 civilians are thought to have been killed. Maseko's art represented how the army tortured civilians by dripping hot melted plastic on them. The exhibition was quickly shut down in an attempt at historical erasure, and like the damnation of memory, to practicse historical amnesia.

Idealized representation

Many paintings and photographs, both of people and places, sanitize or idealize their topics. The first-century Roman Emperor Caesar Augustus had his statues erected throughout the Roman Empire and although he grew old, and he is reported to have gone bald and developed bad teeth, his statues continued to show him as young, handsome and healthy. His statues stand in a long tradition of ancient Greek statues that only appear to conform to actual appearances. Even the most realistic looking statues from ancient Greece are a combination of close observation and what the Greeks considered ideal proportions; proportions that no one in the ancient world actually conformed to.

Today female fashion models are routinely photoshopped. Hairlines are raised, necks are made thinner, skin blemishes are removed, and waists and hips are made leaner, all to conform to today's conception of beauty that, again, very few if anyone actually looks like. And advertising is notorious for idealizing products as well as what might happen to those who purchase and use them. Products are photographed in a golden glow and followed by pictures of users finding their mate, landing their dream job or going on an exotic vacation.

During the eighteenth century, a huge market existed for scenes of Italy's famous cities. Artists constructed highly realistic scenes of Italy's iconic buildings. But instead of painting what could be seen from one particular vantage point, the artists combined the most famous buildings from a whole city into the one picture to produce a fantasy scene of the 'best bits'. Today, in major European cities, artists line the streets selling paintings of their cities, though now they use a kaleidoscope of fully saturated colour that, although quite unrealistic, appeals to a popular taste for beauty as a festival of bright colour.

Sometimes idealization is not just a matter of taste, but public policy. Soviet art under Joseph Stalin was highly idealized. Under the artistic policy of Soviet Socialist Realism, artists depicted ordinary daily life infused with a sense of heroism. Paintings showed daily life as if wrapped in a dream of a wonderful future. Leaders and workers alike were poured into a heroic mould that represented an uplifting, ever optimistic ideal. The goal was not to represent the way things really were, but to show the direction in which Soviet authorities claimed to be leading the population.

Closer to home, family photographs tend to idealize family life. From an early age children are coached by their parents into appropriate photographic behaviour, namely, to smile happily. When children fail to conform, parents tend to wait until the happy smile is elicited, and where the desired smile is not recorded, the pictures tend to be discarded. Photographic evidence of an unhappy child is a reflection on their parenting skills and no parent wants their own parents to think they are not doing the best possible job.

False representation

While some pictures place a gloss on reality, other pictures are deliberately false. Of course some tampering is entirely benign. Minor modification to photographs is a routine matter that compensates for the inadequacies of camera equipment and the small imperfections of real life that we do not ordinarily notice but are picked up in photographs. Cleaning dust or dirt from old negatives, or taking out a distracting element, such as a telegraph pole directly behind someone's head, does not change the meaning of a picture. Subtle retouching reduces these distractions to approximate our real-world experience. This is known as 'image processing' rather than manipulation or fabrication. Some actual manipulation is also done for aesthetic purposes without any intention to mislead. Other examples are intended as merely humorous; for example, a photo of Venice with frozen over canals, or an off-shore cargo vessel with a house sitting atop its helipad. The internet is full of such Photoshop phoniness.

Other examples are anything but benign. Ignoring facts, they represent events that never happened and people as they never were.

People as they never were

Europe has a long history of representing both enemies and marginal groups in dreadful ways. Jews were long depicted as pigs to associate them with filth. The intention was to reveal their allegedly wanton nature and thus lack of political legitimacy. Such depictions culminated in the 1940 Nazi film *The Eternal Jew*. The film also takes one of its tropes from the classic 1922 German Expressionist horror film *Nosferatu* in which the main character, a vampire, is likened to a rat. *The Eternal Jew* juxtaposes images of Jews with images of rats and cockroaches, and the voice over claims that rats, just like Jews, cause dysentery and spread diseases like plague, cholera and leprosy.

War propaganda provides many examples of outright falsity. Consider the Thirty Years' War of seventeenth-century Europe that was fought between Protestants and Catholics. Posters depicted the Pope as a devil with horns, and many images were sexual and/or scatological. The former pictures purported to represent private perversions behind the public mask while the latter represent the most socially levelling of functions. Both represented the direct opposite of the spiritual purity preached by the church. Catholics responded by portraying Luther, the leader of the Protestant movement, as only half-human, with a misshapen and hairy body.

Depicting enemies as wild animals was still used in the early part of the twentieth century. During the First World War, the Allies marshalled support for the war with posters of Germans as barbaric, as fearsome gorillas, dirty swine and mad dogs.

Events that never happened

The origin stories of different countries provide good examples of representations that never happened. Whereas history is replete with inconvenient truths, it is often reworked as pleasant, even heroic, as history becomes heritage – sweet sentiment located in the past. Heritage is history seen through a prism in which disagreeable facts are downplayed or ignored in favour of what is uplifting, wholesome and efficacious; a narrative of noble and brave deeds, idealistic visions and heroic actions. Where history is heavily loaded with despicable motives and atrocious acts, heritage is nostalgic. Heritage consoles us with tradition, rooting us in time-honoured ways of life.

For example, Emanuel Leutze' painting, *Washington Crossing the Delaware*, of 1851 depicts the most critical turning point in the Revolutionary War between what became the United States and Britain. It was a very well received painting, no doubt due in part to being historically inaccurate, much more concerned with heroism than facts (Figure 2.12). Where Washington crossed the river was rather narrow and flat ferries were used, probably fixed to a wire strung across the river. While bitterly cold, there would have been no dangerous icebergs, but like the tiny boat somewhere on what appears a substantial stretch of water, the icebergs heighten the sense of danger and the bravery required. Washington stands majestically, the embodiment of heroism, but he would never have stood up in this tiny boat; he would have capsized this too heavily crowded boat toppling everyone, including himself, into the water. This was a surprise attack; he would have been keeping a low profile. Most likely he was hunched over to protect himself against the freezing cold. He would also have been twenty years younger than depicted here. Here he is at the age he became President. And consider the people accompanying him in the boat. They do not represent his soldiers but a collection of people meant to symbolize the diversity of the United States citizenry. Additionally, although Leutze painted a forbidding sky, the actual attack took place under cover of night. But facts do not matter when creating heritage.

Figure 2.12 Emanuel Leutze, *Washington Crossing the Delaware* (1851).

Disney's animated movie *Pocahontas* (1995) tells the historically untrue but popular story of a romance between a young Indian girl, Pocahontas, and a white settler called John Smith. The film climaxes with a war between the Indians and the white settlers, which the film alleges to be due to nothing more than a failure to get along together. A clash of cultures that later saw the ideology of Manifest Density justifying the forced removal of Indians and multiple attempts at genocide is reduced to the domestic sphere in which siblings fight or neighbours bicker.

Faking photography

When photography was first invented, it was commonly believed that photography, unlike painting, was faithful to nature, an exact replica. Photography appeared to represent nothing but the truth, but from its earliest days photography was replete with examples of deliberate deception. A notable example from the 1870s involved 'spirit photographs' (Figure 2.13) that were faked by double exposing photographs of the dead with living people and passed off to relatives by charlatans to 'prove' the legitimacy of their séances. Some people even attempted to prove the existence of fairies.

Figure 2.13 *Album with Spirit Photographs* (no date).

Photographic manipulation is nothing new, but digital photography is easier to manipulate and the manipulation is much harder to detect than in conventional, film-based photography. On magazine covers, the manipulation of celebrity images has long been routine. Dark skin is lightened to make it more attractive to a predominantly white audience and thereby support, albeit subtly, racial prejudices. Bodies are also slimmed down to conform to media standards of bodily beauty, thereby creating unrealistic expectations of real bodies and viewers with low self-esteem. Even as television news broadcasts use photographic images more and more to imply the truthfulness of their reports, the credibility of the photography is increasingly questionable. Under pressure of time and strong competition from other news agencies, reporters have been found enhancing photographs for extra impact, and some war correspondents have declared that news photographs of war can no longer be trusted. When photographs have lost their credibility, what is one to believe? This is a serious matter when it comes to the verification of incidents by the military and the police.

Web 2.7
Fake News

Fake news, complete with pictures, is also destabilizing social and political discourse. Deliberate hoaxes, propaganda and disinformation are using social media to drive web traffic and amplify their effect. Unlike the satire of news, which seeks only to entertain, fake news intentionally seeks to mislead for either political or financial gain. Insidiously, some fake news bloggers doctor photographs and invent stories with the intention of gaining revenue from advertising; and foreign state actors are now routinely spreading misinformation through fake stories supported by fake imagery. During the 2016 United States presidential election between Donald Trump and Hillary Clinton, many internet sites spread false information that was allegedly confirmed with photographic proof. The Pope was alleged to support Donald Trump, and Hillary Clinton was alleged to be the recipient of millions of dollars from an infamous Mexican drug lord. A photograph of the drug lord and another of Clinton accompanied the latter item, and while the pictures were actually unrelated, the accompanying text implied that they were linked.

Sometimes the fakery is the work of partisan, but misinformed ordinary citizens, making both the ease with which fakery can be achieved and the level of people's gullibility equally dangerous. An example from the 2016 presidential election makes the point. An ordinary citizen took photographs of a large group of buses near the centre of his city and later that day he heard that there were to be protests against Donald Trump. Linking these two things, he posted the photographs on his website with the claim that the protesters were not locals but professional, paid protestors being bussed in from elsewhere. The candidate's opponents picked up his post and it quickly spread among his outraged supporters. However, the two events were unrelated. The buses were in town for an academic convention.

With film-based photography, it was sometimes relatively easy to spot these manipulations. The process of fakery took much longer than it does now with digitalization and the tools were much cruder. Heads would not look quite right when clumsily superimposed on another body, and our human eyes, hardwired for pattern recognition, could often spot anomalies between different lighting, shade, shadow and perspective.

Today, the ability to identify a fake is much more difficult. Manipulation can be achieved at the click of a mouse button: moving subjects around, changing the background, exchanging colours, softening and smoothing surfaces, altering even the angles-of-view. The credibility of photography as a truthful record is now seriously undermined. Can we now believe in the veracity of any photographic image? We should certainly be sceptical.

The posting and sharing of digital fakes is now so common that algorithmic systems have been developed to recognize the tell-tale signs of digital forgeries. It has become big business, given that verifying and certifying photographs as authentic is essential to media editors, the police, the courts and the military. Digital forensics is currently, and likely to remain, a constant battle with the forgers, much like the constant battle waged today between hackers and authorities as each develops ever new levels of sophistication. Such professional image forensics is valuable, but it is not practical or affordable for assessing the hundreds of images we see every day on social media.

Even more problematic than faked still photographs is the use of artificial intelligence to create 'deep fake' videos of people. With perfect synchronization between picture and audio, a 3D image capture is used to transfer the minute detailed movements of one person's eyes, nose, mouth and the angle of their head to another person so that it appears someone is saying something they never said. While useful in bringing actors back from the dead, its use with politicians and other officials is a clear and present danger.

However, although spotting fake photography is more difficult than it was before digitalization it is still possible to train your eyes to detect image manipulations. Questions we can ask include: Could the scene in the picture really have happened the way it is shown? Does something about the picture look too spectacular to be believable? Does the perspective appear to shift somewhere in the image (if so, it is likely that the image is a composite of two or more pictures taken from different angles)? Do the different components of the picture appear to be in proportion to one another; for example, does a person's head seem to be too big for their body or their feet too small for their height? Does furniture seem overly large or windows too small? Examine the people and things in the background. Does the picture repeat or is it reversed to create the impression of a larger number of people or things?

There are now as many internet sites instructing people on how to fake photographs as there are sites indicating how to spot fakes. Educating students on how to spot fake pictures is now one of the most important of all educational tasks. As described in the following chapter on rhetoric, discerning the credibility of a source of information has long been recognized as essential for a functioning democracy.

A final note

Pictures represent all kinds of subjects, real and imagined, true and false, but in every case their making is motivated by beliefs and values. Sometimes pictures act as propaganda, where their preferred meaning is obvious. More commonly, pictures present values and beliefs as if in the order of things, as if they were natural. In the next chapter, this distinction is described as the difference between telling and showing, between arguing explicitly or implicitly.

Questions

1 Why are the formal elements like line, colour and tone and the principles of composition such as balance, dominance and contrast inadequate to describe realistic-style pictures?
2 How does framing and angles-of-view determine our physical position as viewers? Why is this important?
3 Apart from framing and angles-of-view, which elements of realistic style pictures help determine our relationship as viewers with a picture?
4 What is a stereotype and why can they be dangerous?
5 What stereotypes might you hold about other people or other parts of the world? Are they positive, negative or benign?
6 What subjects are commonly *not* represented by pictures?
7 Can you think of examples where pictures have been doctored, situations have been sanitized, or are simply false?

Activities

1 Look up an image bank. Type in your own nationality, e.g., Australian, or some other nationality with which you are familiar. Consider if the images reflect your experience.
2 Take photographs that illustrate each of the elements of still realistic pictures and create a PowerPoint with each labelled. Alternatively, create a PowerPoint drawing upon pictures found on an internet image bank. Consider using a wide variety of picture types, such as photographs and paintings from different historical periods.
3 Collect visual stereotypes from magazines or an image bank and make a collage. Divide them up into demeaning, benign and positive stereotypes.
4 Take a photograph for an advertisement. Consider how each of the elements of realistic pictures contributes to the purpose of the advertisement.
5 Skip ahead to Chapter 10, in which a number of movie making exercises are described to explore the elements of moving pictures.

See Chapter 8 for specific questions on representation: What is the genre? What is represented? Where does it show? When was it made? When does it show? How does the picture represent what is shown?

3

Visual Rhetoric

Pictures argue

Either explicitly or implicitly, pictures attempt to argue pervasively. They are a form of rhetorical practice. Advertisements argue directly: this product brand is better quality or cheaper or safer than other brands; this political candidate has better policies or is more trustworthy than their opponent. Other pictures argue indirectly. Movies, television programmes and video games offer up values and beliefs as givens, as if in the nature of things. Whether explicit or implicit, direct or indirect, pictures make arguments about the world: what it is like, what it should be like or what it should not be like. Pictures are rhetorical.

Web 3.1
Ideas and
Arguments

The first section of this chapter shows how the concept of rhetoric was first proposed and how it was later applied to pictures, and it frames contemporary popular visual culture with an historical perspective. Readers more interested in immediate application may wish to go straight to the second section, entitled 'The elements of rhetoric', which describes how pictures work as rhetoric.

Defining rhetoric

The ancient Greek philosopher Aristotle defined rhetoric as 'the faculty of observing in any given case the available means of persuasion' (2007: 1355). Although many people have written about rhetoric since, his definition remains the most common general definition and all subsequent theorizing on rhetoric constitutes a series of amendments and clarification to his theorizing about it.

Furthermore, the origins of rhetoric remain significant for us today. Ancient Greece was ruled by an early form of democracy where leaders needed to convince each other with words rather than weapons. Even though Aristotle had public speaking in mind when theorizing about rhetoric and this book is about visual rhetoric, the point about the need to persuade remains as pertinent as it was two and a half millennia ago. Today's governments rely upon convincing their citizens of their legitimacy and not just by dint of force; and in order to thrive and prosper, commercial interests must persuade consumers to purchase their goods and services. Modern societies are saturated by rhetoric, both verbal and visual, from both governments and commercial interests.

Dialectics and rhetoric

In defining rhetoric, Aristotle made two critical distinctions. First, he distinguished between rhetoric and what he called 'dialectics'. Dialectics relied entirely on logical deduction. It examined both sides of a question to test rival claims to truth. A purely intellectual enterprise, dialectics was primarily concerned with philosophical inquiry. By contrast, rhetoric involved emotions. Public discourse, of whatever kind, invariably engaged emotion. Arguments advanced by a lawyer in a court of law, or by anyone in the court of public opinion, always involved emotion. Emotions were aroused whenever questions were raised about the expedient use of time, money and other resources; when beliefs and values were shaped by assigning people either praise or blame; and when propounding questions of truth or falsehood.

Rhetoric and the arts

Secondly, Aristotle distinguished between rhetoric and the arts, but only insofar as rhetoric made an argument directly and the arts argued indirectly. A public speaker put forward a proposition in a direct, explicit way, while the arts typically showed a situation that assumed various ideas, beliefs and values that were allowed to argue for themselves. Public speaking involved practical reasoning on particular matters, while the arts as rhetorical practice had the more general intent of educating through representation. It was through the use of emotion, imagination and pleasing forms that the arts represented ideas, beliefs and values. The significance of the arts lay not just in their ability to lift us out of our daily life, but in their power to make pervasive arguments about all kinds of important issues. The arts showed us what is funny, praiseworthy, criminal, sickening and so on. The arts illustrated social norms as well as what society considered abnormal.

With advertising, the intent is to argue in favour of buying a particular brand of shampoo, car, washing machine and so on. Advertising makes specific, direct arguments. By comparison, movies, computer games and television programmes provide sharpened and enlarged visions of life, which argue for things as they are and need to be, or things as they are and need to be changed. One presents and urges, the others represent. One tells; the others show.

Web 3.2
Advertising

What makes rhetoric work?

Aristotle argued that for rhetoric to be successful, that is, to convince an audience of the rightness of an argument, the argument needed to consist of four things: the argument had to have internal coherence, come from a credible source, arouse the emotions of the audience and be delivered in an eloquent manner. By eloquent delivery he had in mind both sensory qualities and aptness; both emotions and sensory qualities tailored to the argument. But first, it was necessary to understand what particular emotions would move a specific audience towards a desired outcome. It was critical to grasp what emotional causes lay behind the concerns of an audience and only then to adapt one's arguments to the emotions of the audience. Does the audience fear the loss of their health, wealth or safety? Is the audience envious of a rival or, more positively, does it wish to emulate a rival? Do the emotions of an audience turn to pity at someone or something, at animals or children for example? Is the audience indignant over a perceived injustice? Can pity be turned to indignation? Can indignation be turned to action? Aristotle claimed that it was only by connecting to the emotions of an audience that it was possible to lead an audience to accept the arguments being made, especially if this involved changing an audience's initial opinions. He thought that understanding the emotions of an audience was so critical to success that his most detailed examination of human emotions is linked to his discussion of rhetoric.

Rhetoric and ethics

Aristotle's theorizing on rhetoric met with strong opposition from his teacher, Plato. Plato warned against rhetoric as a dishonest practice. For Plato, emotions were impediments to reason. By means of emotional appeals, it was all too easy for unscrupulous characters to manipulate an audience to accept false arguments. Some of Plato's and Aristotle's contemporaries did indeed teach rhetoric as a means to win arguments at any cost, irrespective of their truthfulness. But for Aristotle, emotions were basic to human nature; emotions were rational responses to circumstances. Furthermore, he believed that rhetoric could be used for ethical purposes. A knowledge of rhetoric could be used to pursue admirable causes, and, just as importantly, it could be used to defend against bad arguments. By studying rhetoric, an audience could refute misleading and false arguments. Through learning how rhetoric worked, just and truthful arguments had a better chance of prevailing. Why, Aristotle asked, should people be taught to defend themselves when threatened with physical force, and not to defend themselves against injustice and falsehood? Rhetoric could be abused – he was fully aware of this – but used well in the pursuit of truth and justice, rhetoric was an ethical, ennobling enterprise.

Today, we would say that what Aristotle had in mind when addressing indirectly delivered arguments through the arts were ideological arguments; that is, ideas, beliefs and values that help frame the way people understand the world and help determine their behaviour. Ideology has a range of meanings, but it is used here to refer to ideas, beliefs and values that appear to be given, to be in the nature of things, a style of thought, a characteristic way of thinking. Ideological arguments are concerned with the way the world is, or should be, or should not be. They are typically offered as either legitimate social norms or norms in need of reform. In movies, computer games and television narratives, such norms are often merely assumed, lying in the background, and they are all the more powerful for being represented indirectly.

Specific rhetorical techniques

As well as defining rhetoric and arguing for its beneficial use, Aristotle offered specific advice on how best to use it. He advised disposing an audience favourably towards the speaker and unfavourably to the speaker's opponent. One should amplify, even exaggerate, points in favour of one's argument, and minimize and depreciate those against, always moving the listener into emotional reactions. Speakers were advised to use metaphor and simile, especially visual metaphor because it aided learning, but to avoid excess. He advised against hyperbole and signs of superfluity. It can hardly be a surprise that his advice was later applied to interpreting pictures, or that we see such advice applied to the making of pictures every day.

Fine art as rhetoric

Plato and many other philosophers were deeply sceptical about rhetoric, but Aristotle's theorizing not only prevailed, it was developed by many subsequent theorists, notably by two first-century CE Romans, Cicero and Quintilian. Cicero wrote, 'The body talks, so it is all the more necessary to make it agree with the thought ... to indicate the feelings of the mind', and Quintilian described in detail how various gestures and movements of the body 'penetrate into our innermost feelings with such power that at times they seem more eloquent than language itself' (cited in Vickers 1998: 348, 360). Together with Aristotle, their views were enormously influential, so much so that much of the history of Western fine art needs to be understood primarily as a form of rhetoric.

Web 3.3
Elegance and
Emotion

Rhetoric and the Christian church

With the establishment in the early 400s CE of Christianity as the official religion of the Roman Empire, rhetoric was first deliberately applied to visual art. Initially, some early church leaders objected. Rhetoric was pagan knowledge they said, but their objections were overruled. The church adopted rhetoric in the belief that it should be used to serve its own interests. It was too useful to ignore. Consequently, for over a millennium medieval Christian artists painted images that argued for both the rightness of the Christian faith and the legitimacy of the church. Using narratives drawn from the Bible, especially the Book of Revelation, artists painted instructive narratives with savage emotional appeal. The patronage of sadomasochistic frescoes of hell became a primary tool of the Christian message of salvation (Figure 3.1): backslide, and the most dreadful forms of hellfire awaited sinners.

On the other hand, the church also patronized pictures drawn from folk tales of early martyrs who had suffered grievously for their loyalty to the one true faith. Pictures of the martyrs stood as models of correct behaviour, asking of the faithful: What are your sufferings compared to these brave souls? They were devotional images, much like the loving images of Christ hanging from the cross with bleeding open wounds that elicited from believers a mixture of horror and pity as well as gratitude for his suffering on their behalf. Tears were taken as better proof than words of remorse for one's sins and one's love of God. Jesus, his disciples, the Virgin and Mary Magdalene were each represented in tears. Thus it was with a mixture of love and fear, the two emotions often regarded as the most primary, that the medieval church sought to consolidate its community of faithful, prevent backsliding, and deter heretics.

However, while influenced by rhetoric, medieval art was not systemically theorized. Numerous visual conventions were developed to identify specific people – St. John with a book for example – but no catalogue existed of how to represent specific emotional states calculated to arouse horror,

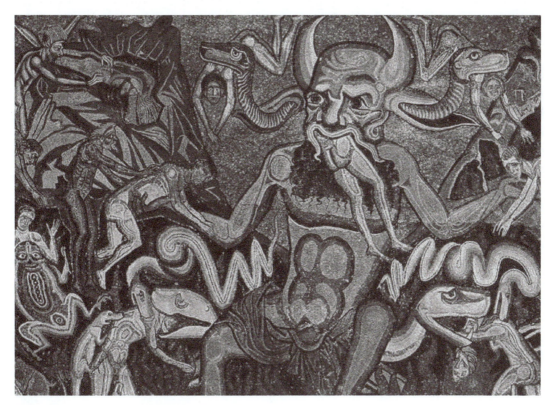

Figure 3.1 Coppo di Marcovaldo, *The Hell* (c.1301).

pity or gratitude, let alone other emotions. It was only during the Renaissance of the 1400s and early 1500s that the first systematic attempts to theorize the visual arts were undertaken, and this included how to represent a whole host of emotions. Theorists naturally turned to the then recently discovered ancient sources on rhetoric because they contained the only complete and integrated system of communication. Drawing on Aristotle as well as Cicero and Quintilian, theorists advised on artistic procedures, appropriate subject matter, stylistic considerations, even the personal character of artists, but above all the necessity to move an audience emotionally. Noting the many visual metaphors evoked by their classical models, theorists and artists alike systematically applied verbal rhetoric to visual imagery. Crucially, they drew on their ancient sources to understand how to move an audience by representing people in emotional states. The Renaissance theorist Alberti advised that nothing moved spectators more than when 'the men painted in a picture outwardly demonstrate their own feelings as clearly as possible [so that]... we mourn with the mourners, laugh with those who laugh and grieve with the grief stricken' (cited in Vickers 1988: 345–6). Like many others who were equally reliant on the classical texts, Alberti described in detail specific gestures, positions and movements of the body that best conveyed specific emotions. He and other theorists were joined in this enterprise by advocates of a system of gestures called *chironomia*. The many *chironomia* manuals illustrated numerous body positions, as well as hand and finger gestures, all with the intent of conveying specific ideas linked to emotional states (Figures 3.2 and 3.3). Although initially intended for public speakers and actors, Renaissance artists also began to use them, and thereafter it became common practice for artists to rely upon them (Figure 3.4.) The manuals were still being published, and still used, well into the 1800s.

The use of rhetorical appeals was especially notable during the heyday of the Baroque style of the 1600s when the visual arts were co-opted by the Counter Reformation. Facing the challenge posed by Protestantism, the initial goal of the Baroque was to reaffirm the Catholic faith. The Vatican sought a simple, direct style that appealed to the greatest number of people, and the artists, intimately familiar with rhetorical theory and practice, responded with highly theatrical exhibitions of extreme emotions. Painting scenes of grief, piteous suffering and religious ecstasy, artists created an audience of primed participants. The artists did not attempt to prove the validity of religious ideas or the legitimacy of the Church. Consistent with Aristotle's advice, artists first drew upon the religious assumptions of believers and then created sharp-edged, concise images intended to move viewers and touch their desires. Whether it was images of horrifying, decapitated heads, violent murders, or classical and biblical stories involving vulnerable, naked flesh, nothing was too extreme to influence faith and secure obedience. Baroque artists relied upon such devices as the mutual gaze, in which a figure in a painting looks out to directly engage the viewer, and they arranged their figures so as to incorporate the viewer within the space of a painting rather than having them appear autonomous and separate from the viewer. They also created scenes without a fixed point of reference so that everything appears in movement. By such visual means viewers were situated as participants in a profound emotional experience.

The two most famous Baroque artists were the painter Peter Paul Rubens and the sculptor Gian Lorenzo Bellini. Rubens twice painted *Massacre of the Innocents*, an event recorded in St. Matthew's gospel, in which King Herod, on hearing of a king born in Bethlehem, had all the new-born children

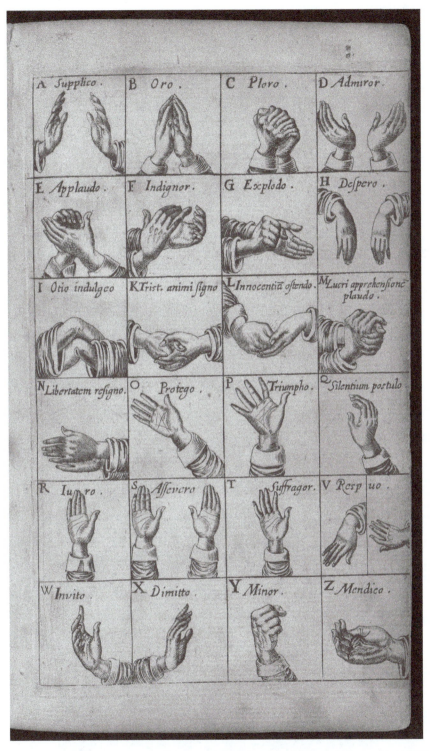

Figure 3.2 From John Bulwer's book *Chironomia, or the Art of Manual Rhetorike* (1648).

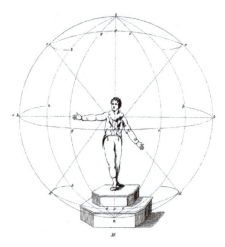

Figure 3.3 From Gilbert Austin's book *Chironomia, or a Treatise on Rhetorical Delivery* (1806).

Figure 3.4 Andrea del Verrocchio and Lorenzo di Credi, *The Virgin and Child and Two Angels* (1476–8).

Figure 3.5 Peter Paul Rubens, *The Massacre of the Innocents* (1616).

slaughtered (Figure 3.5). Rubens' 1616 interpretation shows many naked and near naked people in extremis as they are struck down; one soldier holds a baby over his head ready to dash it while a mother, hands upraised, begs for a mercy that will not be shown.

The single most iconic Baroque sculpture is undoubtedly Bellini's *St Teresa in Ecstasy* (1645–52), an idealized version of a then popular saint whose writings about her mystical experiences were widely known among the laity. She had written that God had repeatedly pierced her heart with a burning arrow. Bellini transfers God to Cupid who, holding up his golden arrow, hovers above the saint. He smiles down as she swoons, so great is her emotional commitment, in an agony of pleasure.

Rhetoric and ordinary people's internal lives

Towards the end of the 1700s some artists were influenced by the first stirrings of democratic agitation on behalf of the politically disenfranchised, and they began to imbue ordinary people with an emotional life. No longer confining emotions to the aristocracy and classical and religious figures, painters depicted the middle and lower social orders as if they too possessed an internal, felt life. Believing that the secrets of the heart could be read on the body, and that the language of

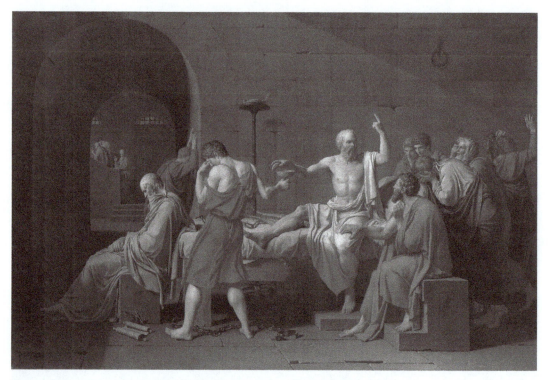

Figure 3.6 Jacques-Louis David, *The Death of Socrates* (1789).

the body was more truthful than words, artists represented everyday people sighing, swooning, exclaiming and, above all, weeping.

In France, this impetus took two different forms: the high theatricality of neo-classicism notably championed by Jacques-Louis David, and the sweet domestic scenes of rural piety and familial affection epitomized by Jean Baptiste Greuze. Intending to arouse patriotic fervour, David employed the full force of classical rhetoric to paint scenes of heroic deeds and sacrifice. He deliberately sought to arouse emotions to win support for revolutionary political struggles by posing his figures in moments of glorious, heroic pathos.

By contrast, Greuze's subjects are entirely absorbed by their own thoughts and feelings. He and his group – they were called the sentimental painters – appealed to the emerging middle class who showed a distinct taste for emotionally involving stories.

Rhetoric and public taste

By the 1800s, the primary patrons of art had shifted from the aristocracy and the church to the middle class, and painting increasingly catered to their taste. This art was known as academic art because would-be-artists were now trained in schools called Academies where they were carefully schooled in visual rhetoric. Each year their work was introduced to the public through annual exhibitions. With large crowds flocking to see what the artists had produced, these exhibitions were at the time the most popular form of visual experience. The public was simultaneously thrilled by the skills of illusion and moved by the wide variety of emotions afforded by the various genres. Paintings and sculptures offered an empire of emotional experience: amusement at the lower classes frolicking and drinking, pity for the poor evicted from their houses and now homeless, pride in victorious battle scenes, horror at disaster scenes, grief at deathbed scenes, anxiety over sick children and joy at pictures of children playing. Viewers were curious about portraits, nostalgic over ways of life now past, charmed by pictures of pretty young women and handsome young men,

Figure 3.7 Alfred Stevens, *The Japanese Parisian* (1872).

calmed by serene landscapes, thrilled by sublime mountain peaks and raging storms, delighted with scenes of happy, domestic life, enchanted by cavorting nymphs, surprised or pleasantly scandalized by the latest trend and so on. Paintings often employed a range of people in different attitudes so that viewers, whoever they were, were likely to find someone with whom to identify affectively. The artists were no longer servants of either church or state, but in seeking custom among an emotionally hungry buying public they continued to employ the rhetorical practices of emotional representation.

An aesthetics of emotion versus a rhetoric of emotion

However, beginning in the 1850s, academic art came under fire from artists who considered themselves to be avant-garde, that is, ahead of other artists as well as society in general. These artists rejected the idea of pandering to the taste of middle-class patrons and instead they saw themselves as expressing their own emotional reactions to what they saw and experienced around them.

The avant-garde break with academic art had been long in the making. Throughout the 1700s, in England, France and Germany, a very different set of ideas about the nature of art and the role of artists gradually took shape in which the rhetoric of emotion was replaced by a modernist aesthetic of emotion. Drawing upon and synthesizing a century of new ideas about art and sensory experience, the German philosopher Immanuel Kant laid down the basic principles of what became known as modernist art theory.

Kant and modernist aesthetics

Kant argued that true artists were divinely inspired geniuses whose role was to serve nothing but art itself. Artists went astray when they sought to serve others. Art was intrinsically valuable; it needed no justification beyond itself. Kant was especially critical of rhetorical practice. Reiterating the complaints of Plato and many others that rhetoric was a dishonest practice, he described it as 'the art of playing for one's own purpose upon the weaknesses of men [and] … merits no *respect* whatsoever' (Kant 1973: 193). Rhetoric existed 'for the purpose of putting a fine gloss or a cloak upon vice and error' and as the means by which one was 'artfully hoodwinked' (193). Where Aristotle had understood emotion and sensation as serving the general purpose of pedagogy and mental health, Kant conceived such aesthetic qualities as valuable in and of themselves. In creating all things anew, art was akin to divine creation. Where the arts expanded the mind by liberating the imagination, rhetoric consisted of nothing but well worn, artificial formulae. Rhetoric was utilitarian in the worst way, while the arts were completely divorced from utility of any kind. Art was utterly disinterested, blind to all practical concerns, a sacred realm that existed without rules.

Romanticism and artists' own emotions

The Romantic artists and poets of the early 1800s were deeply sympathetic to such ideas. In the words of the English Romantic poet William Wordsworth, art was either the outcome of 'a spontaneous overflow of powerful feelings' or 'emotions recollected in tranquillity' (cited in Khatchadourian, 1965: 335, 340). Whether celebrating the glories of nature, political liberation, spiritual belief or modern daily life, the point of cultural production, whether poetry, painting or sculpture, was to express the central emotional core of an artist's or poet's experience. Artists no longer served patrons by imitating the emotions of others; rather, real artists expressed their own emotions in ways that were unique to them. Emotion remained at the core of the artistic enterprise, but now, instead of a rhetoric of emotion, artists, poets and art theorists were focused upon a modernist aesthetic of emotion.

This was not aesthetics as used in the next chapter to refer to the widest possible range of emotions and sensations, but only to those considered refined and ennobling. This was aesthetics as beautiful or sublime as well as unique to each individual artist. Individual artists developed their own idiosyncratic styles, styles that best expressed their unique emotional responses to the world around them.

The ultimate artistic expression of these ideas is found, beginning in the 1870s with Impressionism, how avant-garde artists increasingly downplayed both realism and story-telling. Artists like Vincent Van Gogh and Paula Mendelsohn-Becker abstracted from nature and increasingly stressed the specifically sensory visual means characteristic of their medium (Figure 3.8).

Figure 3.8 Paula Mendelsohn-Becker, *Girl with Rabbit* (1905).

Lines, colours, shapes, tones and their composition became a primary way in which artists communicated their feelings. Then, in the early decades of the 1900s, some members of the avant-garde adopted entirely non-representational styles. Stripped of anything but form and composition, with little or no reference to the external world, their stress was entirely on their own internal life expressed in aesthetic ways.

For some theorists of modernism, it was only in the act of creation that real artists were able to articulate how they felt. Artists did not even know what they wanted to express until they had expressed it. It was the public's privilege to observe the fruits of artists' uniquely individual self-discoveries. Expressing emotion involved individual artists finding out for themselves exactly what emotion was moving them even as they were expressing it. Initially, all a true artist felt was excitement and only in the act of expressing themselves did artists discover what they were experiencing. According to these modernist theorists, it was only during the actual process of creation that artists came to understand how they felt. What the public saw was a record of their emotional journey. And, since artists came to understand their feelings at particular times and in response to particular circumstances, their emotions were particularly fitted to the circumstances that gave rise to them. Consequently, the emotions they expressed were highly individualized. For an artist, an expression of anger was not merely an instance of anger, but a particularized anger, not any expression of love but a highly specific expression of love. All artistic expressions of emotion were said to be differentiated from every other emotion of the same sort.

Such valorization of art and of artists was a response to significant changes, both specific and general, in modes of cultural production. By the middle of the 1800s, photography had taken over one of the traditional functions of fine art, that of imitation, and during the first decade of the 1900s, cinema took over the other age-old function of the fine arts, that of telling stories. Moreover, both photography and cinema largely realized these functions better than traditional fine art media. The new media were quickly used for popular purposes, especially as their emergence coincided with mass production and the unprecedented infiltration of popular culture into most peoples' daily lives. For those invested in fine art, it was essential to find other, new ways to conceptualize and value art; thus, the adoption of the modernist view that art existed for itself alone and was akin to the divine.

Reimagining the history of art as an aesthetics of emotion

Conceptualizing fine art as hovering above social utility, and aesthetic appreciation as quasi-spiritual, had two major consequences. First, it required retrospectively validating the history of art prior to the emergence of the modernist avant-garde in terms of an aesthetics of emotion, not rhetoric. The art of the past was conceived as a succession of great individual artists who stood out from their contemporaries as answerable to no one but their own imagination, artists who had developed their unique, identifiable styles. The fact that most artists, even the great ones, had long served the interests of the aristocracy or the church was wilfully ignored, as was the fact that they had deliberately sought to arouse emotions by well-understood formulae. Constructing the history of art as a history of artists renowned for their idiosyncratic emotional expression meant downplaying all the rhetorical devices they had long and intentionally employed. The fact is that in the long history of Western fine art, the use by artists of a rhetoric of emotions had been the norm; the modernist aesthetic of emotion was a historically specific aberration. This is why it is possible to draw many parallels between the history of fine art and today's popular visual culture. It is the reason this book is able to find numerous connections between the two.

The second consequence of valorizing fine art, past and present alike, led critics to denigrate popular art for its reliance upon a rhetoric of emotion. Modernist critics rightly observed that popular art expressed emotions that popular artists did not always experience themselves. Popular artists deliberately attempted to arouse emotions in others and they served interests other than their own, most commonly commercial interests. But modernist critics did more than merely describe these conditions; they condemned popular art and popular artists in the most forthright terms. Popular was crass, tacky and vulgar. It was in-your-face obvious, appealing to base instincts. When the popular wasn't silly or plain mediocre, it endangered civilized life. A rigid binary was established that strongly separated fine art from popular imagery. Fine art celebrated what was indisputably human: love, passion and an appreciation of beauty. It was set apart from all mundane considerations, an autonomous realm unto itself, while popular pictures were motivated by nothing more than grubby, monetary gain.

However, as indicated above, these distinctions are often quite false. While a clear separation between fine and popular pictures is still held in attenuated form by many people, it does not survive close examination. A clear division between fine art and popular pictures is best understood to belong to a very particular historical period that has now passed away. Postmodern theorizing has replaced modernist theorizing. The once clearly separated categories of fine art versus popular culture now overlap. The divide has imploded, the two categories often being indistinguishable from one another in terms of both their attractions and their social functions.

Thus, in the pages that follow, especially in the following chapter, it is assumed that when we experience cultural sites like theme parks, shopping malls and television, we experience them aesthetically. When we enter fast food restaurants, drive past billboards along the highway, visit casinos, collect souvenirs, surf the net, play video games or watch movies, we are subject to aesthetic appeals no less than in the presence of fine art. For the most part, we enjoy such appeals because they satisfy a basic human greed for pleasure.

The elements of rhetoric

The second section of this chapter examines the four elements Aristotle believed rhetoric relied upon for its success. To succeed in making a persuasive argument it was necessary first for the argument to be internally consistent; secondly, to understand the precise emotions of an audience; third, to deliver the argument eloquently, by which he meant both sensory qualities and aptness; and, fourth, it was critical that the audience perceived the rhetorician as a credible source.

Character and credibility

Aristotle believed that what an audience thought about the rhetorician was critical, while Cicero believed it to be the most important element. Was the rhetorician known to be honest? Intelligent? Knowledgeable? In command of the facts? Were they reliable? Could they be trusted?

Authority

One way to distil these questions into just one question is to ask about the authority of the rhetorician: is the rhetorician authoritative? World religions have long claimed the highest of authority. Judaism, Christianity and Islam base their authority upon a combination of sacred texts as well as their own traditions of belief and practice. Traditional wisdom, passed on from generation to generation, acts as an authoritative way to interpret the sacred texts for practical purposes in daily life. The authority afforded sacred texts is due to the belief that they have been either inspired by God, as in the case of Judaism and Christianity, or directly dictated by God, as in the case of Islam. Similarly, Mao's *Little Red Book* was a source of authority for the Red Guard during the Chinese Cultural Revolution of the 1960s. Whether based on authoritative texts or figures of authority, people tend to accept arguments more readily when they come with an official stamp of authority.

However, popular pictures typically lack such authority, which partly explains why people are often sceptical about arguments offered by them. The people making popular pictures are typically unknown and so lack authority, or they are known but their motives are suspected.

Advertising generally has low credibility because we all know that advertisers are intent on selling us something and that their motive is profit. This is why many product manufactures go to such trouble to appear credible, to offer products that not only fulfil the function for which they are sold, but also products that are safe to use and designed to last; in short, to be good value. Think of a car manufacturer. Do they have a good track record of producing sound, safe, reliable cars? Think of a brand of computer or mobile phone. Are they known for quality products? If the answer to such questions is positive, you will most likely be willing to believe their claims about their most recent product being good value. If their track record is poor, you are likely to be suspicious of their more recent claims. In what is called 'brand management', manufacturers go to great lengths to ensure that people trust them.

However, with movies, most people do not know the producers. We often have nothing to refer to except names of directors and producers we do not recognize. This is why movies rely so heavily on the star system – on celebrity actors who we do recognize from previous movies. Movies are frequently promoted on the basis of the actors' names and what movies they have appeared in previously. While this is no guarantee that a movie is worth watching, it is at least a recommendation by association with a familiar product.

Is anything different on the internet? When purchasing products and services from the internet often the first and only interaction we have as consumers is a company's website. To overcome this lack of brand recognition, companies try to establish credibility by the use of professional looking logo designs that are synergetic with their product and service. To help lend credibility to their claims of reliability they ensure that their website design uses an appropriate colour scheme, which extends and complements the logo design.

Personal authority

Many products and services employ celebrity endorsements. A celebrity may lack authority because they lack full competence to endorse but audiences assume that they would not risk their reputation by endorsing a poor product or service. Yet to succeed, celebrities must appear reliable, believable and informed. Depending upon the particular product or service, they may also need to appear kind, sympathetic, selfless and virtuous, and each of these characteristics is helped by appearing calm rather than anxious, relaxed rather than tense and poised rather than nervous.

The same applies to political advertising. We are much more likely to believe claims made by a politician we already support than from a politician we have not previously supported. When politicians make claims it is now common for fact checkers to run through their claims indicating to what extent, if at all, the claims are true. Too many white lies, fudging or outright untruths, and the credibility of a politician is usually damaged. Such rapid fact checking today is possible because of the availability of so much data on the internet.

Photographic authority

As discussed in the previous chapter, the authority of photographs as evidently true is now seriously undermined by digitalization. Seeing is no longer believing. The character of the source remains as important to us as it was to Aristotle, but it has never been more problematic.

Web 3.4
Photographic
Authority

Ideology or argument

As rhetoric, pictures make arguments. Television advertising, posters for social causes and internet sites for political issues each argue directly. Movies and television programmes argue indirectly. Either way, pictures offer viewpoints about a wide range of issues, and in this sense they are all ideological. *Ideology* is used here in the sense of a characteristic way of thinking, a style of thought, an interpretive scheme employed by us to make the world intelligible to ourselves. For example, today most of us would affirm the idea that men and women are equal; that is, the ideology of gender equality. We reject the ideology of patriarchy in which men are claimed to be inherently superior to women.

The word ideology is derived from the word idea. However, ideology refers not just to ideas, but to big ideas, ideas by which people live. Ideologies frame the way we understand the world and consequently operate within it. They are ideas that most of the time we take for granted, and are also confirmed by our daily life. Ideologies appear to be in the nature of things, to be natural, to be givens. They appear to be true and unarguable. Yet at different times in history and/or in different contemporary societies, every ideology has been, or remains, contested. The equality of men and women, for example, is historically a fairly recent idea, and not everyone accepts it even today. For most of human history and in most societies, men were regarded as superior, the inherent inferiority of women taken for granted. The fact that today gender equality appears to most people to be a foundational truth should not blind us to the fact that it is an ideology. Gender equality may present itself to us as true, but it is important to keep in mind that it is an idea. This applies of all our ideas, values and beliefs. No matter how much ideologies appear to be true, someone, somewhere has held an opposite perspective. Ideologies are not true so much as they are arguments as to what is true.

Ideologies are powerful arguments and pictures are carriers of ideology. Movies, television programmes, newspaper and magazine photographs each communicate ideas, values and beliefs; in short, they embody ideologies. To use Aristotle's language, pictures almost always offer arguments. Pictures offer arguments about the world as it is, should be or should not be. Some ideologies are political, others relate to religion and social issues. Apart from ideas about gender, there are many ideologies concerned with the environment, religion, politics, social norms, war, social organization, children, pedagogy and human nature. Each of these topics is discussed below, but there are many others.

Patriarchy versus gender equality

Patriarchy might be expressed by the following attitudes: a man's job is to earn money whereas a woman's job is to look after the home and family; if jobs are scarce, the wife shouldn't work and even if the wife works, the husband should be the main breadwinner. By contrast, the ideology of gender equality might be expressed by the following beliefs: in a successful marriage, the partners must have the freedom to do what they want individually; and if a husband and wife both work full time, they should share household tasks equally. In the United States both these positions have long been the subject of situation comedies (sit coms) on television. Older sit coms from the 1950s and 1960s typically assumed patriarchy by representing men working and women as homemakers, although much of the humour arose from resistance to this arrangement by showing women as more intelligent and practical than the men. More recent sit coms repeatedly assert gender equity as the accepted norm, with the humour often arising from men who challenge it being the butt of the jokes.

Environmentalism

Environmentalism may be expressed in such terms as: for our survival as a species, it is essential to preserve, restore and improve the natural environment; we must limit pollution; we must protect plant and animal diversity; and it is humanity's role to take responsibility for the caretaking of creation. The argument is often dependent upon exceptionally good photography of sublime landscapes to show how things should be and will remain with help. Alternatively, the photographs highlight environmental degradation and pollution to argue for action against such sights.

Religion

Anti-religious ideologies include the view that religion has a dangerous tendency to promote violence, and in Marx's famous words, that religion is the opiate of the people. For their part, all religious beliefs are ideological; if not always in practice, they help frame ideal ways to think and behave. Both Christianity and Judaism teach that believers should act towards others as they would have them act towards themselves, and Christianity teaches that one should love even one's enemies. Buddhism teaches that one must act with respect, generosity, self-control, honesty and compassion; that it is important to be mindful of one's thoughts, feeling and actions; and that one should not only provide for one's own needs but serve others and improve the human condition. While certain Islamic jihadist sects now teach a radically exclusive doctrine that includes the killing of all non-Muslims, and even Muslims not of their sect, mainstream Islam teaches that drawing closer to God leads one to do good to others and refrain from wrong-doing in daily life. All pictures of Jesus, as a babe in arms or a man hanging on the cross, all the images of the Buddha, sitting or standing, and all the intricate Islamic patterns, embody the arguments for their respective faiths. Consider too the confluence of Confucianism, Buddhism and Daoism in medieval Chinese paintings (Figure 3.9).

Figure 3.9 Li Cheng, *A Solitary Temple Amidst Clearing Peaks* (tenth century).

Landscapes expressed the Confucian sense of ordered relationships, the Daoist renunciation of city life in favour of the natural world and the mystical emotional power of Buddhism. Men of noble character were symbolized by birds and bamboo, pine trees and plum blossoms, chrysanthemums, egrets, gulls, geese and ducks. Peonies and peacocks were symbols of wealth and rank, while tall pine trees and ancient cypresses were symbols of constancy and righteousness. In this way, paintings of the natural world were made to symbolize moral and ethical values. They served the pedagogical purpose of instructing viewers on the social norms of good and wise behaviour.

War

Ideologies about war are often particularly powerful. Whereas in normal civilian life it is a crime to kill someone – it is murder – killing the enemy in war is justified as a necessary evil. What is normally criminal is transformed into a noble, honourable and praiseworthy act. What is condemned in civil life is condoned in war. Similarly, while suicide is normally viewed as pathological, sacrificing one's life in war is viewed as a sacred act. These ideologies can be held so strongly that people are indeed prepared to die for them. They appear threaded though many war movies, especially films made during times of war. During periods of peace, anti-war films emerge, with quite different assumptions about the waste of human life, the corruption of war profiteers and the incompetence of politicians.

Society and government

While ideologies of war and anti-war are similar everywhere, the West and the East have quite different ideologies about social relationships, and these ideologies influence their different ideologies about political and economic arrangements. In Western countries, there is a tendency to stress the ideology of individualism, that is, the view that individuals are of inherent worth and have the right to pursue their own dreams. It is an ideology that is repeatedly asserted in films and television programmes especially from the United States. Individualism undergirds capitalism with its belief that the economy is best owned by individual people and self-governing companies, not by the government.

By contrast, Eastern countries tend to stress the ideology of collectivism, that is, a belief that individuals should forgo their own desires not only for the greater good of their group but for their own happiness. Like Western films that assert the values of individualism, Asian films tend to assume the values of collectivism as self-evident. Collectivism undergirds socialism, with its belief in the collective or governmental ownership and administration of the means of production and the distribution of goods and services. In this way, in both the West and the East, the values expressed in the principal forms of cultural production largely echo the economic arrangements of their respective societies. In each case an ideology regarding social relationships supports and is supported by ideologies on how best to govern and how best to organize the economy. Thus, ideologies support one another, and this kind of mutual support helps them to appear self-evidently natural.

Children and education

That ideologies are mutually supporting is equally illustrated by ideologies held by educators about children and their education. Both children and education are subject to a range of ideological positions that extend to assumptions about political and social systems and beyond, to ideas about human nature itself. These ideologies nestle within each other. A common view about children is that they are by nature essentially innocent and thereby should be given freedom to pursue their own inclinations. On the other hand, others hold that children are essentially bad and need to be disciplined for both their own good and the good of society. Are children inherently good or bad, angels or devils, or are they both? Do children have a natural inclination towards altruism and cooperation, or are they essentially self-centred, even malevolent? If they need constant surveillance, is it because they are vulnerable to influence and need protection from unhealthy social realities or because they are prone to getting themselves into trouble?

Ideologies regarding the essential nature of children help determine ideologies of education. Is the purpose of education to ensure that students acquire understandings about the great ideas of civilization or to acquire a common core of knowledge? Or should education help each student to fulfil his or her own individual potential? Should education serve society by ensuring that students become good citizens? Should education focus on the whole child, not only their intellectual life but also their emotional and spiritual life? Could the purpose of education be to teach students how to address social questions and create a better society?

Each of these question draws upon different pedagogic ideologies. Some questions refer to a didactic pedagogy where knowledge is directly imparted from teacher to student. Others would use a self-discovery pedagogy where children are left to learn by observation and experiment. Others require a combination of didacticism and self-discovery. Movies and television programmes that deal with education invariably reflect one or more of these views; showing teachers struggling with students and/or students misunderstood by their teachers are grounded in these different ideologies.

Many ideological arguments

Below is a list of further ideologies and how they are typically expressed in words, although the statements are only examples. They variously relate to politics, religion, personal philosophies and ways of life. Consider which ones you wholeheartedly believe in, which ones you question and which ones you reject. You may even find some to be abhorrent. But remember that in each case, some people hold the opposite view; there are counter ideologies for each one listed.

(Technological Utopia) Technology will solve our social problems.
(Intuitionalism) When in doubt it is best to trust your instincts.
(Traditionalism) Wisdom is found in previous experience and older ways of doing things.
(Isolationism) We should leave other countries alone.
(Authoritarianism) Authorities know best.
(Totalitarianism) We need leadership from an all-powerful central government.

(Consumerism) A good life is a goods life.

(Fatalism) We are powerless to act; we are in the hands of fate.

(Pragmatism) What works best is best.

(Consequentialism) What is good is whatever is good for the largest number of people.

(Homophobia) Homosexuality is disgusting and/or unnatural.

(Anti-Semitism) The Jews are to blame.

(Anti-ageism) Older people should be treated with respect.

(Racism) Some races are superior to others.

(Racial Equality) All races are equal.

(Puritanism) Idle hands are the devil's playground.

(Xenophobia) Foreigners are suspect/dangerous/dirty, etc.

(Pluralism) We should tolerate all beliefs and values.

(Work ethic) Working hard is its own virtue.

(Sexism) Men are superior to women.

(Reverse Sexism) Women are superior to men.

(Progressivism) Progress is inevitable and good.

These and many other ideologies commonly manifest themselves in popular culture.

Star Wars example

Blockbuster movies typically embody arguments that almost anyone could agree upon. Consider the 2016 Star Wars movie, *The Force Awakens*, which is a sequel to the original trilogy of movies from the 1970s. The more recent film reworks arguments made in the earlier films. It makes at least three major arguments. First, it is both wise and good to respect elders. Luke Skywalker's curmudgeonly uncle, appears to repress the boy, but the older man also keeps Luke safe and raises him to be self-reliant. While Luke sometimes chafes against his uncle's authority, he retains respect for him, which helps establish Luke's sound and virtuous character. Even the primary antagonist, Darth Vader, respects an elder, listens to, and obeys him. This is the ideology of anti-ageism.

A second argument is that co-operation between people of different backgrounds creates good outcomes. Among the other characters in the film are a princess, a scoundrel and a farm boy, and while they each have very different backgrounds, they unite against a common foe. In times of war and/or tyrannical oppression, the characters demonstrate that it is not only working together that enables success but the power of their difference. This is the ideology of pluralism.

A third argument is made that human intuition should not be underestimated because it often trumps technology. In a critical, climatic scene Luke realizes that a technological solution is inadequate and that instead he should trust his own intuition and rely on the mysterious quasi-spiritual 'force'. This is the ideology of intuitionism.

Emotion

Emotion is the third essential element of rhetoric. As indicated in the first half of this chapter, emotions have been used to persuade people about ideas, beliefs and values since ancient times. Arguments are so much more persuasive when emotions are stirred. But why? What are emotions that they should be so powerful? And why are pictures capable of drawing us in through emotional appeals, let alone able to undermine reason and accept arguments we might easily reject if they were not so laden with emotion? The remainder of this chapter addresses each of these questions. It considers what emotions are and how important they are to us; how much pleasure we derive from the arousal of emotions by pictures, as well as a range of specific reasons why pictures are able to arouse emotion and so act as rhetorical forms of communication.

Defining emotion

First, what exactly are emotions? A typical, general definition is that emotions are conscious mental states experienced as strong feelings directed towards a specific object and typically accompanied by physiological and behavioural changes in the body. Emotions are coping mechanisms for situations that have triggered the emotion, and they help us appraise the significance of an event to our own well-being. Emotions also help determine how we view the world. When sad, everything around us looks grey and it is difficult to focus; when in love, the whole world seems to be in love.

Emotions are closely related to feelings, but usually feelings are considered milder than emotions, more diffuse, and less publicly expressed. However, the line between emotions and feelings is often unclear, as the above definition indicates, in which emotions are defined in part as strong feelings. Consequently, most discussions of emotion use *feeling* as a synonym, and this practice is followed here.

Emotions motivate action. Some people claim that at the root of all our numerous motivations there are only two emotions: love and fear. Yet we commonly experience love, hate, joy and sorrow, and there are many others besides. The following is only one list. Feel free to add your own.

Joyful	Tender	Helpless	Defeated	Enraged
Cheerful	Curious	Powerless	Bored	Outraged
Content	Adoring	Dreading	Rejected	Hostile
Proud	Fond	Distrustful	Disillusioned	Bitter
Satisfied	Receptive	Suspicious	Inferior	Hateful
Excited	Delighted	Disturbed	Grieving	Spiteful
Amused	Shocked	Overwhelmed	Helpless	Vengeful
Elated	Interested	Uncomfortable	Isolated	Disliked
Enthusiastic	Exhilarated	Guilty	Numb	Resentful
Optimistic	Dismayed	Hurt	Ambivalent	Alienated
Elated	Amazed	Lonely	Exhausted	Bitter
Delighted	Confused	Melancholic	Regretful	Indifferent

Calm	Stunned	Depressed	Ambivalent	Insulated
Relaxed	Intrigued	Hopeless	Exhausted	Distrustful
Hopeful	Absorbed	Sad	Insecure	Scornful
Pleased	Eager	Sorrowful	Preoccupied	
Confident	Hesitant	Uncertain	Angry	
Brave	Worried	Anguished	Jealous	
Comfortable	Anxious	Disappointed	Annoyed	
Compassionate	Insecure	Self-conscious	Humiliated	
Aroused	Horrified	Shamed	Irritated	

Web 3.5
Emotional
Persuasion

Emotions and physiological reactions

Some psychologists claim that physiological changes cause emotions; others claim that emotions cause physiological changes; and still others believe that emotions and physiological changes provide feedback to each other. What can be said with indisputable certainty is that emotional reactions are made apparent to both ourselves and others through a very wide range of physical changes. These physiological changes can occur in numerous combinations, so that there may be as many manifestations of emotion as there are emotions. Just a few include heart pounding, trembling, laughing, frowning, as well as smirking, sniggering, smiling, snarling, striking and sweating. Consider how various visceral reactions interact when crying. They might begin with a familiar burning in the back of your throat, a momentary tightening of the muscles behind your palate, a tingling in the sinuses, and then your eyes might suddenly begin stinging as they fill and gush with tears. This is only one possibility for there are many ways to cry, including cackling, bleating, braying, howling, screeching, shrilling, sobbing, weeping and wailing. One can also cry quietly, out loud, bitterly or with joy. The Oxford English Dictionary lists ninety-seven ways to cry.

Emotion and cognition

Recent neurological research indicates that emotion is not a single and separate system of our brains, but rather emotions activate neural circuits across our entire brains. Contrary to the long-held Western belief in a separation between the head and the heart, emotions cannot be separated from cognition. We use emotions to help us think and we use cognition to help us feel. Consider voting patterns. In elections, it is apparent that people do not make rational choices based upon their economic interests, but rather on how candidates affirm their emotional lives. Successful candidates are not those who are necessarily expected to deliver on promises but those who make voters feel as though they are understood by them because they share similar emotional responses.

Pictures and emotion

Whether pictures are conventionally considered fine art or popular art, and whether still like a painting or moving like a movie, an emotional response is frequently elicited. Emotion is typically aroused by love vanquishing evil, good triumphing over evil, self-sacrifice, the contraction of a serious disease, and death. We cheer, loathe, feel the pain of, and weep for characters like us, or who we recognize we have become, or not become, may never become, or fear we might become. We cry with characters that remind us of the relationships in our lives that we lack, and we are filled with gratitude for the relationships we do have. We are moved when pictures take us somewhere we do not expect. But often we are especially shaken up when characters are unable to articulate their own feelings. They unsettle us, making us shift through our own personal histories knowing that the characters hint at feelings we ourselves may not be able to name.

Aristotle long ago noted that narrative structures are driven by turnarounds, discoveries and the occasional catastrophe, and, furthermore, that these are the most emotionally charged parts of any narrative. Turnarounds typically occur when a hard heart is suddenly softened, where a character who has displayed nothing but resistance finally relents, or where something is revealed about characters that makes their actions explicable. Much as we are in real life, we are shocked when there is an unexpected death of a sympathetic figure, and we rejoice when we are led to expect death and there is a recovery. Moreover, sometimes we can be deeply moved, even cry, at pictures we know to be manipulative, even while resenting their effect upon us. Even the stalest formulae can sometimes work havoc on our hearts.

Why do our emotions affect us?

None of the above descriptions addresses the question: Why are we attracted to pictures that arouse our emotions? This includes emotions we may not fully recognize or understand, or, in recognizing them, wish we did not? Why do we weep? Or conversely, why does our blood boil? While it makes intuitive sense that we seek entertainment that maximizes pleasure and minimizes pain, what sense is there in choosing entertainment with counter hedonistic emotions like fear and sadness? It is clearly pleasant to feel love, joy and happiness, but why is it also pleasant to feel fear, sadness, to grieve and even to cry? These are important questions because understanding what arouses emotion leads to understanding how we can be manipulated by arguments couched in emotional terms.

Perhaps there is no single reason. Just as there are many emotions, and many emotions that pictures arouse, there appear to be different reasons for responding emotionally. In what follows, a number of reasons are described.

Escape through distance

Highly emotional pictures can act to help us escape from our own actual circumstances. We may seek to experience pain that is about, yet not about, our own losses, of the pain of love lost, roads not taken, of romances kindled and failed. We may even use popular media to sustain feeling blue in the belief that by such means we will learn from the experience, thus avoiding immediate pleasure for the sake of a longer-term positive outcome. Think of someone undergoing a trauma like a major surgery with all of its physical pain and anxiety; in watching a movie about the suffering of other people, one's own world might be dissolved in tears and virtually disappear.

For this to work, however, they would need some distance from the experience, and this is just what mediated experience provides. It is often called 'aesthetic distance', in which we are both simultaneously involved emotionally and yet not wholly involved.

As viewers, we strike a balance between being both a participant in, and an observer of, mediated experience. Too much distance and we feel nothing; too little distance and the experience remains overwhelming. By establishing an optimum distance, we may simultaneously retain our own identity yet also identify with the pain of others. Consider a soap opera character whose love life suddenly turns sour or a fine art devotional picture, for example, of Jesus cruelly and unjustly crucified.

Identity and identification

Pictures offer the opportunity to imagine ourselves in them. While fictional characters in movies and television programmes are known to be constructed, to be products of writers and realized by actors, we tend to follow them as if they were real people and feel able to imaginatively enter into their worlds. We empathize. It is comforting to realize that others experience similar things and respond with similar emotions as ourselves. To this end we often cultivate emotional experiences in order to have our emotional attachment about the world confirmed. For example, many people believe that ultimately justice prevails, and numerous popular narratives reinforce this view by ending happily. Viewers suffer along with the protagonist on the understanding that eventually the tables will turn. Alternatively, many current US television dramas like *Law & Order* and the *CSI* series usually end ambiguously, which appears to echo the now pervasive lack of moral certitude that characterizes much of today's world. Either way, whether seeing the world in terms of the ultimate triumph of justice or of ambiguity, there is comfort in having one's worldview confirmed.

Consider soap operas. Women are the primary audience, and surveys suggest that many women tend to regard the most realistic narratives as those that contain events similar to their own lives. Furthermore, narratives that evoke the strongest emotions are those that replicate viewers' own family dynamics. Soaps are a major television genre, with many countries producing their own indigenous kinds, but despite national differences, soaps typically employ the same conventions: multiple, convoluted plots involving romance, secret relationships, extra-marital affairs, real love, chance meetings, coincidences, mysterious strangers, unexpected calamities, crime and last-minute rescues. Viewers identify with the characters by seeing in them something of themselves; and viewers participate in the fictional characters' lives by making ongoing decisions about their behaviour. Has a character made the right decision? Should he or she have left that relationship, made that offer, taken that job, started that affair?

Identification can also be highly personal, and sometimes we may not initially understand our emotional reactions. Our tears may seem inexplicable, with no apparent connection between our lives and a particular movie or television programme. Only on reflection will it emerge that a common emotional core links our lives to fictional figures and/or a fictional situation. For some people, such links are to scenes of death and departure, such as members of families saying goodbye. For others, who have survived terrible circumstances, the link may not be to death but to the determination to live. For still others, the link may be to the pain experienced by those left behind, cut off from the love of family.

Human attachment

Emotional expression is not only an individual behaviour; it is also reciprocal. Emoting is often intended to call forth a response from others and usually it succeeds. Emotions are critically important to our species every bit as much as logical reasoning, perhaps even more so, and showing emotion is part of an inherited, inborn method of establishing and maintaining bonds between people. Crying, for example, helps develop child/parent bonds, and this symbiotic relationship thereafter continues throughout our lives by means of shedding tears. The hardwired cry of infants finds its adult counterpart in calling out to friends and family for support and the corresponding response of caregivers to an infant's cry is replayed by adults as empathy towards others. We humans are highly dependent on the support of others, not only at birth, but also throughout our lives, so it is biologically sensible that in healthy humans closeness is pleasurable and separation is painful. We rely on behaviours that incline us towards each other and keep us there; or alternatively, considering this idea from a purely hedonistic perspective, feeling compassionate for a suffering victim or empathizing at another's loss means being able to feel a desirable social trait.

Almost anything can make us cry, and like other emotional expressions, crying is almost always in some way related to attachment, either gaining it or losing it. People cry over images that are either too full of emotion or empty of emotion. Either images overflow with emotion and overwhelm us, or there is a deficit of emotion and we feel bereft. In Christian theology, this equates to being either overwhelmed by the gift of God's grace, an undeserved but unconditional acceptance for which believers feel profoundly grateful, or its opposite, a realization by believers of their separation from love, a sense of being cast out, a stranger to God's love and protection.

In today's rationally ordered society, one of the few places it is socially permissible to cry is in front of mass media. Crying helps establish bonds of community through a mutual recognition of love and loss. Classic melodrama worked on alternating between these polar opposites; one minute characters were connected with each other and the next minute they were torn apart, and often just as quickly they were reunited. In the many forms that melodrama takes today, this oscillation continues to work because it dramatizes both attachment and its lack, the foundation of our very being, the basic tension that structures our lives as both individuals and social animals.

Participation

Although emotional scenes dramatize our own need for attachment, they also call forth an emotional reciprocity from viewers. The reciprocal relationship between characters represented in pictures is repeated between them and ourselves as viewers. We fall into the imagery; we participate. We become absorbed. Watching an emotionally moving scene we may slip into acting in it.

Pictures welcome our participation as viewers, and, in turn, we play an active part, entering into the picture's emotional reality. Like Baroque paintings discussed earlier, photographs, movies and television dramas are often structured with a space to allow us to fall into. A space is deliberately left open for us to enter in and participate. Sometimes fictional characters engage us with a mutual gaze, though more often figures appear self-absorbed in their own lives, in which the absorption of the characters acts as an invitation to step into the scene with our own emotions, to empathically join in the scene and engage with the characters.

Television soap operas offer a clear example. While the programmes are often simplistic and excessive, viewers' emotional responses are not necessarily those of the programmes. Soaps follow a wave pattern, building affective peaks, followed by an undertow, but although the emotions of the audience also typically follow waves, they are often quite different waves. The response to characters expressing angst is often irritation, impatience, or annoyance, not empathy. While soaps structure the affective responses of the audience, they do not dictate them.

This is why a textual analysis of pictures is never adequate to understand them. It is easy to dismiss the hyper-emotional register of soap operas and other melodramatic forms as simplistic and manipulative without an understanding of what they call forth in viewers. When audience response is considered, melodrama invariably turns out to be infinitely more complex, ambiguous, and multi-layered than one would gather from a purely textural study.

Tearing up, tearing away and tearing down

In melodramatic narratives tears are often used as a turning point in a plot. Sometimes they bring closure; at other times they signal that further revelations are to come. The narratives develop to a point where either characters tear up or, alternatively, motivated by their deep emotion, characters tear away to tear down their antagonist. Think of action movies in which, typically, a sequence of events starts strong to arouse interest. The hero and the villain are each introduced along with the cause of the conflict. The plot develops as the villain obstructs the hero in his or her goal, the hero fights back but only to be cut down by the villainy of the villain. As audience members we are taken on a roller coaster of positive and negative emotions, love and sympathy for the hero and contempt for the villain, as well as the desire to see the hero's final comeback. We revel in deploring the villain's evil deeds and then cheer as the hero overcomes seemingly insurmountable odds to demolish the villain.

No matter what form melodrama takes today it is at root an excessive mode that articulates moral conflicts in a secular, post-sacred society. Melodrama is a sensibility where a lack of faith in a divine order has been replaced by a sensibility where the private and personal spheres have become a major realm of personal significance.

Yet long before the invention of melodrama as a genre the essential idea of the genre, suffering virtue, had been employed for millennia. Numerous paintings and narratives have been based on innocents betrayed, undeserved pain, unrecognized worthiness and so on, including many exemplars from Greek tragic drama and much of Shakespeare among them. In fiction, we reverse the values we hold in life. We enjoy the spectacle of virtue undergoing great ordeals, even the most dreadful efforts directed against virtue.

Aesthetic eloquence

Aristotle's final feature of rhetoric he called 'the eloquence of the delivery', what in the next chapter is referred to as aesthetics. With aesthetics, not only is emotion activated in the cause of persuasion but many kinds of sensory pleasures.

Summary

The chapter applied the ancient concept of rhetoric to pictures, past and present, to fine art as well as contemporary popular mass media pictures. Rhetoric involves persuading people of arguments. While advertising pitches its arguments directly, paintings, movies and television programmes alike make their arguments indirectly by representing people and situations imbued with beliefs and values that appear natural. Learning the tricks of rhetorical practice enables viewers to critique and when necessary, to better resist arguments laden with emotion. The chapter envisaged much of the history of fine art as rhetoric. It also focused on the kinds of ideological arguments that pictures commonly make as well as two of the three elements that rhetoric relies upon for success, namely the appearance of a reliable source and strong emotional appeals.

Questions

1 The study of rhetoric arose at a particular time and place. Why was this?
2 How is it possible to use the theory of rhetoric to study both fine art and popular mass media?
3 What are the differences between a rhetoric of emotion and an aesthetic of emotion?
4 From the list of ideologies, which ones do you agree with, are unsure of, and reject?
5 What ideologies do you hold about education? How do these ideologies relate to ideologies about students and beyond, to human nature in general?
6 Why do emotions have such a strong hold on us?
7 What emotional connections do you find between your life and your favourite movie or television programme?

Activities

1 Choose a picture (still or moving) and first identify what argument or arguments the picture appears to be trying to make. Then ask the following questions: Does the picture argue directly or indirectly? How is the argument or arguments made? Does the source of the picture appear credible? If credible, is credibility based on authority, celebrity association, or some other means? Does the picture attempt to engage you emotionally? Using the list of emotions provided in this chapter, can you identify which emotions are expressed? Are you persuaded? Why? Why not? If there is more than one argument, do they support one another? Are the arguments based on some basic ideology about human nature? Does the argument(s) rely on downplaying or refusing to acknowledge other points of view? To refer back to the previous chapter, does the argument involve idealization? To what extent does the argument(s) rely upon factors that are not pictured but instead require a knowledge of the maker's intentions and/or other contextual considerations?

2 Choose a picture that appears confusing or a puzzle. Consider how the argument could be made clearer. Do some aspects of the picture need to be emphasized, deemphasized or eliminated? Does something not included need to be introduced?

3 Collect pictures that make a similar argument. For example, collect pictures that have as their underlying argument the benefits of technology or family or leadership.

4 Collect pictures that make different arguments about the same topic that offer quite different, even opposing views.

5 Choose a picture and ask what emotions you think you are feeling in response to the picture. Again, use the above list of emotions to identify what emotions are aroused. What features of the picture appear to be evoking such emotions? Consider why there can be a disjunction between emotions expressed and our reactions as viewers.

10 Make your own advertisement trying to argue as clearly as possible for your product or service using 'all the available means of persuasion'.

See Chapter 8 for specific questions on rhetoric: Who is the picture intended for? Why was the picture made? How does the picture attempt to seduce? What use is made of emotions?

The Pleasures of Aesthetic Seduction

Aesthetics defined

The term *aesthetics* has a long and complicated history and it is currently used in different ways, so it is important, first, to understand how it is being used here. Aesthetics refers here to a wide range of sensory and emotional lures. By contrast, aesthetics is still commonly equated with beauty and considered to be entirely positive and equated with high moral purpose. This latter view, first developed in Europe during the eighteenth century, was until recently highly influential; it informed theorizing about modernist art for two centuries. A postmodern view of aesthetics – the one used here – is very much more inclusive. A postmodern view refers to all kinds of visual appearances, their effects upon us, and the desires we bring to pictures. Although the modernist equation of aesthetics with just beauty is still widely employed in art, art education and literature, outside these specialized areas, aesthetics today commonly refers to many more forms of appearance than beauty and many experiences other than moral or spiritual uplift.

Today, aesthetics has returned to the original ancient Greek sense of *aesthesis*, from which the word aesthetics is derived. The ancient Greeks used *aesthesis* to refer to things that could be perceived, by contrast to things like unicorns that could only be imagined. This means that today aesthetics refers to things that are not only attractive and life enhancing but also to things that are repugnant and life damaging. For the Greeks, *aesthesis* was an inclusive concept that incorporated all perceptions and their effects, not just the beautiful and its appreciation, but also the unpleasant, the crude and rude, as well as their effects upon us. This means considering the effects on our guts as much as on our minds, of both the disquieting and the uplifting. As viewers, we can be pleasantly seduced as well as hit over the head, bored, and lulled to sleep by pictures. Pictures can heighten sensory awareness, but also dull it. All the sense perceptions that were deliberately excluded from consideration by modernist art theory are hereby reintroduced into consideration as aesthetic. While modernist aesthetics was based on a deliberate suppression of bodily sensations in favour of mindful activity, postmodern aesthetics abandons this separation of mind and body in favour of their integration. Modernists were concerned with what they considered good taste, or restrained responses, a concern that was based primarily in middle class disgust at the vulgar pleasures of the working class. But from a postmodern perspective, aesthetics refers to all kinds of sensory and emotional pleasures.

A pluralist view of aesthetics

Consider the following ways in which aesthetics is used today. The aesthetics of the weather refers to all the many manifestations of the weather, though especially the sublime nature of features such as

Figure 4.1 Charles-Andre van Loo, *Sultante* (1753).

thunderstorms and rainbows. Sport aesthetics refers to especially fit bodies making eloquent moves; camp aesthetics to deliberate ostentation, to an exaggerated, affected theatricality; kitsch aesthetics to mass-produced sentimental, cheesy pictures that surprise; grotesque aesthetics to exaggerated strange, weird things that can be disquieting or even disgusting. Aesthetic dentistry refers to shiny white and perfect teeth; the aesthetics of plastic surgery to the enhancement of the body to conform to conventional standards of attractiveness; cute aesthetics primarily to young animals and humans that charm. Trash aesthetics uses bright, garish colours and crude representational skills. Today, cool aesthetics can refer to just about anything, though originally it referred to carefully composed restraint. Domestic aesthetics refers to how we decorate our own living spaces, of which there is an infinite variety.

Additionally, just as we can refer to art styles as having a particular aesthetic, so various kinds of popular culture have their own aesthetic styles. European fine art styles include the Renaissance aesthetic of restraint and the Baroque style of exaggerated and heightened emotion. *Turquerie* was a European fine art style that was popular during the eighteenth and nineteenth centuries, in which Europeans adopted Turkish clothes and furnishings (Figure 4.1). But there is also a manga comic aesthetic, a video game aesthetic, and even an aesthetic of Japanese and Korean lunchboxes.

Seductive pleasures

There are many forms of visual seduction and those introduced below are only examples of how pictures seduce, of how we are enchanted, charmed, fascinated and bewitched. In each case, the pleasure is described, examples are provided, the critical discourse associated with it is noted and reasons are suggested for its attraction. Serious problems with some of these pleasures are discussed in the following chapter.

The bright and the busy

Bright pictures use colours that are strong, vivid or brilliant. Brilliant pictures can shine brightly, sparkle, glitter or be lustrous, radiant, splendid or reflecting. A busy image is ornate or characterized by activity, full of action and interest.

From prehistoric times and across many cultures there has been a taste for bright and/or busy images. Palaeolithic peoples loved bright things like fossil resin amber with its varieties of golden yellow, orange, red, green and violet, and the first Neolithic peoples employed copper for jewellery and later gold and silver. Neolithic peoples also used precious gemstones, shiny metals and shells of many kinds for beads, headdresses and necklaces. Pre-dynastic Egyptians employed the bright blue and apple green of turquoise, the many shades of emerald green quartz, and the deep blue of lapis lazuli. Such items decorated our ancestors' bodies in life and accompanied them in death.

Today, souvenir shops exemplify both the bright and the busy; they brim with shiny, multicoloured trinkets. Supermarkets' shelves are lined with thousands of competing products, almost all packaged in fully saturated colour. Consider shopping malls, with their spectacular, kaleidoscopic stimuli, or

Figure 4.2 Author, *A Japanese Pachinko Parlour* (2019).

a Japanese Pachinko parlour with all its glitter, shine, sparkle and flashing lights (Figure 4.2). Think of firework displays, torchlight parades, flashing disco lights, streets lined with neon signs and the cacophony of market stalls. Each signals excitement, the time and place to be, now, in the moment.

In the West, elite opinion has often looked askance at bright and busy imagery, condemning things bright as garish, gaudy and lurid and busy pictures as over-ornate, fussy or cluttered. Only when bright and busy imagery served a serious purpose were they deemed acceptable. Plato claimed that pleasure without serious purpose weakened resistance to base instincts, and he set the tone that many have followed. The Roman philosopher Cicero called for visual restraint in what has ever since been known as 'the doctrine of decorum'. Decorum has long been harnessed to battle against perceived excess, no more so than by early modernists with their desire for the clean lines and muted colours of a geometric, minimalist aesthetic.

In light of this persistent call for restraint by cultural elites, why does a taste for the bright and busy continue unabated? Is it cultural? Or could it be part of our evolutionary inheritance? Could it be both?

First, a preference for bright and busy imagery does appear to be cultural. Over time there has been a great deal of variability as to what elites have considered too bright and too busy. But elites have consistently called for restraint as a political act. They deliberately and regularly used restraint versus excess as a cultural marker of class. The bright and busy has been a way to identify and marginalize lower classes, but also it appears as though lower classes have responded by using it to assert their own taste. Just as sober restraint has been lauded by cultural elites as a maker of good taste, others have used a taste for the unrestrained as a mark of social resistance. Consciously or unconsciously, a taste for the bright and busy has been used to establish a resistant and even transgressive identity. Finding their tastes denigrated, a taste for what elites condemn as garish, gaudy and lurid, fussy and cluttered, has been frequently adopted as a badge of honour.

Secondly, a taste for busy detail may also be rooted in our evolutionary history, specifically in our ancestors' need to pick out essential detail from a complex pattern of stimuli (Coss, 2003). In the distant past, failure to perceive danger in the distant approach of a predator in an otherwise benign visual field would have been disastrous. The same would have applied to any failure to discern danger in the smallest detail of a predator in foliage close by.

With regard to bright and shiny surfaces, consider that there exists a universal association of glossy surfaces with something wet. Children make this association as early as six months, the significance of which is a further association they make between wet and water. The dispersal of early hominids was restricted to areas and climatic conditions that offered regular supplies of water. Preventing dehydration by the ability to find drinking water on a daily basis would have sensitized our forebears to both the static and the dynamic optical properties of water. Still water can act as a natural mirror, a glassy surface reflecting the overhead environment. Turbulent water is foamy and luminous because it appears white. The glinting properties of the smooth rippling surface of a pond or stream would have attracted attention, as would the glittering dew on leaves in the early morning. In short, the sparkling properties of water constitute a historically consistent recognition cue that was easily detected at a distance both in full view and when partly occluded.

A taste for the bright and/or busy appears both cultural and innate. It acts as a cultural marker either of bad taste or a form of cultural resistance. But a taste for the bright and/or busy appears also to be built into our genes, a residue from a time when our survival as a species required our attention to such visual characteristics.

The spectacular

The spectacular refers to spectacles on an exceptionally large scale; they are grand, lavish, magnificent or marvellous. Very large things make a huge impression; they shock, thrill and awe. They induce chills, shallow breathing and increased heart rate. Palms may get sweaty, and goose bumps may appear on the skin. We may shiver and gasp in disbelief.

There are many and varied kinds of spectacular scenes: natural, human-built, ancient and modern. Each of the seven natural wonders of the world is spectacular, like the Grand Canyon of the United States or the Great Barrier Reef off the east coast of Australia. Each of the seven wonders of the ancient world was renowned for being spectacular, like the Great Pyramid of Giza in Egypt and the Hanging Gardens of Babylon. Similarly spectacular are the seven wonders of the modern world, including the Great Wall of China and the Taj Mahal in India. Of the sites still extant, each is a major tourist attraction and reproduced in countless photographs.

Even as we view movies on ever smaller electronic devices (though also on ever larger television screens), the popular draw of the spectacular is undiminished. The Mount Rushmore National Memorial is a sculpture carved into the granite face of Mount Rushmore in the Black Hills of South Dakota, in the United States (Figure 4.3). It portrays four of the more notable United States presidents. Each face is approximately sixty feet high, their mouths approximately eighteen feet wide. It took around 400 workers between 1927 and 1941 to realize its present state. It now draws about 3 million visitors a year – the principal tourist attraction of the state.

Imperial powers have always favoured the spectacular. A sculpture of the Roman Emperor Constantine stood about thirteen metres high. Stalin envisaged the tallest buildings in the world while Hitler compensated with the largest dome. The latter was to be four times the size of St. Peter's dome in Rome, so large that in inclement weather clouds would have formed inside it. Hitler also favoured spectacularly large sculptures. A Nazi sculptor created such giant figures that when one visitor to his studio was asked about the whereabouts of the artist, an assistant replied, 'Up in the left ear of the horse' (cited in Lehmann-Haupt 1954: p. 98).

The spectacular conforms to the aesthetic category of the sublime. The sublime refers to things that are too big to take in all at once, that overwhelm and might even induce terror if not for being viewed at a safe distance. Kant distinguished between two kinds of the sublime: the mathematical and the dynamic. The mathematical sublime impressed through multiplication; the dynamic, through sheer force.

Figure 4.3 Author, *Mount Rushmore, South Dakota, United States* (1927–42).

Of the mathematical sublime, think of the Taj Mahal; it is not only large, it is covered in such an extraordinary amount of intricate decoration it is impossible to grasp it. The same applies to many Islamic Mosques. They overwhelm by their size and by their intricacy. And while spectacular things are spectral, they also impress by the extraordinary extent of their production. As with the Mount Rushmore sculptures, recounting the length of time and the very great number of people required to build them is an inseparable part of their attraction.

The dynamical sublime impresses by force. Think of witnessing massive natural disasters such as lightning storms, massive floods, volcanic explosions, raging fires and tsunamis. These are the stuff of disaster films, and so long as we feel at a safe or mediated distance, the experience is one of awe. Fireworks are an ever-popular pyrotechnic display and are bright, busy and large, but also fast paced. Military parades are extravagant, calculated, showy displays that can be also relentless.

Whether mathematical or dynamic, the spectacular makes a huge impression, and we often recall experiences of them long afterwards. They are often among the highlights of our lives. But why should this be the case? Why should being overwhelmed be so attractive?

With the spectacular, we tend to lose a sense of ourselves as separate beings. Our individuality is transcended. If only momentarily, we escape from ourselves. In Freudian terms, we experience ego loss or ego death, a pleasant sense of being but a small entity in a very much larger scheme of things. We feel at one with something well beyond our small and insignificant selves, be it a crowd, the universe, or the belief that we are in the presence of God. Either way, it is a blissful state, one of astonishment, of wonderment.

Sentimentality

Sentimentality refers to feelings of compassion, sympathy, empathy, love, sadness and nostalgia. These are often called the tender emotions. Sentimentality typically adopts a soft and decorative style, and it employs a sensibility of innocence. It views everything as essentially uncontaminated, as pure and good. It induces tears and sighing, and 'oohing' and 'aahing'.

Sentimentality prefers certain subject matter, typically soft, furry animals (especially puppies and kittens); wide-eyed children, both naughty and nice; flowers; sunny, idealized landscapes; hearts; decorative borders; cherubs; angels; and cute figurines. It celebrates old men, old women, orphans, mothers and motherhood itself. These subjects find a ready home on cards and mementos for births, christenings, birthdays, weddings, special holidays, illnesses and deaths – all the major events of our lives.

As a style, today's sentimental imagery frequently employs a pastel or sepia palette, with an intimate scale, and much use is made of repetition, pattern and decorative intricacy. Sentimental aesthetics typically value clarity, cleanliness, purity, harmony, symmetry and a highly skilful finish. Traditional ideas of beauty prevail and technical perfection is prized (Figure 4.4).

As a sensibility, sentimentality is marked by benevolence. Everything is viewed through rose-tinted glasses even when the subject matter is sad or the actual reality is unpleasant. Melancholy and nostalgia are two of its major attributes.

Figure 4.4 Anonymous, *Scrapbooking Sample* (no date).

A precursor to today's sentimental imagery is the Rococo fine art style of the 1700s. The Rococo did not pretend to show life in all its colours. It was an opulent, graceful style, preferring delicate, shell like curves, pastel colours and vague, atmospheric effects. Artists painted scenes of a carefree aristocracy playing at romance in idyllic, flower-strewn landscapes. All the women have perfect, beautiful skin, all the men are handsome and all the lovers are elegant. The Rococo was light-hearted, optimistic and, above all, it was charming.

Today, among the most obvious examples of a sentimental aesthetic are the photographs of vulnerable babies, both human and other animals. Campaigns seeking to protect endangered species almost always use baby or young animals, not adult animals. Advertisements show baby bears cavorting happily in snow, bunnies rubbing noses and fluffy ducklings tentatively taking their first swim.

Yet sentimentality is commonly condemned in quite furious terms. It is attacked as exaggerated, self-indulgent and accused of beautifying lies. Many prejudicial synonyms are used to damn it, including mawkish, maudlin, mushy, sappy, syrupy, schmaltzy, gushy, corny, weepy and, simply, over-emotional.

However, the degree to which sentimentality is condemned appears in direct inverse proportion to its popularity, for there appear to be many reasons for its popularity. There are times when escape into an aestheticized sanctuary is entirely beneficial for mental health. Who wants always to be confronted with unpleasant realities? The idealization of a subject may even help rather than hinder coming to terms with painful realities. Sometimes recalling a full account of an experience can be so painful it is completely avoided. Airbrushing a subject may help, piecemeal or in part, to recall and address what would otherwise be met with absolute suppression.

Sentimentality satisfies a yearning for a pleasant past, one innocent of present and past difficulties alike. History is replete with inconvenient truths, but reworked as pleasant, history becomes heritage. Heritage is history seen through a prism in which disagreeable facts are downplayed or altogether ignored in favour of what is uplifting and efficacious. Where history is loaded with despicable motives and atrocious acts, heritage is filled with noble and brave deeds, idealistic visions and heroic actions. Heritage clarifies the past so that it can serve our present purposes. The flag, war memorials, statues of heroes, re-enactments, iconic buildings, gardens, paintings, family photographs and heirlooms, all play a part in maintaining present-day emotional attachments with the past. There is comfort in a pleasant past, and there is even the pleasure of melancholy in longing for it.

Web 4.1
Heritage

Sentimentality evokes loving, compassionate relationships, and love and compassion are their own rewards. By loving and showing compassion, we give of ourselves and in giving we receive the comfort of knowing that we are profoundly and positively connected to others. By loving we are loved; by offering comfort we are comforted, not alone, but part of a community capable of feeling as we do.

Such emotions, no less than negative ones, are grounded in our biological inheritance. We are genetically programmed to care for babies with their large heads, large eyes and small mouths. This appears to extend to some animals with their big eyes, and to baby animals with their big heads. This has long been known to the inventors of cartoon characters; Mickey Mouse and Manga characters alike draw upon our sympathy for big heads and oversized eyes.

In an uncertain world, sentimentality offers a sense of comfort and security, and when located in the past, sentimentality offers a sense of wellbeing in the present.

The exotic

The exotic refers to things of foreign origin or character that are regarded as striking or unusual in their effect or appearance. It refers to artefacts from cultures other than our own and specifically valued for their otherness. Almost anything can be exotic: people, animals, plants, buildings, landscapes, locations, objects and situations. Exoticism works through a combination of selection, exaggeration and domestication. To be regarded as exotic, something must be sufficiently different from one's own culture to fascinate while also to be readily assimilated; too much difference and items from the other culture are regarded as repugnant. The exotic is always a mix of something unusual but not too unusual, something distanced, but not enough to threaten. It always involves decontextualizing artefacts from one culture and recontextualizing them in another, ripping them out of the way of life of which they are constitutive and then planting them somewhere new. Often the exotic involves

Web 4.2
Celebrating
Place

exaggerating difference, making difference appear even more different. Alternatively, it involves toning down difference, domesticating the difference so that it is acceptable.

Exoticism is far from a recent phenomenon. *Turquerie* was mentioned earlier, but the appeal more generally of the Orient for Europeans went far deeper than a taste for clothes and furnishings. For centuries, painters, then photographers, then cinematographers represented the Orient as a place of striking, unfamiliar customs. Men were represented smoking a hookah, riding on camels, playing strange musical instruments and charming snakes. Women carry large jugs on their heads or shoulders, and they lounge about in luxurious, bedazzling clothes and jewellery. Whether painted, photographed or filmed, the highly intricate Islamic decorations found on wall hangings, carpets and buildings are emphasized, as well as the brilliant sun as it hits the buildings and creates deep shadows, so unlike the soft light of Europe. Equally depicted are the spectacle of the desert landscape and the excitement of market places full of colour and strange items for sale.

Today's tourism is no different. It is one of the largest industries in the world and it is entirely based on exoticism. Promotional material emphasizes the otherness of other countries. England is commonly represented by the Houses of Parliament and Beefeaters; Italy by the Leaning Tower of Pisa and Vatican Guards.

New World countries, which lack a distant European past, typically feature motifs derived from the artwork of their indigenous populations: Canada by motifs derived from First Nations People, in New Zealand from Maori, and in Australia, from Aborigines.

Tourism is highly selective, but it also domesticates what it selects. Package tours ensure that the exotic is controllable, manageable and easily consumable. Tourists tread well-worn paths according to finely coordinated schedules that are interspersed with ordinary, familiar experiences. They experience the exotic by taking photographs at pre-determined stops, eating exotic food and shopping.

But why should the exotic enchant? Wherein lies the attraction of otherness?

On a personal level, the exotic provides spice seasoning to one's own dull life, and on a broader level it rejuvenates one's own culture. The fascination of eighteenth- and nineteenth-century Europeans with the exotic Orient lay in trying to escape from what they considered the stupefying banality of their own lives. Today, tourism equally provides an escape from the mundane routine of home and habit, tourism being a no-work, no-care situation.

The exotic can also clarify how we value our own culture. We may see in the strangeness of another culture something better than our own, or, alternatively, something less worthy. Or the exotic can just delight.

Eroticism

Erotic pictures are defined here as those involving sexual arousal or interest. They are perennial, and though long repressed, today they are as pervasive as they are public. Like violence and abject aspects of horror, discussed below, sexual imagery bypasses cognitive control and triggers the central nervous system. We are hardwired for erotic representations to focus our attention, a fact that research now finds applies equally to people of all sexual orientations.

Perhaps more than any other kind of popular aesthetic, eroticism attracts heated debate. Nude paintings have been lauded as the embodiment of perfection, nothing less than celebrations of the divine remade in human form, while detractors of eroticism castigate it as decadent, debauched and depraved. The consequence of such damnation is that erotic pictures are subject to social censorship and, more than any other kind of picture, fall into a public versus private domain.

Acceptance of erotic imagery often hangs on whether pictures are considered to be art or pornography, the two categories often being understood as mutually exclusive. But a great deal of premodern fine art was no less than what today is commonly considered soft pornography.

Drawing upon scenes and figures from ancient pagan sources, as well as the Bible and early Christianity, nudes appeared in a variety of premodern art genre, and almost always they were justified in terms of classical learning and moral injunctions to a virtuous life. Artists, patrons, historians and critics alike either traded on the cultural cache of ancient Greek and Roman sources or evoked the moral authority of the Bible. Venus, for example, goddess of love and ironically an icon of chastity, was a favourite subject. In numerous paintings, she arises from the sea, lies asleep watched over by Cupid, kisses Cupid, bathes, undresses or just lies on a couch; but she is always youthful and either partly or fully nude. Homoerotic desire is equally evident in numerous muscular male nudes. Favourites of premodern painters include David from the Bible, and from ancient mythology they include Pan, Hercules, Mars and Perseus. That sexual desire found such ready decoys has been variously described as 'the traditional high-status alibi' or 'the classical alibi.' Western fine art nudes compare directly with photographic pornography. In particular, the same gazes and poses are used as well as the same attempt to establish an intimate relationship between pictures and viewers. In both pornography and traditions of Western painting, women not only display their bodies for the viewer's gaze, but also engage the viewer with a mutually desiring gaze. Thus, today's mainstream culture has returned to that of premodern times, although without the felt need to disguise desire.

The pleasures of erotic imagery include voyeurism, which refers to taking pleasure in watching people unaware that they are being watched and, thereby, the pleasure of being in a position of power to them. As discussed in Chapter 6 on the gaze, voyeurism turns the subjects of a gaze into objects, and in the case of erotic imagery into objects of sexual interest and arousal. Voyeurism is taken further with fetishism. Instead of showing a whole body, either only one part of a body is shown or only one part is emphasized. Over the decades Hollywood alternated its particular fetishes. In the 1920s it was legs, with any number of movies involving lines of dancing chorus girls, and in the 1930s it was breasts with actresses 'forgetting' to wear bras and so enabling their nipples to show. In the 1940s legs returned, and in the 1950s breasts made a comeback with displays of ample cleavage, tight fitting sweaters and torpedo-like bras. The most extreme form of visual fetishism is undoubtedly found in pornography, a visual form that specializes in making visible body parts that are usually hidden from view. Whereas for classic era Hollywood, eroticism was largely the art of concealment, pornography is explicit.

There is also pleasure to be derived from fantasizing that the desirable erotic subject of a picture desires them; through the power of a mutual, desiring gaze, the sexual figure of the image and the viewer lock into recognition of each other as both enjoying simultaneously the pleasures of looking and of exhibiting themselves. This is as true of classical paintings as it is of today's pornography. These combined pleasures of exhibitionism and spectatorship are also manifestly engaged with the current phenomenon of sexting, by which couples send sexually explicit photographs of themselves to each other.

Echoing the multiple and fragmented nature of sexuality, none of the associated pleasures described above are strictly dictated by one's own gender or sexual orientation. Images can be queered, where male and female homosexuals gain pleasure from erotically charged representations of their own gender. Moreover, in proportion to the degree to which queering was and remains socially taboo, an extra erotic charge may be experienced precisely because it is clandestine. For example, an erotic image of a woman intended for what in Chapter 6 is called a male gaze, may be enjoyed not only by a woman's queer gaze but especially so for being illicit. Ironically, the social injunctions against queer pleasures may only increase them. The Hollywood biblical epics of the 1950s were once a favourite of gay men because of the many beefcake actors who bared their chests and muscular arms and legs.

Sexual imagery, whether explicit or veiled, championed or repressed, is of great longstanding, a feature of indigenous art, Greek and Roman art and Western painting and photography thereafter, and it is now mainstream. Whether we respond with mere curious interest or arousal, disgust and horror, we are genetically programmed for erotic imagery to grab our attention.

Violence

Violence refers here to intentional physical harm. Among popular violent entertainment there are basically four kinds: comic, transgressive, retaliatory or gratuitous. Comic violence includes the knockdown antics of clowns, comedians and animated cartoons, while action dramas often involve the transgressive violence of antagonists and the retaliatory violence of protagonists. Transgressive violence ruptures the peaceful status quo while retaliatory violence re-establishes the status quo.

Web 4.3
Violence

Gratuitous violence exists for its own sake, has no narrative relevance, a mere spectacle, and is enjoyed without regard to moral questions or the fate of the protagonist.

Pictures of violence can also be sanitized or visceral, and realistic or stylized. Sanitized violence dominated United States mass media until the late 1960s in which the bodies of victims remained whole. Victims merely clutched their chests, covered where they had been shot, and keeled over. By contrast, today's mass media violence is often visceral. Blood splatters everywhere, internal organs spill out, and we respond at a pre-cognitive, gut-level. Realistic violence appears real, while stylized violence involves obvious artifice, which is commonly achieved today with special effects. Today's screen bodies routinely explode, spurt blood and spew guts, but the frenetic-paced editing of contemporary media violence renders many such scenes quite divorced from anything plausibly life-like, and thus for many viewers they are not even considered violent.

Many social critics are alarmed at the amount of mediated violence to which we – and especially children – are exposed. Yet pictures of violence have been common since ancient times. Assyrian relief sculptures of warfare and Roman gladiatorial games bear witness to a long-standing fascination with violent entertainment. Consider too how much of the history of European painting contains scenes of battles on both land and sea (Figure 4.5). Horses charge, guns discharge, the wounded fall to their knees and bodies lie face down leaking blood. Ships fire their guns, others explode and sailors are thrown into the sea. Some battle scenes represented transgressive violence intended to arouse patriotic indignation. Others still, simply represented general mayhem.

The very first full-length feature film, *The Kelly Gang* (1906), recreated the story of the Australian bushrangers. It featured a number of shootouts, setting a precedent for many to follow. Today, film critics describe much of violent entertainment as a brand of fun; as a blood and bullets ballet, an exuberant celebration of fight choreography or even a cheerful orgy of the gratuitous. Video game manufacturers claim they are under pressure to intensify the level of violence and producers of movies and television series see their job as pushing the violence envelope as far as they can so that their audiences do not get bored, knowing that for many in their audience the violence is where the fun peaks.

Yet not everyone is attracted to mediated violence; many people recoil. We do not therefore appear to be hardwired to enjoy violence. We are hardwired to react to visceral violence, but not to be attracted to it. If a love of violence is not part of our archaic makeup, left over from our evolutionary history, why are so many people attracted to it? What is so seductive about the thrill of blood spilt?

Aristotle (1952) thought violent entertainment was cathartic. He famously wrote that tragedy must 'contain incidents arousing pity and fear, wherewith to accomplish its catharsis of such emotions' (p. 1149b). For Aristotle, violent entertainment purged aggressive, destructive emotions.

Figure 4.5 W. V. Velde, *The Burning of the 'Royal James' at the Battle of Solebay, 28 May 1672* (1672–1707).

His view has been highly influential, not only with media critics keen to justify it, but with Freud, who viewed violent entertainment as a form of sublimation, a way to positively channel and relieve the unhealthy emotions of frustration, fear and anxiety.

However, volumes of empirical evidence now suggest that exposure to violent dramatic performances results in audiences being more anxious and fearful, not less so. Aristotle appears to have been entirely wrong on the purgative value of fictional violence. Catharsis may operate in relation to the evocation of sorrow as discussed above on the sentimental, but it does not appear to operate with frustration, anxiety or fear.

Researchers suggest that we enjoy violence because it triggers a moral code grounded in our perception of fairness and justice. This idea is supported by how audiences define violence. Most people do not consider all pictures that represent intentional physical harm to be violent. Rather, most audiences consider physical action to be violent only when there is an unequal use of force; for example, when a participant introduces a weapon or when a participant possesses greater strength than their opponent. Additionally, the degree to which an action is deemed violent is determined by how real the violence appears. Even when violence involves blood and gore it may be deemed mild if it appears unreal and, alternatively, a relatively mild assault can be considered very violent when it appears to be for real.

We tend to make moral judgments about the characters represented, which is especially marked when protagonists unjustly suffer physical harm. We adopt a witness perspective and respond to fictional characters, cognitively and emotionally, much as we do in real life. We adopt the position of observers, who, as third parties, allow ourselves to succumb to the illusion of watching real events unfold before us. As in real life, we assume favourable and unfavourable dispositions towards different characters depending upon our interpretation of their appearance and behaviour. When a character towards whom we adopt a positive disposition is threatened with violence, especially when it is utterly undeserved, we suffer as we would in real life, though with this difference: it is experienced as pleasurable because the experience occurs within a safe, protected zone.

But this begs the question: why do we find pleasure in violence towards protagonists? Is it that we experience a kind of forepleasure due to the anticipation that however unlikely it is made to seem, the tables will turn? Is it that while the antagonist has the upper hand, we anticipate a just resolution, feeling anxiety on behalf of the protagonist yet knowing from previous experience of narrative formulas that there will be a turnabout?

However, this begs another question: why is pain pleasurable? Pleasure and pain are activated in the same regions of the brain, so could it be that they are not experienced as opposites but as complementary? The brain is generally hardwired for pleasure, and since those areas of the brain assigned to pleasure evolved to co-ordinate basic survival functions, perhaps all normal behaviour is directed at evoking electrical activity in the pleasure areas of the brain.

The thrill of violence is especially noticeable when the tables turn. As viewers, we experience what psychologists call excitation-transfer, in which one state of excitement transfers to another. Emotional arousal often lingers after the cause of it has ceased. Although we may adjust cognitively to a new situation, our emotional reactions lag behind cognitive reactions. Our head moves forward but our bodies do not immediately follow. Furthermore, if there remain residues of our initial emotional response at the time of a second emotional stimulus, our second response will be greater than if the residue did not exist. An arousal residue from prior distress intensifies our enjoyment, making gruesome, transgressive violence an essential prelude to the joy from the emotional override of retaliatory violence. The more we suffer through an early round of transgressive violence, the greater our euphoria. Film makers have long known how to take advantage of this phenomenon.

Perhaps exposure to violent entertainment is also an attempt to confront fear and anxiety and so master it. Vicarious violence allows us to test our reactions to violence without running actual risks. Entering into the thrill of violence, we simultaneously confront our fears. This appears to apply especially to certain adolescent males, who are the only major demographic who report enjoying gratuitous violence. By viewing high levels of violence, they may appear to master their fears, and consequently they are led to play their socially assigned, gendered role as emotionally detached and fearless. Male adolescents are typically in search of a social identity where watching violent entertainment enables bonding with peers; it acts as a rite of passage.

More generally, and for a wide cross-section of the public, violent imagery is used for mood management, to regulate levels of excitement or arousal. Stimulus seeking applies to all of us today who live within the limits imposed by the orderly arrangements created by the institutions of government, education, law, medicine and so on, by all the minutiae of bureaucracy that curtail individual expression. Societies today often fail to provide sufficient stimulation. In this context, the transgressive but also safe characteristics of highly stylized, exaggerated violence appear as a kind of liberation. Highly structured, rationally ordered societies make us vulnerable to the appeal of the unstructured, irrationality of bodily excess. In highly regulated societies, wild, indulgence offers welcome relief.

Additionally, as with any form of mediated violence, there is much more to like than the violence. People who love violent entertainment point to music, editing, setting, the exaggeration and distortion of reality, sexually explicit imagery, comedy, movement, energy and novelty. In particular, violent video games are found attractive because they involve special effects, fantasy, challenge, stimulation, scorekeeping, feedback, graphics, sound effects, freedom of movement and above all, the exhilaration of hurtling through infinite space. Video games also frequently involve a combination of competition and collaboration. With single-player games players compete against time to acquire points and so achieve a higher level of attainment. With multiple player games like *StarCraft* and *World of Warcraft* many players, often from many countries, not only compete with other teams, they also collaborate with their own team members. *StarCraft* intentionally incorporates camaraderie as a key element. In a game with a do-or-die ethos, players must trade stories and work together to be successful. The games provide a virtual space in which players meet, hang out together and share experiences, and by celebrating triumphs and commiserating over failures, players come to feel that they matter to one another. Playing at mediated violence helps build social identities and social competence.

Violent entertainment enables the pleasure of making moral judgments so that we can enjoy even transgressive violence in the expectation that the tables will turn. Mass media violence is pleasurable because pain and pleasure are closely related, because it provides liberation in an under-stimulating environment and because it is linked to many other pleasures.

Destruction

While the previous section focused on violence to people, destruction here refers to large-scale damage and ruin caused by sudden, violent action to non-human things like cars, buildings and even the entire planet. Most mediated disaster is spectacular, and like the spectacular, meditated disaster conforms to both Kant's categories of the sublime: the mathematical and dynamic. Being violent and colossal, destruction relates to the pleasures of violence and the spectacular. Watching destruction, we are wide-eyed in amazement, half relishing it, half horrified.

Just as violence appeared at the very outset of narrative cinema, so did scenes of disaster. The 1908 Italian film *The Last Days of Pompeii* depicted massive destruction and the annihilation of an entire population. Destruction has remained a staple ever since, becoming its own genre: disaster films, in which giant monsters like King Kong and Godzilla tear down bridges, push over skyscrapers and send people flying through the air in every direction.

Naturally caused destruction is equally popular: tsunamis, planetary collisions, the heating of the earth's core, tornadoes, hurricanes, fire, flood and earthquakes. The eruption of Vesuvius, Italy, was virtually a subgenre for centuries (Figure 4.6). Or the cause can be small but the effect large scale, like numerous marauding creatures that behave like locusts, devouring everything in their path: rats, lobsters, carnivorous plants and even unspecified jelly like substances. Yet as spectacular as the special effects used in today's disaster films are, they are only latter-day versions of annihilation imagery that has appeared in all corners of the globe for millennia. Among the earliest images of utter devastation is the approximately 650 BCE Assyrian stone relief *The Sack of the City of Hamanu by Ashurbanipal*. The relief depicts soldiers with pickaxes and crowbars demolishing the city, buildings on fire, and timber and bricks falling in mid-air. Each of the world's major religious traditions has visions of the calamitous, horrendous end times. The film *2012* is loosely based on the Mayan prophesy that the world would end in 2012.

But wherein lies the delight of witnessing the destruction of cities, the death of millions and even the annihilation of almost the entire human race?

Since images of destruction relate to both the spectacular and the violent, images of destruction share much the same pleasures as these two other aesthetic lures. Like the dynamic sublime of the spectacular in which, overpowered, we momentarily lose ourselves, watching destruction we get caught up in something far larger than our own concerns. And like the pleasures of violence by which we enjoy both transgressive and retaliation violence, anticipating and then relishing wrongdoers getting their comeuppance, images of massive destruction allow us to take the moral high ground. Like violence, destruction is a thrill ride that relieves the tension of living in a highly regulated society.

With pictures of destruction, though, is there an extra pleasure? Is it that images of massive destruction return us to our most primordial and biological state, that of babies, a time of crying in profound rage, pain and with a lust for destruction? When frustrated, babies lash out and cry with a fury quite unlike anything else. In enjoying destruction, do we relive this early experience?

Alternatively, does the pleasure of destruction derive from knowing that the destruction of the established order is only temporary? Almost always, destruction is followed by restoration and even the renewal of the status quo, as well as the chance that things will be better next time. Destruction paves the way for a return to a simpler, happier time beyond present-day strife and suffering. In the

Figure 4.6 Pierre-Jacques Volaire, *The Eruption of Vesuvius* (detail) (1771).

film *2012* the survivors begin anew in South Africa, where our species began. Destruction opens the door to renewal, the necessary means to eliminate the status quo before a new dawn can commence. The pleasures of massive destruction are linked to the pleasure of restoration.

Destruction appears to be enjoyed for multiple reasons, all the pleasures of the spectacular and violence, but also other pleasures specific to it. Destruction offers a return to our primary state as wrathful creatures while also offering the promise of renewal.

Horror

The horrific is whatever excites a sense of terror and/or dread. Terror is a sharp, intense, overmastering fear. Terror causes a shock, a sudden and violent disturbance of the mind, emotions or sensibilities. Dread is an apprehension of something terrifying in the future.

Often our reactions to horror are marked by physical as well as psychological effects, psychological fears realized in physical terms. Horror confronts us with images of the body in extremis that affect our own bodies, reaching down into our glands, skin, muscles and circulatory system. Finding horror shocking, we may squirm, shudder, shiver, shout and scream; we may tremble, stop breathing and suddenly take in or exhale air. Our skin may crawl, the hair on the back of our necks may bristle and we may involuntarily avert our eyes. We may be rendered motionless, or even ridged, with fear.

Many people do not like horror films, but many others do. Whether it is shambling, flesh-eating zombies, werewolves, slimy monsters or unspecified evil forces, the lure of the horrific is as strong as it ever has been. Vampires may be undead, but in the imagination of the horrific they are as alive today as similar figures have been in many societies since ancient times.

Horror engages our primal fears, our worst nightmares. Some of these fears are personal and perennial, such as a fear of the dark, bodily deterioration, death, dismemberment, loss of identity, the non-human, mental and physical deviance and sexual dysfunction. With horror films fears of castration, separation and abandonment, being devoured, loss of identity and being subsumed by another, are each played out in a form that permits their enactment in a safe, controlled way (see Figure 2.9).

Other fears are social. Hollywood science fiction horror of the 1950s variously addressed the fear of nuclear annihilation and the threat posed by science and technology. Horror films of the 1960s dealt with the breakdown of sexual taboos, the assertiveness of women and the consequent diminution of the power of men. Some Japanese films from the 1950s in which a monster destroys a city evidently echo the horror of nuclear devastation (Figure 4.6). Recently, horror has haunted our vulnerability in ordinary living and working places by terrorist attacks. While social fears take specific forms at particular times and places they invariably seem to arise from a fear of social upheaval and anarchy. Whether arising from passing social issues or from our inescapable condition as human bodies and minds, horrified responses are typically triggered by a violation of cultural categories as well as entities that inspire revulsion and disgust.

Since horror is possibly the most unpleasant of popular pleasures, wherein lies its attraction? What is pleasant about high levels of apprehension, dread, panic and alarm at the ghastly, grisly and gruesome?

Does the attraction lie partly in the same conditions, noted above, that operate with violence and destruction: that is, an escape from the banality of a too well-ordered daily life? Does horror fascinate because real life is so orderly, peaceful and predictable? If so, perhaps no form of entertainment is as successful as horror at providing escape because horror provides an imaginary inversion of ordinary life like no other.

Perhaps the attraction to the shock of horror may also have evolutionary origins associated with protective vigilance and curiosity. We are hardwired to focus our attention on cues to danger, such as horrific events, and our emotional reactions have not significantly changed since our hunter-gatherer days. Perhaps today's civil life fails to provide the threats and the challenges to overcome that characterized the lives of our ancestors.

Like pictures of gratuitous violence, horror films have a particular appeal among male youth for whom they provide a means of both mastering their fears and demonstrating mastery of their traditional gender role. This powerfully determines the appeal of these films. Watching horror movies is an endurance test, and sharing it in the company of other males has the additional advantage of engendering male bonding.

Furthermore, when male and female youth watch horror movies together the movies enable age-old, gender-specific role-play with one another. While adolescent males teach themselves to be unfazed by horror, adolescent females are socialized to display discomfort. Horror films provide a venue to enact mutually supporting male/female identities whereby adolescent males demonstrate their manliness and females their vulnerability. By playing out their expected roles with one another, both genders feel equally empowered, ironically, through misattribution. Females routinely attribute greater mastery to males than they actually feel, and males routinely attribute more distress to females than they actually experience. Each gender also misattributes their liking for each other to the films themselves. This is known as the 'snuggle theory' of horror. The ancient Romans observed the same phenomenon: the more terrified women were of the mayhem in the gladiatorial arena where people and animals were torn apart, the more they sought comfort from their male companions.

Nor are the tropes of horror movies new. Horror was a staple of medieval Christian Europe. Murals of hell were populated by ugly demons, hideous tortures and a foul-looking, animalistic Satan. Sinners fell into stinking rivers, pits of pitch or boiling oil. Gluttons were force fed and hacked to pieces; the lustful were inflicted with emaciation and running sores, their rotting flesh penetrated with serpents (Figure 3.1).

Moreover, human responses have remained consistent. Disgust is a knee-jerk emotion, an immediate, straight to the nervous system response. Although specific instances of disgust are culturally determined, disgust exists in all societies. It is a biologically determined human response. Repugnance is a universal.

Monsters disgust, but they also fascinate because they confuse cultural boundaries. They are the abject made flesh, us, but not us; and ambiguity in any form threatens our common desire for identifiable boundaries. Monsters exist somewhere between being alive and dead, or somewhere between human and not human. They threaten our fundamental identities as alive and human.

Horror also engages any number of social taboos. Either explicitly or covertly, horror includes cannibalism, incest, torture, murder, sadism, masochism and necrophilia. Necrophilia and incest may only be implied by vampire movies, but murder, torture and other sadistic acts are now commonly depicted in the same gory, graphic detail as medieval frescos.

So, again, wherein lies the fascination? According to psychoanalytical theory, horror presents us with primary aspects of ourselves. In watching horror we unconsciously recognize aspects of our own natures that we cannot consciously acknowledge. Mediated horror is nothing more than the unconscious writ large. The unconscious is not an unknowable territory forever hidden; it is made manifest in dramatic form in all its complex and powerful darkness, at the movies, up on the big screen for all to see.

Psychoanalytical theory claims that the pleasure of horror lies in recognizing very real and powerful parts of ourselves we normally repress or ignore. While consciously we cannot accept that we may wish to indulge in taboo practices, as in dreams, horror fulfils our wishes in a disguised form. Instead of accepting these desires as our own, they are projected onto others as monstrous. Consciously, we are

Figure 4.7 Carniphage. *Female Vampire at Trade E3 Show* (2000).

revolted at horrific imagery; unconsciously, we welcome them. We may protest that we are horrified by monstrosity, but this is a dodge. We deceive ourselves. The lure of horror lies in permitting the satisfaction of what we wish for but cannot acknowledge. Appearances notwithstanding, what makes horror attractive is our disgust, for disgust serves our need to repress our actual wishes and anxieties. In horror, as in dreams, our deepest, inescapable anxieties, conflicts and desires find expression.

Horror may also offer a glimpse of alternative, even oppositional, ways of life. It certainly challenges the status quo in ways that otherwise go unexpressed. Perhaps horror's appeal lies in offering liberatory alternatives to elements of mainstream life. To a socially disenfranchised audience, could monsters act as a kind of superhero wielding power in their name? Consider the European lesbian vampires movies of the 1970s. While arising from a fear of both women's emancipation and alternative sexualities, these vampires could also be read as role models of strong, independent women. Consider that marginalized groups might find in monsters, heroes wielding the power to destroy the status quo. Could this explain the interest in cosplay, whereby people cease to be viewers and become participants (Figure 4.7)?

Speculation aside, horror both disgusts and fascinates. For some, horror acts as a rite of passage, and it can facilitate gender identity. It also simultaneously confronts us with our fears and anxieties and it appears to fulfil unconscious desires. Horror may also act as a form of transgressive liberation.

Humour

Humour is either an expression or an appreciation of what is amusing or comical. It is not the same thing as mirth or laughter, though they are often confused. Mirth refers to observable expressions of gaiety, happiness or joy, including laughter. Joy and laughter can exist without humour. Mirth is genetically programmed, but a sense of humour is learned. Babies and young children laugh a great deal because they are happy, but they do not have the mental equipment to have acquired a sense of humour. It is ironic that as a species we laugh most at the very time of our lives when we lack an understanding of what makes something funny. Moreover, as adults we sometimes laugh in social situations because it eases strained relationships, not because we find something amusing. We may laugh precisely because we are not amused.

Genuine amusement causes a wide variety of physical manifestations, including smiling and smirking, and, in more extreme forms, we may slap our sides, hold our stomach and even roll around helplessly. We may laugh, chuckle, snigger and snort. Wit may raise little more than a smile, while a pratfall can cause a prolonged belly laugh.

There are many kinds of humour; for example, clowning, irony, jests, jokes, kidding, mockery, puns, repartee, riddles, ridicule, satire, slapstick, teasing and wit. In addition, caricature involves the ludicrous exaggeration of characteristic features of a subject; burlesque involves mockery and exaggeration; parody involves exaggerated imitation intended to destroy an illusion; and travesty involves a ludicrous incongruity of style or subject matter.

A great deal of humour is verbal, but much is visual as captured, in part, by the phrase 'sight gag,' and found, for example, in political cartoons, animated cartoons, circus clowns and situation comedies. Visual humour is found in ineffable facial expressions and in bodily movements that defy scripting, and much humour also arises from an incongruity between speech and visual appearance.

Unlike some other popular pleasures, it seems obvious as to why we enjoy humour. We need only to connect what particular pleasures align with particular forms of humour. With ridicule and mockery we find pleasure in the misfortune of others. We feel superior, and our vanity is gratified that we ourselves are not in the predicament observed. Ridicule and mockery subjugate and disparage; their tone is aggressive, hostile and negative.

Ridicule and mockery are often directed at figures of authority, notably by political cartoonists and satirical programmes. With more genteel forms of humour, pleasure arises more from a surprising juxtaposition of unlike, incongruent things. In place of the evident nastiness of ridicule, the ludicrous puts us into an easy, happy state. We delight at silly mistakes, strongly aroused emotions for no good reason, ridiculous errors, preposterous situations and absurd statements. Consider horror movie monsters; when they fail to horrify, we find them ridiculous.

Often, it is not just any incongruity we find funny, but a descending incongruity, that is, one involving high and low status, where the high is brought low or the low gets above itself. We laugh when someone acting haughty is found to be clumsy or stupid and, conversely, where someone known to be stupid attempts to act smart. We find it funny when the serious is juxtaposed with the ridiculous, the elevated with the petty, the great with the insignificant. In each case, there is a sudden transfer from big and important matters to the small and trivial. Parody is based on this principle. During the nineteenth century, Shakespeare was a favourite target. His famous lines were turned into puns, often rhyming, and snippets of his tragedies were performed in outrageous music hall costumes. Political satire also operates on the basis of descending incongruity of the high brought low.

Humour also offers an emotional respite. Cultural producers of serious material have long understood the need for such release, obliging us by offering 'comic relief'. If horror turns the screw, comedy releases it.

Emotional release can extend to broad, social constraints. For Freud, humour acted as relief from the repressions of the social order. Humour was a momentary mutiny against social taboos, a rebellion against decorum, even against constraints that are necessary for civil life. In fact, we take particular pleasure in mocking what should not be mocked. Humour for Freud condensed and substituted for pent up, aggressive energies. It acted as a form of mood repair, substituting what would otherwise be expressed in physical violence. Rebellious humour was a defence against authority, the pleasure lying in a momentary liberation, and specially thrilling when it was transgressive.

Web 4.4
Humour

The humour of European medieval carnivals provides a perfect example of emotional release. Medieval Europe was highly repressive, with order imposed from above by both the medieval church and feudal authorities. Yet it was under such strict control that an outrageously transgressive culture of misrule developed. In large European cities up to three months of the year were devoted to carnival. Medieval people lived in two worlds, the official world of church and state repression and a second, unofficial, transgressive world of folk humour. Where people were commanded to be clean, during carnival, they were dirty; where chaste, promiscuous; where restrained, outlandish. Where they were expected to be civil, they were offensive. In turning authority upside down, for a time at least, otherwise powerless people could feel powerful.

The humour was vulgar. By contrast to the closed, smooth body of classical fine art, carnival celebrated the open, grotesque body. Body parts were invariably either too large or too small, principally the belly, the buttocks, and the genitals. Carnival humour was a deliberate affront to all that was considered right and decent by both religious and secular authorities. Yet it reminded everyone of their essential humanity, because the humour dealt substantially with the body parts and bodily functions that everyone had in common. The bawdy, scatological and outrageous humour of carnival represented a victory of laughter over fear, and given that medieval life was nasty, brutish and short, carnival humour offered at least temporary release.

Today, vulgar, carnivalesque humour is a staple of many US television animated cartoons series, such as *Beavis and Butt-Head* and *The Simpsons*. Homer Simpson is an anti-role-model father. He guzzles beer, gorges food, is primarily motivated by a desire for leisure, takes pride in his ignorance and frequently throttles his mischievous son Bart. US tabloid newspapers like the *World Weekly News* and *The Sun* regularly feature photographs of bodily excess: people who are too fat, or too tall, or hideously ugly. And World Federation television wrestling is a highly flamboyant theatrical spectacle of corporeal excess, grotesque, sexual and scatological.

Humour offers many pleasures. With ridicule we are able to feel superior to others. With the incongruities of wit, we are surprised by unexpected connections; and with many forms of humour there is a release of emotional tension.

Illusion

Visual illusions involve deception. They are the opposite of illumination, which means to throw light upon, to enlighten. To enlighten is the purpose of realistic pictures, to be discussed below. By contrast, illusions deceive the eye, confusing and confounding us into mistaking illusions for things real. Illusions delight and surprise. With widened eyes, shaking heads and open months we find we have been fooled, and we ask: how was an illusion created?

Illusions are an age-old delight. The current revival of 3D movies and the introduction of 3D television and Augmented Reality is only the most recent example in a long history of attempts at visual deceit. In the ancient world, the Egyptians were renowned for their illusionistic tricks and the Greeks invented the genre of painting called *trompe l'oeil* that deliberately attempted to cheat the eye. Stories of ancient Greek artists focus on how, allegedly, artists could fool not only other artists but even animals. The Romans introduced *trompe l'oeil* onto the walls of their homes to create the illusion of nature outside. In Europe, *trompe l'oeil* reached the height of its popularity in the seventeenth century, though it never disappeared (Figure 4.8).

Figure 4.8 Cornelis Norbertus Gysbrechts, *Trompe l'oeil with Violin, Painter's Implements and Self-Portrait* (1674).

With realism, a scene is placed behind the surface on which the image is created, whereas with *trompe-l'oeil*, the illusion also appears to come forward, standing out from the material surface of the image, projecting out into real space. An especially confounding example of *trompe-l'oeil* is achieved when used in combination with ordinary realism; for example, when a painting of a scene that is clearly situated behind its material surface appears to have a fly resting upon it.

And yet, we are not quite fooled. If *trompe-l'oeil* was entirely integrated into the real world it would pass unnoticed. At first glance *trompe-l'oeil* deceives, but on further consideration doubts arise and as viewers we typically put out a hand to verify by touch and only then to find for certain that we have been hoodwinked. *Trompe-l'oeil* confounds the real with appearance; it creates an ambiguity between life and artifice.

Magicians are masters of illusion. They have relied on basically the same repertoire of deception for thousands of years: surprising appearances and disappearances, things being destroyed and then reincarnated as whole, inexhaustible supplies of something from a small container, and defiance of gravity through levitation. When practised well, magic tricks appear to defy the rules of nature.

Ordinarily we do not like to be fooled. Where then does the pleasure lie in being fooled by illusionistic tricks?

Part of the pleasure lies in our admiration for the skills involved. Illusion makes us doubt our own powers of perception, but our cognitive dissonance is rewarded with a feeling of gratification for, once understood, we invariably appreciate the illusionist's skill. Illusion is a practical joke, a 'gotcha game', the pleasure of it being to find that we have been its victim.

Much of the pleasure in a magic show also lies in thinking we know how a trick is, or could be, managed, and then being bewildered when what we think is shown to be impossible. Knowing that an audience is looking to see behind the magic, magicians often misdirect by showing, for example, that nothing is up their sleeves, or by having an audience volunteer testify that they have had no prior experience with the performer. When the illusion is managed in spite of these proofs the pleasure of amazement is that much greater. The desire to be confounded works even when one knows it is chicanery.

Counter to the delight in being deceived, there is also the joy of being in the know about how illusions are created, of seeing behind the curtain. In the first century CE, the Greek engineer Heron exposed the mechanisms of the magic long practised in Ancient Egypt; for example, of how fire could be made to suddenly appear and disappear with the use of certain chemicals, and how things could be made to appear and disappear using rods, pulleys and trapdoors. Today, these and similar tricks are available in the numerous books that take readers behind the magic to reveal how tricks are achieved. It is hard not to be impressed at how elaborate the set ups are, and, once the secret is out, how obvious it was.

Illusions surprise and delight. We love being momentarily fooled, and then we love finding out how we were fooled and solving the mystery, but we also enjoy continuing to be baffled.

A realistic style

Realism refers to styles that approximate the actual appearance of real life. This is not illusion as discussed above where the aim was to deceive. Although *trompe l'oeil* was common throughout much of Western art history, it was never more than a footnote to the more usual practice of mimicking the veridical world. To mimic is to imitate or copy, to simulate or resemble closely in such a way that, as viewers, we are happy to make believe that the imitation stands in for the thing represented. This is verisimilitude, a faithful rendering of the appearance of something without any intent to confuse reality with representation. We may be drawn in, but we are not taken in.

Among painters and sculptors, the attempt is clearly evident in Ancient Greece, and while it later declined under the influence of early Christianity, it was rediscovered in twelfth-century Europe and has continued unabated ever since. Towards the end of the nineteenth century, modernist, avant-garde artists turned their backs on the then centuries-old tradition of pictorial realism, but popular taste has remained decidedly grounded in faithful, realistic representation. Since the twelfth century, the history of Western pictures has been a steady search for ever more realism as well as more kinds of realism. Always there was a desire to pour more detail into a given space.

In painting, the use of oils on canvas greatly increased the degree of realism possible with murals on plaster. Painting was understood as a window on the world. With other visual media, the same desire for ever-greater realism is apparent. With printmaking, woodcut was superseded by etching and engraving, which in turn was superseded by lithography and then photolithography. While artists have continued to paint, painting was long ago superseded by photography as the dominant visual cultural form. From its invention in 1839, the success of photography was phenomenal. Everyone wanted their photograph taken and within decades of its invention, photographers had ventured into many parts of the world to satisfy the publics' hunger for accurate representations of the world beyond their own locality (Figure 4.9).

Figure 4.9 Carleton Watkins, *Merced River, Yosemite, California* (1865).

As the dominant cultural form, photography was in turn superseded by film. With film, increasingly better stock provided ever more detail, and silent film was replaced by sound to make pictures multimodal. With printmaking, photography and film alike, black and white was superseded with colour and then ever better colour; and today, digital has superseded analogue to provide even greater detail and colour reproduction.

It is easy to understand the attraction of realism. Everyone understands a realistic image. Commercial enterprises employ pictorial realism to relate to the broadest possible number of consumers just as governments use photographic realism to communicate with the largest number of their citizens. Realism has been considered democratic because everyone understands it.

Think of how important photographic realism is to family photography, and how crucial it is to family life. Family photography, especially of children, is one of the most common forms of image making in the world, and family photographs are often the most prized possession among older family members, being the first to be rescued from the threat of fire or flood. Many household items can be repurchased, but a record of one's family life is irreplaceable. Family photography is the focus of profound emotions, of all the trials and joys of lives spent together. However ordinary they are to others, they are endlessly fascinating to ourselves.

Realistic images bring to mind those who are loved but absent; facilitate an emotional connection with fictional characters; and show parts of the world that are otherwise inaccessible. With painting we delight in realism because of the artist's skill, and with all forms of realism. We enjoy both comparing the image to the original and discovering the original from the copy.

Formulae

A formula is a prescription followed in order to achieve a predictable result. They are synonymous with conventions in being widely understood by viewers. The great virtue of visual formulae is that they are immediately recognizable, which is important where either the audience is illiterate or the time to develop characters and situations is limited.

Modernists, who championed originality, attacked formulae for a lack of imagination. Both image-makers and viewers were condemned as uncreative. This is despite the fact that, as discussed in the previous chapter on rhetoric, fine art paintings relied heavily on formulae for millennia. For example, the Holy Family and major Christian saints were all readily identifiable through easily recognizable attributes of age, dress and accompaniments.

Today, film genres like action adventure, romantic comedies and horror are synonymous with formulae. The formulae are like road maps in which one is able to tell not only where the roads are but also where they will lead. They are also like cooking recipes that contain all the ingredients that must be used, and which to be successful are then mixed in a step-by-step process.

Characters, conventions and plots are reworked over and over. The characters, often called archetypal types or stock characters, represent a whole class of people by means of a single prominent trait. The ancient Greek playwright Theophrastus introduced thirty character types; for example, the flatterer, the fabricator, the penny-pincher, the coward, the insincere show-off and the faultfinder. Today's genre movies similarly rely upon a range of stock characters such as the wise old man; the yokel, an unsophisticated country person; the jock, a muscular but not very intelligent male athlete; the nerd, a socially impaired, obsessive and overly intellectual person; the boy next door, an average nice guy; the girl next door, an average girl with a wholesome outlook; and the mad scientist, who is insane or highly eccentric and often villainous (Figure 4.10).

Genres rely upon readily identified conventions, some of which are ages old. Consider horror movies. The conventions of decapitated heads, walking dead, hideous monsters and cannibalism have been reused from century to century. Twenty-first-century horror entertainment recycles conventions of twentieth-century comic books and cinema, which reused conventions drawn from the nineteenth-century stage, which recycled eighteenth-century gothic novels, which reworked conventions of seventeenth-century paintings, which repackaged medieval imagery, which took their cue from the biblical Book of Revelation and Ancient Greek theatre.

Web 4.5
Formulae

Genre movies rely upon plots to drive their stories rather than the idiosyncrasies of individual characters. They are plot rather than character driven, characters being used primarily to serve the plot.

So formulaic are these characters and plots, is it curious that they remain popular? If we know what to expect, why do we still choose to watch the same old thing?

Narrative formulae have the great advantage of reducing life's confounding complexity. Real life is invariably complicated, often nasty and rarely with clear resolutions. Narratives compress all the

Figure 4.10 J.J. *Mad Scientist Caricature* (2003).

world's complexity by neatly dividing it into a beginning, a middle and an end that closes off the conflict. Whatever happens, however nasty, resolutions are provided; moreover, with genre stories, resolutions are often happy. Knowing what we are about to see we can anticipate the pleasures to come, so much so that we may feel frustrated when our expectations are not realized.

Formulae are familiar and familiarity is comforting; they reassure, and given the ongoing complexities of the world and our anxious responses, narrative formulae provide repeated reassurance. Just as children want to hear the same story over and over in order to fully assimilate lessons and to feel safe, adults seek security through repetition. Children's play is involuntarily caught up in repetitive acts that demonstrate an instinct for mastery over the conflicts and anxieties that give rise to their play. Their repetitive play is at the same time pleasurable and indicative of the persistence of anxiety. Formula fiction is a dramatization that is similarly part pleasure and part trauma. The incentive for repeatedly exposing ourselves to stories of essentially the same kind involves an ongoing mixture of pleasure and anxiety.

The fact that romantic comedies repeatedly end happily suggests that we know relationships do not always end this way, but we prefer to return to, or look forward to, a time during courtship which, despite its own complications, is a giddy time filled with possibilities. The action genre with its stories of unstoppable heroes, or superhero stories with invincible heroes, suggests we acknowledge that we are rarely heroic, but we seek to feel heroic.

Yet we equally enjoy innovation. We enjoy finding out how a new film reinterprets the formulae. Consider the single most famous 'rags to riches' story, the tale of Cinderella. Disney's 2012 remake of its animated 1942 version used lived actors, but this was not the only significant change. Although the new version used similar costumes and followed the older one almost scene for scene, scenes were also added that made Cinderella appear more complex and powerful than her previous incarnation. The earlier version of a demure Cinderella who quietly accepted her fate would not have been welcomed. We enjoy seeing how current values are positively acknowledged and incorporated. With formulae, convention and innovation go hand in hand.

Finally, some movies and television programmes go further than updating formulae; they deliberately work against formulae, where interest is peaked by seeing the familiar determinedly turned on its head. This happened with westerns. As the formulae grew stale, new westerns were made that revisioned the genre; heroes became anti-heroes, Indians were humanized, and clearly defined conflicts between good versus bad were blurred.

Formulae reassure. They reduce complexity, and their repetition addresses an ongoing need for reassurance. And the pleasure of the familiar goes hand in hand with the pleasure of what is new or innovative.

The many pleasures of pictures

There are many pleasures to pictures. Depending upon who we are and the kind of pictures we view, these pleasures include being awed, taken out of ourselves, stimulated, fascinated, temporarily deceived, comparing pictures with reality, comforted, connected to other people, liberated, transgressing social norms, facing our demons, spicing up our lives or simply indulging in our human love of looking. All such experiences are either morally benign or life giving.

However, as discussed in the next chapter, some of the aesthetic pleasures discussed above are also deeply problematic. Many of them can be used against us to further the ends of other people. And some of them require us to think through whether our own enjoyment is also morally compromised. Pictures are not always innocent.

Questions

1 Can you think of pleasures that are not covered in the above chapter?
2 To what extent do the above descriptions of the above pleasures describe your own experience? Do some of the descriptions of the attractions appear exaggerated or not even valid at all?
3 Among the above pleasures some appear obvious but others might at first glance appear not at all obvious. Which is which?
4 Why do some people like horror movies and/or violent action movies and/or sentimental movies and some people do not like them? Consider other kinds of movies or television programmes and consider why they are not liked by everyone.
5 Are there any common threads among the attractions to different pleasures?

Activities

1 Create a PowerPoint using pictures from the Internet that exemplify one or more of the pleasures of pictures. Choose pictures from the past and present and across cultures. Some of the pictures you choose could be drawn from examples given in this chapter but feel free to introduce your own examples.
2 Alternatively, instead of starting with the pleasures described above, look for the particular attractions such as awe or comfort, and find pleasures that arouse such emotional reactions. Then create a PowerPoint.
3 Alternatively, create a collage of either activities 1 or 2.
4 After reading Chapter 7 on intertextuality, start with one pleasure, or a specific example of one pleasure, and create an intertext showing how the pleasures can relate to one another.
5 Choose a picture that exemplifies one of the pleasures discussed above and examine it in terms of the points made about it in the section on that pleasure. For example, if choosing an example of the exotic, is its attraction due to spicing up your culture, your own life, because you feel superior to it, or do you desire it as something superior to your own culture or your own life?

See Chapter 8 for specific questions on aesthetic seduction: Why do people look at it? What use is made of emotions? What use is made of sensory qualities? What of moral criteria?

5

Some Problems of Pleasure

Everyday pleasures and their problems

The harm pictures can do is partly a matter of their ability to undermine critical thinking through their emotional sensory nature, and partly a matter of their everyday nature. It is everyday life that provides the basis from which spring all our conceptualizations, definitions and life stories. Everyday routines, the repetitive taken-for-granted experiences, ground in our beliefs and values, and today more than at any time in history, pictures are an integral part of everyday life.

We learn very little through self-discovery; mostly we learn through repeated exposure to the world around us and assimilating through osmosis, and more often than not, learning is unconscious. We appreciate powerful, isolated learning experiences, but they are usually poor indicators of what constitutes learning as a whole. Most learning is prosaic. Day in and day out the same lessons are repeated until skills come automatically, knowledge appears incontestable, and beliefs and values seem unassailable; and there is now nothing more everyday than pictures.

In education, no one doubts the significance of the so-called 'hidden curriculum' wherein students learn at a deep, unconscious level social values that are never explicitly taught and are often unconscious even to teachers. It follows that learning about the world is achieved mainly through everyday rather than special experiences, partly because the lessons of the everyday are ground in through repetition and partly because the lessons go unrecognized as lessons. When the lessons come enfolded in aesthetic pleasure, it is hard to resist.

The bright and the busy

The bright and busy often delight us but they can also make us vulnerable to persuasion. This is noticeably true in commercial environments. When supermarkets were first developed it was thought that people appeared to purchase more than they would over a counter because confronted with an abundance of stimuli, they became anxious, but research indicated the opposite. Blinking eyes is a sound indication of anxiety, and researchers found that instead of the rate going up to indicate anxiety as predicted, the rate went down. Normally we blink around thirty-two times per minute, but hidden cameras indicated that walking down the aisles of a supermarket, women blinked only half as much, about fourteen times per minute. This is just short of being in a trance or hypnotic state, a state in which one is especially vulnerable to suggestion. Supermarkets, of course, are carefully designed to make suggestions. Shelves stacked with numerous competing products almost all employing the emotive element of fully saturated colour call out 'buy me'. Most people report that they do buy items in supermarkets that they never had any intention of buying upon entering, so that among the many other means of enticing people to purchase, a hard-wired attraction to the bright and busy seems cunningly exploited by commercial interests. In short, colour and clutter has the distinct purpose of selling goods, a phenomenon known to ancient market vendors as much as supermarket operators today. Far from being superficial, a matter of mere surface, for retailers there is nothing so serious as a bright and busy aesthetic.

The seduction of the bright and busy is part of a larger concern with highly attractive visual phenomenon. For example, Disney animated cartoons are beautifully colourful with wonderfully sinuous, ever moving lines and shapes, yet they are notorious for offering sexist, racist and xenophobic ideas. Consider the aesthetics and values of *Build-A-Bear Workshop* (Figure 5.1). This is a retail franchise with branches all over the United States, Europe and Asia. It is a cultural site of particular interest to education, for it is targeted at K-6 children. Instead of selling ready-made stuffed toys, *Build-A-Bear* allows a child to choose unstuffed animals, have them stuffed to a child's preferred level of 'huggability', choose clothes for the toys – there is a vast selection – and perform a birth ritual by dressing and fluffing up the toys. The stores are laid out to facilitate this process with seven successive individual booths named Choose Me, Hear Me, Stuff Me/Stitch Me, Fluff Me, Dress Me, Name Me and Take Me Home. Children are encouraged to commit to their stuffed animal with the promise to make their toy 'their #1 pal', which can be demonstrated by buying clothes – otherwise the bear would be naked – and accessories (all of which have stratified price tickets). The stores are brightly coloured and children dance about playfully as they proceed through the purchasing process. The tender emotions of caring, compassion and empathy, of nurturance, are activated to ensure financial reward, and children are taught that love and materialism go hand in hand. A store sign reads, 'Clothes make a bear feel really special', thus encouraging children to believe that if they buy clothes for their bear they demonstrate love; and, further, the truly pernicious, general message that it is through the buying and gifting of material goods that love is shown. Here, a bright and busy aesthetic is combined with sentimentality to create consumer demand, and thereby promote the ideology of consumer capitalism of continual consumption.

Build-A-Bear illustrates the connection between aesthetics and social cohesion, for without aesthetic seduction consumer capitalism would be seriously disabled. It illustrates just how early

Figure 5.1 Aolden23, *Build-A-Bear Workshop, Potomac Mills, Virginia, United States* (2018).

the basic lesson of contemporary capitalism – to consume – is taught through aesthetic experience. However, if children are to learn that love, joy, compassion, empathy and so on can be expressed by many means, they need exposure to more than the cultural sites of corporate capitalism; they need loving parents and teachers, including teachers who will address the tension that so often exists between pleasure and ideas, beliefs and values.

The spectacular

The spectacular is often described in a negative light; for example, theatrical and glitzy. A theatrical spectacular means an extravagant or irrelevantly histrionic display, a calculated and/or showy display. Glitzy describes an extravagant, ostentatious or a glamorous display in poor taste. The spectacular is thereby accused of being devoid of serious purpose, to be sensationalist: sensation without good purpose. The spectacular is constantly on a knife edge between wowing and being silly: of pomp turned into pompous; grand into grandiosity; glorious into vainglory, and gigantic into gargantuan, in which the former impresses and the latter appears a vacuous overreach. Along these lines, spectacle is often criticized in movies as a cosmetic thrill, offering scale over subtlety, eliminating character development and reducing narrative to a succession of spills and thrills. Each of these criticisms relates either to taste or to the undermining of intention by overreach.

A more serious problem lies in the ability of the spectacular when it actually works, that is, when it overwhelms us. While losing oneself is uplifting, a liberating experience in which we feel part of something beyond our own mere existence, it also makes us vulnerable to suggestion. Due to sheer size, spectacles can suggest that might makes right.

Consider how the Nazis used their annual rallies with up to 700,000 highly drilled participants. The rallies were filmed, most famously by Leni Riefenstahl. Her 1935 *Triumph of the Will* interweaves close-ups of people with vast panoramas of massed troops and lengthy parades of troops filing past Hitler. At the time Germans had not witnessed images of military power since the end of the First World War in 1918 so the rallies demonstrated that with Hitler as leader Germany was once again becoming a great power. The rallies were intended to cement the relationship between ordinary Germans and the Nazi party, while the massed troops also acted as a warning to dissidents not to resist. The message was clear: the Nazi party was all-powerful; it was foolish to think otherwise.

The fact that scale matters when setting out to impress was known to many ancient civilizations. The Babylonians, Mayans, Aztecs and Chinese each built on a grand scale. Monumental structures aided the elite of ancient Egypt in maintaining a largely slave society (Figure 5.2). Hierarchy, power, and spectacle have long been connected.

Figure 5.2 Musik Animal. *Pillars of the Great Hypostyle Hall in Karnak, Luxor, Egypt* (1290–1224 BCE).

Another difficulty lies in how a love of spectacular scenery can affect environmental sustainability. Spectacular landscapes that conform to the eighteenth-century aesthetic of the sublime see some landscapes protected, and others deemed boring and consequently unworthy of protection. Wetlands and prairies have historically had little chance over mountain ranges and waterfalls. Our aesthetic sensibilities act to marginalize geographic areas that lack the awe-inspiring wonderment of the spectacular but that nevertheless serve critical ecological functions. The protection of non-scenic, unspectacular environments on ecological grounds is often met with derision. We form emotional attachments with what we find aesthetically pleasing, but conversely what we consider dreary or just ugly we are prepared to see destroyed.

In summary, the spectacular is a matter of great delight, but also it can overreach, be used to manipulate us and work against environments that are not spectacular.

Sentimentality

As described in the previous chapter, sentimentality also has been attacked on grounds of taste, but it too can have serious consequences that go far beyond taste. First, in viewing subjects as sweetly innocent, sentimentality can disempower its subjects. For example, seeing children as simply innocents in need of adult protection robs them of the rights they might otherwise be thought to possess. Worse, it may also beget a crude reaction when other realities intrude. Sentimental images of children as perfect angels cast children who break the stereotype as devils. An ideal of perfectly innocent children sets up a fantasy that real children can never match, which leads to disappointment at best and may at worst be associated with abuse. The truth is that children are neither angels nor devils, but like adults, a complex mixture of characteristics neither wholly good nor wholly bad. Additionally, sentimental images can distract from social realities. Consider how children were pictured as sweetly innocent during the nineteenth century at the very time that child labour was widespread (Figure 5.3). They are the forerunners of today's cards and calendars of sweetly aesthetized children in a world of child labour and child soldiers.

The bifurcation of stereotypes is also apparent with ethnicities. Sentimental stereotypes are sometimes offered to counter negative ones, but in offering a patronizing perspective they too are disempowering. Being stereotyped as sweet and harmless, even cute, strips people of their complex humanity and encourages patronizing and disempowering public policies that treat them as if they were helpless children rather than possessing their own agency.

Sentimentality can be equally disempowering of viewers. While sentimental images can sometimes be used to challenge the status quo in the cause of social justice, they can also lead to nothing more than an indulgence of emotional sympathy. It is always easier, and certainly safer, to shed a tear than confront injustice. By means of sentimentality, one can be false to oneself, a way of feeling good about oneself as a sympathetic, sensitive soul without the expense involved in taking action.

Furthermore, when the victims of trauma embrace sentimentality, it can simultaneously act to comfort them while encouraging their own infantilization. The cheerful embrace by cancer sufferers of their status as survivors through the purchase of teddy bears and other similar items constructs them as infants in a way that negates their fear and rage.

Figure 5.3 Amalia Lindegren, *Breakfast* (1866).

One can be sentimental about many things: a country, a social cause, other people, even war. Used in the service of political and social causes the effects of sentimentality can be grave. Countless millions have died in wars as a consequence of failing to see though sentimental appeals with little if any direct relevance to the issues at hand. During World War I the Allies were motivated by posters and other propaganda that claimed the Germans had killed Belgian babies. No doubt people were more willing to believe the Germans were brutes because it was babies they were alleged to have killed rather than adults. The powerful emotional attachment we all feel towards defenceless, vulnerable babies managed to subvert scepticism to the propaganda claims, claims that consequently were shown to be completely false.

The mischaracterization of something as sweetness and light results in an equally brutish mischaracterization that too often ends in violence and oppression. Consider how Americans reacted following the 2001 attack on the World Trade Center in New York. Deeply committed to the view of their own history as wholesome, family-friendly fare, they consequently cast

Figure 5.4 Sheila Lau, *Seven Month Old Panda Cub at the Wolong Nature Reserve, Sichuan, China* (2006).

themselves when attacked as innocent victims. Understanding themselves as innocent, they had neither the motive nor any basis for self-reflection. They lacked the grounds on which to consider how their own actions in the world might have contributed to their being attacked.

Not even our sentimental attachments to soft and furry, cute animals are entirely innocent (Figure 5.4). Just as an aesthetic of the spectacular can marginalize unspectacular but ecologically important environments, so a sentimental aesthetic can sideline the protection of animals over which we tend not to be sentimental. Our love of soft and furry, especially baby, animals helps to protect them against eradication, but it can also mean the neglect of other less alluring animals with equally significant ecological roles to play. Baby pandas get protected; lizards and snakes do not. Conversely, a love of baby animals means that the ecologically justified culling of adult animals can be obstructed. The phenomenon is known as 'the Bambi effect'. Whether in under- or overprotecting these animals, our sentimental preferences may stand in the way of environmental sustainability. Our sentimental associations pit us against sustaining the environment.

In dealing with sentimental appeals, to the tender emotions of love and compassion, we always need to be aware of how our heartstrings are being worked upon. When the stakes are high, it is important to examine the facts and face reality rather than retreat into a nostalgic past or avoid reality by viewing it in warm, sentimental terms.

The exotic

The use of the exotic to cast some people as other than ourselves helps to establish our own cultural identity, but exoticism invariably involves exaggeration, domestication or even outright invention. Consequently, the referenced culture always suffers some degree of distortion. In the early 1700s, England began to take an interest in many things Chinese. The initial interest lay in the belief that they represented a social and political continuity (Figure 5.5). In China, they represented a period of history that had already passed; they represented change. At the time England sought status by associating itself with a culture considered superior. But why should any culture feel that another is superior and inversely one's own culture to be inferior? The question arises today as so many Asians, especially the Japanese, undergo eye surgery in order to look more western. Similarly, many Korean women use hand gestures to mask their typically wide faces in an effort to appear to have western-like oval faces. Why should western standards of beauty be regarded as superior? Rather than viewing one culture as better than another, why are different cultures regarded, and celebrated, as simply different?

Web 5.1
Exoticism

Perhaps the most common relation of one culture to another is not to feel inferior to the other but to indulge in a sense of superiority. Exoticism has often been used in order to make a culture feel good about itself by denigrating the other culture. Today tourism can also shrink the mind as well as open it. Tourists often complain about cultures other than their own for not having the amenities with which they are familiar, for being less efficient, more dangerous than home or simply being incomprehensible. Tourists often complain that foreign countries are a rip off, a tourist trap. Foreign countries are thereby rendered less evolved and less honest than one's own and thus on a moral scale, less worthy.

The pleasures of exoticism are further complicated when the dominant culture projects onto the other its own dark side, failing to see in its projection a mirror of itself. When negative stereotypes are used over and over and go uncontested, shown as if in the nature of things, they establish a view of the other that invites denigration, and real-world consequences can be catastrophic. Going to war has been so much easier because the other is understood to be inherently inferior. Was the selling of the US invasion of Iraq in 2003 to the US public made easy because for centuries the Middle East had been represented in paintings, photographs and films as degenerate, a fantasy realm in which Europeans located their own anxieties, desires and social preoccupations? While purporting to be an image of all that the West was not, many of the conventions used to represent the Orient were a projection of the darker, unacceptable side of European life. The Orient was an imaginary place into which seamy, violent passions and frustrations could be projected and enjoyed while simultaneously denying their existence at home.

Irrespective of the media, Orientalist conventions were consistent from the eighteenth to the twentieth century. Compare Figures 2.10 and 4.1. As described in chapter 2, Orientalist stereotypes were invariably negative. Arab women were almost always alluring, and Arab men were typically villainous. As buffoons they were forever stumbling over themselves, as oversexed they consistently took a licentious interest in Western women, and as violent they fought and killed every sort of foe. They were quintessentially evil. Thus did the West project its own unrecognized and unfulfilled desires onto the other, justify its exploitation of the resources of the Middle East, and fail to confront its own cultural limitations. While claiming superiority, Europeans adopted amnesia towards their own culture. The processes of projection and denial went hand in hand. Not only was the referenced culture demeaned, but also the dominant culture avoided self-examination. It refused to take responsibility for its own limitations and was thereby rendered helpless to address them.

Denigrating others by imagining them as monsters seems characteristic of societies deeply troubled by their own bad dreams. It is far more pleasurable to enjoy the monster in others than to recognize it in oneself. This explains the lure of the exotic but does not excuse it.

A further difficulty with exoticism is that sometimes the referenced culture is a willing participant in its own exoticism. A marginalized culture that has long been ignored, rendered invisible to anyone but itself, is sometimes easily seduced by the promise of recognition. This applies even when in order to gain attention the marginalized culture must deny its own everyday reality and concoct itself as exotic. In the early 1980s, Hong Kong revitalized its then ailing film industry by producing Kung Fu movies. This established a taste in the West for Chinese films, though only insofar as they mixed Hollywood narratives with breath-taking action and were set in China's distant past. The East has long been willing to play the piper to Western taste. As mentioned earlier, an interest in Chinese goods led to the development of *Chinoiserie*, a completely hybrid style invented specifically for the European market that bore little or no resemblance to anything produced in China for its own home market (Figure 5.5). Chinese craftsmen produced wallpapers, furniture and porcelain sets to order from European designs that were European conceptions of Chineseness that no one in China would have recognized as Chinese.

Today, as many parts of the world struggle financially, they are willing to turn themselves into exotic sites, emphasizing not what is typical about them but what is atypical. All over the world, modern-day tourism is enabled by communities recreating themselves as exotic destinations.

The pleasures of the exotic are many, but so are its problems. Exotic images enchant, but the exotic always involves a relationship of power in which a referenced culture is used for one's own purposes. A culture can feel inferior to another, or more seriously, it can feel superior, and a marginal culture, seeking recognition and/or financial support can turn itself into something it is not.

Eroticism

Compared to only a few decades ago, our times are characterized by a highly sexualized media. Some describe our society as pornified, in which the tropes of pornography have become mainstream. To justify such permissiveness, the media positon themselves as socially progressive, champions of civil liberties and free speech. Eroticization is cast as a war on the one hand against the prudery of a bygone era dominated by organized religion and old-fashioned family values, and on the other hand by the politically correct liberal and feminist police. But does this mean that we are finally liberated or are we under a new form of repression? Having thrown off the repression of

Figure 5.5 Unknown, *Vase Decorated with Chinoiserie Figures* (eighteenth century).

Web 5.2
Sexuality religion, have we imposed upon ourselves the repression of the market place? As Foucault suggested decades ago, just as the prohibitive practices of the past had grave consequences, so the consequences of a highly sexualized media are deeply problematic. The problems of permissiveness are different from prohibition, but just as consequential.

For Freud, fetishizing a woman's body represented 'a token of triumph over the threat' that women posed (cited in Williams, 1989, p. 104). It was a strategy of control. By viewing women as a collection of body parts, men attempted to turn women into something reassuring rather than dangerous. Consider advertising in which a body or body parts are turned into the advertised product. Such imagery reinforces misogyny.

Additionally, a great deal of evidence suggests that for many people, mostly for women but also for men, highly sexualized imagery causes self-objectification, an internalizing of oneself as primarily a mere sex object. People acquire a sense of themselves as sexual commodities that moreover can never live up to the body images offered by the media. Advertising, for example, has reinvented the smooth perfection of the closed bodies of fine art nudes, and also, like fine art nudes, pornography has now eliminated pubic hair. Thus, considered by the impossible standards of popular media, people are shamed and disgusted by their own appearance, which in turn leads to eating disorders to become or stay slim, sexual dysfunction, and the trivialization of intimacy and consequent depression. Women now spend millions on Botox, laser and eyelid surgery, breast implants and liposuction, and there is an epidemic of eating disorders. Men feel the need to beef up in a form of reverse anorexia. And many observers are most troubled by the media's sexualization of children, what some call corporate paedophilia.

Highly sexualized imagery is not a concern because it is too sexy, but because it offers no alternatives. To represent bodies as sexual is no more problematic than acknowledging that we are sexual beings. The problem is that some media, especially advertising, music videos and fashion, are so influenced by pornography that they often represent people as no more than sexual commodities. The erotic permissiveness of the marketplace is as much an exercise of power as earlier forms of prohibition and, as with any form of power, there are winners and losers. For many observers, ordinary viewers of today's highly eroticized popular culture are, ultimately, the losers.

Violence

Researchers firmly reject any direct causal relationship between mediated violence and actual violence, but entertainment violence does appear to have real-world consequences. Only mentally disturbed people watch violent media and then act violently. And while mediated violence is not alone in being responsible for real-world violence, it does appear to be at least a contributing factor. From a theoretical perspective, it could not be otherwise. As discussed in Chapter 1, pictures are not separate from the rest of society, a mere passive expression or reflection of an otherwise constituted reality. Pictures are an integral part of the real world, both a reflection of it and a lively contributor to it. Pictures help to frame our beliefs and values. They draw upon our existing views and, in turn, create powerful mental maps to understand the world, and such mental maps then provide scripts for real world behaviour. Visual images thereby play an active role in helping to determine the nature of the real world.

Web 5.3
Bullying

A wealth of research studies bear out this general theoretical point with regard to violence (e.g. Goldstein, 1998). Contrary to the theory of catharsis, media violence does not reduce fear and anxiety, but induces them, cognitively and affectively. And when people are anxious they tend to think in simple black and white terms, seeing themselves versus others in terms of good versus bad. People view themselves as good and innocent and others as evildoers. Through the inducement of apprehension and fear, media violence creates a general framework for viewing the real world in terms of actual threats, and fearful of being victims of violence, people tend to be drawn towards retaliatory violence. Violent images thereby contribute to hostile constructs and mental scripts. While not violent themselves, people are more willing than they would otherwise be to allow the police and armed services to use violence on their behalf. While they would never themselves harm another person, they are more prepared to sanction violence on their behalf. Such violence is justified as legal violence, violence mediated through the state as a third party. Perpetrated by the state, legal violence is considered necessary for the common good.

Driven by fear and anxiety, a cycle of violence is created. Repeated representations of violence raise levels of fear and anxiety that, in turn, create a view of the real world in terms of actual threats, which leads to sanctioning real violence, which is then enacted by the state, which is then recycled in violent media fantasies, which are then justified as no more than reflecting real life. Thus, popular media violence and real-life violence feed off and reflect each other.

Paradoxically, it is the desire to live in a safe, stable and predictable world, especially when feeling threatened, that influences the acceptance of violence to secure safety. This dynamic is repeated ad nauseam in popular media fantasies. Antagonists invariably threaten the status quo while protagonists re-establish the status quo, but consider that protagonists typically use a great deal more violence than the antagonists. In innumerable action movies, protagonists are often sociopaths who, given licence to right wrongs, go on a killing spree.

Consider also the idea that factious protagonists and antagonists are stand-ins for the social fabric. In this case the protagonists would represent the state and social stability, and antagonists would represent the forces of social disorder such as anarchy, subversion, crime and terrorism. In one violent spectacle after another, the state, represented by the hero, defends social stability against the disorderly forces that threaten it. Media violence is thereby a means through which the cornerstone of social cohesion is maintained. Moreover, typically the hero perpetrates more violence than the villain. If we continue to think of fictional heroes and villains as stand-ins for whole societies, this means that social stability is defended by violence more often than threatened by it. Any amount or kind of real life violence is justified in defence of social stability.

Violence in popular entertainment is exceedingly complex. There are many kinds of violent entertainment and much of it is probably benign. Violence is often humorous, and some of it might be necessary in a generally mediated and rationalized society for stimulation. Some is undoubtedly legitimized by serious narrative purposes. Yet today societies all over the world routinely indulge in massive and visceral media violence that is only nominally required by a plot.

Fear is a universal of the human condition and it is easy to arouse, and symbolic violence may be the easiest way to cultivate it effectively. This suggests that a violence-saturated media plays a role in maintaining social order. Fearful of terrorism and feeling frustrated about the limits to freedom in overly rationalized, sanitized societies, people all over the world turn to media fantasies of violent retribution. Violent media help create and maintain a culture of fear and anxiety, which, in turn, serves the socioeconomic and sociopolitical status quo. It is perhaps a shocking idea that popular media violence is an important factor in the maintenance of the social fabric. It is especially troubling to note that the violence perpetrated by the protagonists in retribution against the forces of chaos are greater than those perpetrated by the antagonists in their creation of disorder.

Given the ongoing connection between media and real world violence, the question is: what are we to do? Should media violence be banned or tuned down? In any event, it is precisely because media violence helps engender fear and anxiety with real world consequences that violent entertainment is a profoundly problematic issue.

Destruction and horror

The problems with violence similarly plague images of destruction and horror. They raise levels of anxiety that feed into the splitting of actual people into good and bad. Destruction raises fear of our own destruction. Such images arise from our fears of destruction and then feed into them, giving them a tangible reality. And abject monsters of horror movies and horrific spilling of guts remind us of our own vulnerability. Both images of destruction and horror remind us of our tenuous hold on normal, everyday life, which creates anxiety, which then leads to the sanctioning of violence on our behalf in order to maintain our own peaceful way of life.

Web 5.4
Horror and Hate

There is a long history of picturing enemies as horrific monsters, monsters that break social taboos and wreak havoc on a vast scale. They have long been used to motivate commitment to wars on both sides (Figure 5.6). They appeal to our base instincts. We respond viscerally and are consequently highly vulnerable to suggestion.

Figure 5.6 DPA Ludwig 90054, *Anti-Soviet, Anti-Semite German World War II Propaganda Poster* (1939–45).

Humour

Today there is such a profoundly positive view of humour that to suggest humour is problematic runs the risk of appearing to be a churlish killjoy. Both popular self-help literature and academic researchers laud the positive benefits of humour to those both physically and psychologically ill. Pedagogues laud its value in creating an atmosphere conducive to learning and business managers recommend it to ease relationships in the workplace. A sense of humour is now regarded as a vital human quality; someone without a sense of humour is thought of as boring, even suspect. In short, there is a pervasive belief in the warm-heartedness of humour. It is part of an optimistic, can-do outlook in which no matter what happens to people, they are encouraged to accentuate the positive.

However, humour is riddled with contradictions. While humour provides uplift, and not just for some people but for everyone, the most life-sustaining of popular pleasures, helping people to survive in the most dire circumstances, it can also be profoundly destructive of others. Indeed, humour may be the most problematic of all our pleasures.

Even mild forms of humour necessitate at least a temporary postponement of empathy. As the nineteenth-century French philosopher Henri Bergson wrote, humour requires 'a momentary anaesthesia of the heart'. When we laugh, 'we must, for the moment, put our affections out of court and impose silence upon our pity' (Billig, 2005, p. 120). A major topic of humour is other peoples' foibles of character, such as jealousies, childish fondness, vanity and self-conceit. Thus humour is frequently accompanied by a degree of contempt. Although disguised as warm-hearted and innocent, humour often involves a streak of malice. It is often anti-social and malign. It is ironic that the aesthetic of humour involves its exact opposite, a partial anaesthesia.

Moreover, an anaesthesia of the heart is not necessarily only a thing of the moment. It can also be a deep disposition towards people of another race, religion, gender, sexual orientation, and who are differently abled and so on. How else to explain the numerous websites of humour directed towards Jews, Arabs, homosexuals, lesbians and so on? (Figure 5.7) These websites contain hundreds, sometimes many thousands, of jokes, often redirected from one target to another. The fact is that a great deal of comedy comes from terribly dark places, from horrific pain and consequently humour can take some very ugly forms.

Furthermore, humour generally, though ridicule especially, plays a critical role in teaching and imposing the disciplinary codes of social life. As such, humour is simultaneously instructive and persuasive. Humour imparts the normative values of society, and by means of the pleasure it offers, it helps to persuade us to accept such values. This can be entirely beneficial to social life.

Sometimes, humour can facilitate progressive social change. The history of US television sitcoms provides a clear example. Since their inception in the early 1950s they have charted many of the social conflicts in US society: civil rights, women's rights in the home and in the workplace, children's rights, immigration and multiculturalism, as well as evolving conceptions of the family. Each of these issues has been addressed through humour in a way that has helped to make more progressive values more acceptable than hitherto. Often a character, usually someone marked as a bigot, resisted one or more of these developments and was then made to appear ridiculous. They were cut down either through their own stupidity, the one-liner chiding of others, or both. In this

Figure 5.7 Author, *Screen Grab of Internet Racist Memes* (2017).

way, the humour of sit coms acted as a cost-effective means to encourage acceptance of a more pluralistic and tolerant society.

However, as a pedagogic tool humour can also be used to repress social progress and engender intolerance. Freud explained this insight by reference to jokes. With jokes ideas come wrapped in the pleasure of humour in such a way that the ideas recommend themselves to our acceptance. We are inclined to give the ideas the benefit of the doubt because they are offered in a form we find pleasing. We are inclined to find nothing wrong in what has given us enjoyment because that would be to spoil the source of our pleasure. Finding pleasure in a joke, and not wishing to reject its pleasure, it is harder than it would otherwise be to refuse the idea the joke contains. If a joke is directed at a minority to which we do not belong, and especially if the joke is clever, it may be hard not to find some pleasure in it. At the very least, cognitive dissonance is established between rejecting the idea the joke contains and still enjoying it.

Perhaps the universality of humour, especially ridicule, is based on the universal need of parents to discipline their children. Parents almost instinctively employ mockery as a disciplinary tool; it is part of their repertoire of both pedagogic techniques and control mechanisms. Smiling knowingly, teasing and even laughing at a child's mistakes are each a part of a parent's instructional and disciplinary tool kit. Children learn not only what is funny and not funny, but also what is deemed more generally appropriate and appreciated as well as what is inappropriate and to be avoided. Being the subject of other people's humour, children learn how to think and behave towards others. The lessons can be genteel, as in teasing, or aggressive, as in the form of hostile sarcasm.

Humour can be powerfully persuasive, and as pedagogy it may have no more powerful peer. Ridicule can be deeply hurtful and cause not only an immediate flood of tears; it can scar for life. Sometimes being laughed at can be worse than death. People prefer to be hated rather than the target of ridicule, for it is easier to hate back than to ridicule in return. Thus does humour help bind people together into social groups and simultaneously divide people from one another.

Disciplinary humour mocks those who transgress social codes and thereby helps to maintain the social order, and rebellious humour can facilitate social change. Rebellious humour mocks social codes and lays a claim to challenge the social order.

However, rebellious, transgressive humour does not necessarily equate to social progress. It can work to cement the social order. From a psychological perspective, a sense of liberation undoubtedly fuels a great deal of humour, but what can feel like rebellious liberation is, from a wider social perspective, often merely a reinforcement of existing social values. Rebellion can make us feel good, but its consequences are usually limited. So it is with transgressive humour because media humour is always carefully curtailed; it is always authorized rebellion.

Consider the carnivals of medieval Europe. Medieval carnival turned all the social norms upside down, but only at certain prescribed times of the year. However much carnival transgressed social norms, when it was over, the social order was reimposed.

Today, watching *The Simpsons* and its like offers the thrill of transgression, an opportunity to thumb a nose at authority, but no avenue to act against it. Nor should we expect such programmes to do so. Television humour is produced by the same global corporations of rationally ordered societies that make transgression so attractive. The more we laugh at mass marketed rebellious humour and imagine ourselves free from social constraints, the more they hold us captive. Rebellious humour directly aids the rational order of society that produces it.

Moreover, those who ridicule in the name of rebellion may also be highly reactionary. In sitcoms, a character who habitually resists social progress can be read not as ridiculous but right, a character with whom to be identified. Transgressive pleasure is not confined to social rebellion; it is equally at home with social repression. In the US today reactionary forces frequently mock social progressives for being 'politically correct'; that is, for avoiding sexist, racist and xenophobic language.

However, undoubtedly the clearest example of rebellious but reactionary humour is Hitler's humour in regard to the Holocaust. Many explanations have been offered to explain Hitler's motivation in the genocide against the Jews. Was he a lunatic or a monster? One researcher has offered evidence for the deeply troubling idea that Hitler's evil resided in his sense of mockery (Rosenbaum, 1998). Hitler frequently shared laughter at the fate of his enemies, and it is clear from transcripts of private conversations that he enjoyed getting his own back on people who he perceived had laughed at him. His laugher is of someone who knows what he is doing and relishes getting away with it. Hitler laughed not only at the exquisite joy of revenge for perceived insults, but also at how deeply transgressive he and his comrades were being, of how illicit were their actions. This must surely be the ultimate transgression, of laughing at one's own atrocious acts.

The idea of bigots and tyrants enjoying a sense of humour at other people's expense is deeply disturbing, but only because today we normally think of humour as completely benign. The fact is that no one has a monopoly on what they consider funny. Humour does not pick sides. Like other popular pleasures, it serves whoever uses it.

A realistic style

Realistic pictures, especially photographs, are problematic because they possess evidential force. Despite their selective and carefully constructed nature, realistic pictures can appear to present irrefutable proof about people and situations. Realistic images offer a seemingly veridical view of life in which seeing is believing. Although what realistic images offer is a mediation or filtering of real life, they appear unmediated and unfiltered, a mere mechanical copy of reality, innocent of human intervention. Yet any number of examples demonstrate that it is precisely because they appear unmediated, to present nothing but the literal truth, that they are so effective in conveying falsehoods, fabricating facts and offering suspect ideas and values. For centuries, painters idealized people's appearance, represented heroic acts that in reality were anything but, and recorded events that never happened. Today photographs appear to present the truth but as described in Chapter 2 on representation, they are carefully constructed, and as described in Chapter 3 on rhetoric, one must always be sceptical about the source of images, especially today when digital manipulation is so easy.

Our relation to realistic images today is not entirely unlike medieval European's view of realistic imagery as idolatry. Medieval Europeans condemned realism, fearing that believers would mistake the image for what was represented; for example, that a picture of Jesus was in fact literally Jesus. They feared people would collapse the sign with the signifier. Today the problem is not idolatry, but fake news, that is, that people conflate photographic imagery, still or moving, with what things actually looked like or with what actually happened. The fact that images can appear so realistic is both their great value and why they remain problematic.

Formulae

The problem with formulae is simple. Formulae can be comforting, but they can also become boring. When formulae are not spiced up with novel interpretations, they soon lose their value. In the US, westerns, both movies and television series, were once very popular; in the 1950s they outnumbered all other genres. Plots of early classic westerns involved the simple goal of maintaining law and order on the western frontier with fast paced action, but westerns proved to be a very flexible genre with numerous variants of protagonists and antagonists, locations and conflicts. Heroes could be sheriffs, army officers, ranchers or a quick draw gunslinger, though villains could also be ranchers and gunslingers as well as cattle rustlers. Locations varied; they could be isolated homesteads, the desert, and/or small frontier towns. Conflicts could involve white settlers versus Indians, humanity versus nature, civilization versus wilderness and lawlessness, and rugged individualism versus community, and more generally good versus bad. Other typical elements included horses, stagecoaches, long-horned cattle, cowboy hats, spurs and saddles. Despite its enormous variety, so common did westerns become that eventually audiences became tired of them. Although there have been attempts to revive the genre with movies that deconstruct the formulae with less mythology and protagonists as antiheroes, at the present time the genre appears exhausted. Presumably the same will eventually happen to all the detective programmes and the so-called reality shows that are now a staple of television in the many countries.

Summary and implications

In the section above on humour, Freud was mentioned explaining the relationship between the pleasure of jokes and ideology, of how a joke wraps an idea, belief or value in pleasure and thereby makes it more difficult to reject the ideology than if it was offered without pleasure. This basic insight into jokes applies not only to an aesthetic of humour but more broadly to all forms of aesthetic enjoyment. Put simply, the problem with aesthetic pleasures is that they can involve more than pleasure. Each of the aesthetic pleasures listed above is capable of wrapping suspect ideologies in such a way that to enjoy the pleasure while rejecting the ideology is to set up cognitive dissonance, and many people find this unpleasant. It is so much harder to reject the pleasure than the ideology, so that in a conflict between pleasure and ideology, the pleasure is the more likely to win out.

Everyday visual experiences are highly influential in structuring thought, feelings and actions precisely because they are everyday. It is because they are so ordinary that they are so significant. The very special importance of aesthetic experiences lies precisely in their ubiquity.

There are many kinds of aesthetic pleasures, many of which are benign and can be enjoyed without a moment's thought. Others can be problematic. As educators, we need to reject an innocent view of aesthetics as a kind of magical, uplifting experience and understand how aesthetics can be used to draw us into and make acceptable arguments about the way societies are structured and lived. We may accept the lessons offered by images, but we need to do so consciously and not merely be seduced, lulled or overwhelmed. A major role of education should be to examine how aesthetic features of visual imagery offer up ideologies as natural and seductive and how they work to achieve assent.

Questions

1 Among the issues raised in this chapter, which ones do you think are a matter of taste and which ones do you think are moral issues?
2 Do you think that any of the issues raised above actually do pose a problem? If so, which ones and why?
3 Most of the examples offered here are from the West? To what extent do you think they have parallels in other parts of the world?
4 Do the pleasures of popular culture outweigh the problems or do the problems outweigh the pleasures? Is it possible to hold both in balance?
5 Considering the problems of popular visual culture, do you experience cognitive dissonance, that is, a sense that you are enjoying something but feel that you shouldn't? Why is this?
6 Have you ever watched a movie or television programme and thought: I am tired of seeing this kind of thing? In other words, has a formula run its course for you?

Activities

1 Visit a supermarket or a mall and take note of what colours are used and whether they are bright. Try to count them. What is their effect on you?

2 Watch an action genre movie, noting who the protagonists and antagonists are. Make a timeline of their interactions and consider the relative amount and kind of violence perpetrated by each.

3 Choose one of the popular pleasures. Make a two-sided collage from magazines and/or printed out from the internet. On one side celebrate the pleasure, and on the other side illustrate its problems.

4 Consider what your reactions might have been to a situation where you were daily exposed to pictures of your country's enemies as a horrid, animalistic monster.

5 Watch a comedy and take note of when you and others laugh. Consider what made you laugh? What kind of laughter were you using? How did it make you feel? On reflection, how do you feel about your laughter?

See Chapter 8 for specific questions on problems with pleasure: What of moral criteria?

6

Gazing and Glancing

The concept of the spectator's gaze

The word *gaze* in its ordinary sense means a prolonged, mindful examination, but it also has another meaning – the one used in this chapter – in which the spectator's gaze refers to all kinds of looking. As a concept rather than just one way to look, the gaze extends and complements the concepts covered in previous chapters. When discussing representation, ideology, or aesthetics in previous chapters, it often did not matter who was looking or the circumstances under which they looked. It was as if the meaning of pictures was an objective fact, and to find the meaning all anybody needed to do was look carefully because meaning lay within the pictures themselves. But this is never the case. The concept of the spectator's gaze draws attention to the fact that the meaning of pictures always involves three things: what is looked at, who is looking, and the circumstances under which they look.

As a concept, the spectator's gaze assumes that meaning is determined not only by a picture, but an interaction between the picture, what we as viewers bring to pictures, essentially, who we are, and also the context surrounding our viewing. Meaning is found through a symbiotic relationship between the picture, ourselves and our circumstances. Picture analysis should never be just of pictures as visible objects.

The significance of the gaze is primarily to reflect upon our own ways of looking for how we look tells us about ourselves. Put another way, one way to understand ourselves is to consider how we look, especially how we look at pictures of other people. This is because looking and being are so closely linked; how we look at other people in pictures is being ourselves. For example, looking at pictures of indigenous people in a curious, engaged way is being curious and engaged, at least at that moment. Looking at a picture of someone in an erotic way is acknowledging that one is a sexual being and, at least at that moment, considering the person in the picture in a limited, objectified way, not as a whole person.

Employing the concept of the spectator's gaze involves the need for reflexivity, to reflect on our own viewing, and thereby to consider who we are. The gaze involves looking inwards, of accepting that we are implicated by our own interpretation of pictures. To this extent, interpreting images is always autobiographical. Furthermore, when considering the interpretation of pictures by other people, we should consider who *they* are and the conditions of *their* looking. We need to keep in mind their gaze, be they professional media critics, historians, art connoisseurs or lay people, and how their gaze influences their interpretation.

Among the many ways to look

There are many ways to look. As noted above we may *gaze* in the conventional sense of a prolonged examination, though today we are more likely to merely *glance*, to take a quick, cursory, or intermittent look, to grab a momentary, passing glimpse. Glancing and glimpsing are perhaps the most common ways we look today as we flip through multiple television stations, surf the internet or scroll through our news feed. We may also *stare*, which means to look with wide eyes in surprise, wonder, stupidity or impertinence. We may *gape*, which is to stare with an open month, often in ignorance, wonderment or with curiosity. We may *glare*, which is to stare fiercely or angrily. We may also *peer*, *peep* and *peek* (Figure 6.1). To peer means to look with curiosity but narrowly; to peep means to look slyly or furtively, curiously or playfully; and to peek means a brief or furtive look, often from a concealed position. We may *watch*, in which we look attentively or observe something being done, maintain a guard or vigil, or keep under surveillance. We may *behold*, which has religious or spiritual connotations, or *scrutinize* which suggests engaging the intellect. More colloquially, we may *feast our eyes*, *look ardently*, or *look daggers*.

The picture, people and place dynamic

Each of the above ways of looking is determined by three factors already mentioned: pictures, people and places. They are discussed below in greater detail, and although they are discussed separately, even when separated their boundaries bleed into each other.

The picture's share

Previous chapters examined different ways in which pictures can help to determine their meaning. Such factors as lighting, camera lens, framing and angles-of-view were described. In considering

Figure 6.1 Heather Cowper, *Looking through the Keyhole at the Villa of the Knights of Malta* (no date).

body language, the intradiegetic gaze was also discussed; that is, the gaze of figures in a picture, how they appear to look and how they appear to be seen by others in the picture (Figures 2.3, 2.4, 2.5). This is not the kind of gaze being discussed here, although the intradiegetic gaze sometimes implicates the spectator's gaze. The two cannot be wholly separated because gazes within a picture often suggest how an image-maker has intended an image to be viewed; an intradiegetic gaze is often effectively a form of pedagogy for the spectator. With still pictures, a figure's gaze is sometimes a way of saying, 'you the viewer should look where I am looking'. With moving pictures, the way in which people look in one scene at another scene will often suggest how we should look. In Chapter 2 this was called *anchoring* by means of related pictures.

By contrast, this chapter deals with the audience's or spectator's gaze, our gaze as viewers. Early studies of the gaze noted that pictures in the past had been constructed in patriarchal societies in which pictures had been primarily made by men for men. Berger noted that in numerous Western fine art paintings, women were represented adopting their gender-assigned role, variously demure, coquettish and cute, and moreover that the same tropes were then being used in mainstream advertising. Berger (1972) wrote, '*Men act* and *women appear*. Men look at women. Women watch themselves being looked at' (p. 47) (Figures 2.10, 6.3). Similarly, Mulvey (1985/1988) observed that in Hollywood films from the 1930s and 1940s men carried the burden of the narrative while women were treated as spectacle; the role of men was to act while the role of women was to be looked at. She wrote of 'women as image, men as bearer of the look … In their traditional exhibitionist role women are simultaneously looked at and displayed, with their appearance coded for strong visual and erotic impact so that they can be said to connote *to-be-looked-at-ness*' (p. 62). Women were shown with lighting (and Vaseline on the camera lens) that made their faces luminous and ethereal, while men in close-up were shown in deep focus. Men existed in a sense of real space; women existed on the surface of the screen, which reduced their role primarily to spectacle and thereby lacking agency. The inevitable tension between the need to tell a story and spectacle was only overcome by building spectacle into the narrative itself, where, according to Mulvey, camera angles and editing ensured that a scene was viewed through the eyes of male protagonists and by extension, a male audience. Mulvey went so far as to claim that women were forced to adopt the male gaze.

While there is no doubting the fact that patriarchy was inscribed into many pictures in the past, and some still are, these early studies had two limitations. First, they assumed a so-called ideal male gaze, that is, a gaze that all men share, by which they meant a heterosexual male gaze. Clearly, not all men are the same. Secondly, they assumed that the gaze people used was determined by the picture and that viewers were passive. In short, these early studies did not acknowledge the degree to which we as viewers are different from one another.

The people's share

We all come to any picture already with a subject position, that is, already with beliefs and values that predispose us to view a picture through the lens of these predispositions. How we look is determined by who we are: our gender, our sexual orientation, ethnicity, class, ableness, age, experience and the extent to which we respond to the times through which we live. Consequently, many subject positions need to be acknowledged.

A distinction needs to be kept in mind between pictures made with a particular gaze in mind and how actual people view them. Images constructed with a male gaze can be read against the grain; for example, from a feminist perspective that views female nudes as sexist or just plain silly. Contrary to Mulvey's view, Hollywood films always seemed to have catered to a female gaze. In the 1920s, silent star Rudolf Valentino is said to have set women swooning and from 1918 successive Tarzans appeared near naked.

Beefcake as well as cheesecake has long been a feature of Hollywood. Today, men are as likely as women to be offered up as erotic spectacle. Consider the numerous half naked men advertising Calvin Klein jeans.

Furthermore, gender and sexual orientation are not identical and in addition to a male heterosexual gaze, we need to acknowledge a male homosexual gaze and also a female gaze that can be either heterosexual or homosexual; dislocating gender from sexual orientation means acknowledging both a straight and queer gaze. We should also acknowledge a transgender gaze. In short, a homosexual female may readily enjoy the erotic charge of images of women intended for men, and homosexual males may enjoy the images of men intended for females. No doubt this has always been the case. Consider all the nude and near nude men in the history of art that have no doubt appealed to both queer men and straight women just as much as nude or near nude women have appealed to both straight men and queer women (Figures 2.10, 6.2 and 6.3).

Regarding ethnicity, we also need to acknowledge that during the nineteenth and early twentieth centuries there existed a colonial gaze in which Europeans regarded colonized people as inherently inferior. Today, pictures of former colonial peoples can be viewed with a post-colonial gaze in which the latter interprets the former gaze as racist (Figure 6.6).

Figure 6.2 Antonio Canova, *Perseus with Medusa's Head* (1804–6).

Regarding social class, the middle class often employ a moralizing gaze by which they govern themselves and judge others as morally suspect, a gaze that is preoccupied with self-improvement and the accrual of certain forms of cultural and economic capital. On the other hand a middle-class gaze defines itself in opposition to an imagined working-class project of disinvestment of the self. By contrast, a working-class gaze tends to see in incidents the hand of fate and is resistant to middle-class moralizing.

Ableness is also a factor in how we gaze; we need to distinguish between a disabled gaze versus an able-bodied gaze. Age and experience are also factors in the way we gaze. Young children focus on details and separate parts of a picture; they are as yet unable or uninterested in relationships between parts. They take a liking to a picture if it represents a particular subject they like, effectively thinking, 'I like this picture because it is a picture of a dog and I like dogs'. Content to accept fairly abstract pictures, they will typically delight in unrealistic colours, especially if they are bright. Theirs is a culturally uninitiated or a culturally naïve gaze. Older children, who are more attuned to the values of their culture, tend to be attracted to pictures that are realistic. They operate on the basis that a picture of a dog is good primarily if the dog looks real. They tend to turn away from abstraction. In a culture where most pictures are photographically real, they are keen to value what appears the norm and to reject what is not. However, many adolescents will appreciate not only realistic but expressive pictures, especially if they have been taught to appreciate them through an art education focused upon expression. When people are also introduced to one of the many histories of pictures – of art, movies, video games and so on – they are also able to make comparative judgments between a picture and similar pictures, to situate them in terms of individual contributors, movements, national styles and so on. At the most sophisticated level of experience, that of a connoisseur, a person is able to not only gaze with a comparative eye, but also a reflexive gaze; they are able to distinguish between the value of a picture and their own preferences and prejudices, to take into consideration not only the picture upon which their eyes fall but how they might be feeling on a particular day. A connoisseur's gaze is based on looking both outwards at the picture and inwards at themselves.

Unfortunately, today another kind of gaze has become necessary. In response to terrorist attacks, many people have adopted an actuarial gaze, a gaze that is alert to risk and the possible need for escape. Posted government warnings to report suspicious behaviour no doubt reinforce the need to be habitually scanning a crowd of people to assess danger that in turn influences the way we now view pictures of crowds. An actuarial gaze is also typically used whenever walking alone in a city late at night, especially by women, by police at a crime scene, and by troops out on patrol.

The place's share

Places can refer to environmental, institutional or social settings, as well as all three. Each imposes levels of control over how we are able to look.

Regarding environmental contexts, consider the differences involved in driving past a highway billboard and studying the same billboard in a library book. Billboards are designed to be taken in at a glance; viewing a reproduction of it in a book allows us to take our time, to subject it to critical scrutiny. Consider the experience of watching a movie in a darkened theatre where we can do nothing but continue to watch, and watching the same movie at home where we are free to stop it, and return to it later, or only half watch while doing other things. In a darkened theatre, we have no choice other than to watch the screen in front of us; at home our watching can be integrated into a range of other activities. Most people don't just watch television. Research has found that rather than watching programmes from beginning to end, most people have the television on in the background allowing the auditory track to cue them in on when to watch. For most people, watching television is a highly intermittent affair, interspersed with washing up, doing homework, playing with pets, and so on. Contrary to popular opinion, when television is considered in its domestic context, it is less a visual medium than an auditory one.

Institutional contexts of looking also make a difference to the meaning of pictures. A painting in an art gallery might be viewed purely for pleasure while looking at it in an art class as a student always assumes an additional educational purpose. Both the gallery and the classroom are institutional contexts that help establish viewers' different roles and expectations for viewing. In art galleries, most people tend to use an appreciative gaze, the modernist aesthetic gaze that is looking for beauty and uplift. In class, teachers hope that students use a curious gaze.

Many institutional gazes are managerial; they involve surveillance, regulation and categorization. In hospitals, professional staff look at people as either patients or visitors. Their medical gaze is a normalizing and an inspecting gaze. In police line-ups, witnesses look at suspects of crime in terms of innocent or guilty. In law courts jurists look at the accused in the same light. And in schools there is the teacher's gaze, one that is habitually alert to students who are struggling or misbehaving.

With regard to social circumstances, viewing can be public or private. Consider the difference between watching a television programme with friends and watching the same programme alone. With friends, watching television involves viewing not only through one's own eyes but also with the aid of the ongoing comments made by others. Staring at images on a mobile phone on a busy subway where you may not want others to be looking at what you are looking at is different than looking at the same images in a deserted library or at home alone. Most people do not like watching horror movies by themselves, but as described in Chapter 4, many are happy to do so with friends where experiencing fear and dread often serves as a rite of passage among peers.

The social context of our looking extends to broader issues of how we live now. The pressures of a busy life tend to leave no time for prolonged gazing in the ordinary sense of the word; as noted earlier, today we typically just glance at pictures. We flip through magazines, drive past billboards, channel surf, and speed through our news feeds. In a darkened movie theatre we are transfixed by the big screen, and in art museums we may also take our time to deliberately look contemplatively, but mostly we are forced by time and circumstances to employ a hasty glance. A slow, languid examination is out of tempo with the way we live now. We typically view pictures as if we are tourists, as if we are always hopping off a bus to quickly snap scenes before quickly returning to the bus to move on to the next site. This is a perfunctory look, motivated by a perpetual dissatisfaction with what we are looking at, and a perpetual moving on. Tourists are always moving on to see something else, to see ever more sites rather than taking time to understand them. Today we are inclined almost always to look at all pictures as if we are tourists, not only when we are actual tourists, but also for most of our everyday viewing. Today, while viewing an image, we are also often looking forward to seeing something else.

Perhaps an even better metaphor than the tourist gaze, at least for much of our viewing, would be the anticipatory gaze employed by players of video games. The pace of games is so fast that players are only partially conscious of what they are seeing on the screen; to be successful in the game, players must be focused on anticipating what they might be about to see.

Neither the tourist nor the anticipatory gaze is anything like the way pictures were commonly viewed in the past. Pictures received a prolonged examination. Artists made pictures with this expectation in mind, and, although different theorists gave different advice on how to look at pictures, no one ever thought that viewers would not take their time. Today, in art museums it is still possible to find people employing a contemplative, mindful gaze; the culturally hallowed sanctuary of art museums continues to facilitate quiet contemplation. But even in art museums this is an exception. Many galleries are crowded, and crowded moreover by tourists. Research indicates that most people spend only a few seconds in front of any one artwork. Even in art museums, people typically look only momentarily at an artwork.

Below, interaction between pictures, people and places to make meaning is illustrated, first by reference to the various pleasures of the gaze, and secondly by noting the limits to the power of the gaze. Many image makers intend their audience to use a particular gaze but as discussed above, we viewers can be contrary.

The pleasures of the gaze

The spectator's gaze is almost always experienced as pleasurable, with pleasure derived from at least six major experiences of the gaze: scopophilia, voyeurism, sadism, identification, exhibitionism and transgression. Reflecting the dynamic interaction between pictures, people and places, actual cases of gazing often involve various combinations of these experiences.

Scopophilia

Scopophilia means a love of looking, *scopo* meaning looking, *philia* meaning love. Freud regarded scopophilia as nothing less than an instinctive drive, and as noted in Chapter 4, today we know that the visual and pleasure centres of the brain are very closely related. That they are linked makes good evolutionary sense. Lacking a good sense of smell, that looking was pleasurable would have been essential to the early survival of our species.

Today, there remains a continuing connection between survival and vision. Success in social situations is often dependent upon visual cues. And from an evolutionary perspective it continues to make sense to link vision with the motivation afforded by pleasure. Thus, we have an inbuilt love of visual things even when survival is not at issue: a curious interest in the appearance of other people but also a love of sunsets, saturated colour, graceful movements, elaborate decoration, bright and shiny surfaces and so on.

Voyeurism

Voyeurism combines the simple pleasure of looking at things with the pleasure of being in a position of power in relation to the object of the gaze. Voyeurism refers to taking pleasure in watching people unaware that they are the object of a gaze, subjecting them to a curious gaze, but also to a controlling gaze. Since looking at any picture of people usually involves the absence of the people being viewed, the pleasure of looking at a picture is typically combined with the pleasure of voyeurism. With Figure 6.1, we are ourselves spying on someone who is spying on someone else. Voyeurism turns the subject of the gaze into an object. While scopophilia may be enjoyed in real life without any sense of power, looking at an image typically involves the power inherent in voyeurism. Voyeurism is especially inscribed into the very act of looking at movies in darkened theatres where an entire audience looks at the screen in front of them while virtually unable to be seen seeing. Here, voyeurism is unavoidable and socially acceptable.

On the other hand, voyeurism is usually considered a form of perversion, and where its status has remained ambiguous, a need to justify it has been felt. This is most notable with Western fine art paintings and sculptures of nude women. In a patriarchal society where men were in charge of cultural production and its patronage and yet also a society that adhered to values of modesty, it was necessary to mask erotic desire with decoys.

A number of justifications were developed. As described in Chapter 4, 'the classical alibi' was to view paintings and sculptures of nude figures in terms of classical learning and moral injunctions to a virtuous life (Figures 2.10, 6.2, 6.3).

Figure 6.3 also illustrates a second justification, that of looking through the eyes of one of the figures in the picture. The viewer imaginatively views through the intradiegetic gaze. The viewer is able to say, 'I am only doing what is already happening in the picture.' This combines two pleasures, identification as well as voyeurism, and identification is discussed below.

A third justification is based on evoking the so-called 'third body'. If the first body is that of the figure represented, the second that of the spectator, the third body is that of the unseen but presumed-to-be-present photographer, artist, or film crew; viewers can legitimatize their pleasure in presuming merely to share the original gaze of its producer.

A fourth justification involves pointing to figures gazing at themselves as signifiers of vanity. It will come as no surprise that in a patriarchal society the most common examples are of women narcissistically examining themselves in a mirror (Figure 3.7). The women were thereby condemned by their own objectification. Viewers could mask their voyeurism, not in this case so much as spiritual enlightenment as moral condemnation of women.

Sadism

Sadism occurs when the pleasure of voyeurism morphs into the pleasure of watching someone being harmed. It involves gratification obtained by the infliction of physical or mental pain, of cruelty to others. With sadism, objectification is extreme. Many pictures of violation ostensibly meant to outrage (Figure 3.5) or to evoke fear (Figure 3.1) can just as easily be viewed sadistically.

Figure 6.3 In the Manner of Raphael, *The Judgement of Paris* (1483–1520).

In the movies, sadism is usually legitimatized as just punishment for an immoral antagonist. As noted in Chapter 4, audiences suffer through the abuse inflicted on innocent protagonists while anticipating and then enjoying a violent retribution. It is noteworthy that retaliatory violence often far exceeds the original, transgressive abuse.

Just as with the socially taboo nature of voyeurism, the even more socially taboo nature of sadism is typically masked by moral justifications. The antagonist's grisly comeuppance is legitimized as getting only what the antagonist deserves, righting wrongs and, thereby, bringing order to the social fabric.

Identification

On the other hand, many gazes appear innocent of sadism or even of the objectification of voyeurism. Gazes can also form the basis of identification where, as spectators, we project ourselves onto a figure in a picture. Inhabiting a figure, we imagine ourselves to be that figure. Consider how females sometimes identify with another female in a picture – desiring to be wearing those clothes perhaps, that jewellery, or on the arm of that handsome male. And abandoning traditional roles, females fantasize about being able to wield a weapon fearlessly and fight alongside men as their equal. Consider how males often desire to be the hero of a story, able to endure hardship, act courageously, win the beautiful female, and so on. Think of how youth identify with outsiders, with the misunderstood rebel, and of how children often identify with the irrepressibly naughty cartoon figure. Think too of how followers identify with pictures of their leaders (Figure 2.5).

The French psychiatrist Lacan's (2001) theory of the mirror phase is frequently employed to understand these kinds of identification. Lacan regards identification as a re-enactment of an event that he believed occurs around six months of age when we as babies, seeing ourselves in a mirror, understand for the first time that we are simultaneously our own bodies and our image. Since this happens at a time when our motor control is limited and outstripped by our physical ambitions, we imagine our image to be more complete, more perfect, than what we know our bodies to be. At this age, we experience our bodies as an uncoordinated collection of separate parts: a head, a leg, an arm and so on. While our bodily experiences are fragmented, the image of ourselves appears to us to be whole, to be complete. The joy of recognizing ourselves in a mirror therefore comes with the understanding that we and our image are separate as well as the misrecognition that the mirror image is superior. The mirror image is simultaneously that of a separate self and an ideal self, which leaves the real self of our actual body fragmented and feeling both inferior and desiring to be united with our ideal body. This early experience is then repeated throughout our lives; always there is a sense of fragmentation, of lack and of a desire for the completeness that is felt to be lacking. Always we experience ourselves as less than our ideal. We experience ourselves as fragmented, but imagine that our ideal self is whole, and consequently we are fated to be forever in search of an ideal of wholeness. Unable to find wholeness within ourselves, we develop a desire for completeness through identification with others.

According to this theory, it is a sense of incompleteness within ourselves that lays the foundations for the intense identification that exists between celebrated actors and cinema audiences. In popular films this projection of the self in an idealized form is especially notable in the celebrity star system, in actors whose looks we typically consider superior to our own and whose own real life seems ideal, being characterized by fame, wealth and glamour.

A more positive way of understanding identification with figures in pictures is that identification is motivated by a desire for human connectedness. Instead of a lack, of something missing within ourselves, identification aligns with empathy and compassion for others. According to this view, identification is based on a push to establish links to, and share with, others; identification is part of an inbuilt, genetic inheritance as social beings that are dependent upon others for survival.

Whichever of the above theories you prefer, voyeurism and identification often work together, as addressed above in relation to Figure 6.3. Today, pictures of male and female celebrity couples are common; they are found in magazines everywhere. A heterosexual female viewer might identify with the female celebrity while gazing as herself at the male with both desire and envy. Alternatively, she might imagine herself hanging on the arm of her handsome male companion and looking at him through the eyes of the female celebrity with whom she is identifying. A heterosexual male might look at the very same image of the celebrity couple and imagine himself as the male celebrity while also looking at the female celebrity, either through his own eyes or the eyes of the celebrity with whom he is identifying.

Exhibitionism

Exhibitionism involves the pleasure of fantasizing in two alternative ways. Consider looking at a picture of a figure you find especially attractive and who is attracting your attention with a mutual gaze. First, you might simply look at the figure in the picture, returning their gaze, but then you might also imagine the figure in the picture is exhibiting themselves specifically for you. You might then respond by imaginatively exhibiting yourself for the figure in the picture. In your imagination you might effectively say, 'You there in the picture, you are very attractive. What do you think of me? Am I also attractive?' (Figures 1.5, 2.10).

Secondly, you might go further into the realm of fantasy by combining identification with your own exhibitionism. You might imagine yourself to be the figure in the picture; that is, identifying with the figure, and then seeing yourself through the figure's eyes. You might effectively say, 'As the figure in this picture, I think you, the viewer, are attractive'. In this case you and the pictured figure are locked into recognition of each other as simultaneously enjoying the pleasures of voyeurism and exhibitionism.

Pictures that clearly lend themselves to this kind of exhibitionism are offered by the many pre-modern Western fine art paintings in which women not only display their bodies for the presumed male gaze but engage the male viewer with a mutually desiring gaze. But this can also work with female viewers and other sexual orientations.

Moreover, today's social networking and sharing sites represent an unprecedented confluence of exhibitionism and technology. Exhibitionism has greatly expanded through the ubiquity of the selfie. Youth also take numerous photographs of themselves, and they mime and dance to music in prolonged performances that once were private but are now posted on the internet.

Transgression

In actual cases of viewing, none of the associated pleasures described above are strictly dictated by one's gender, sexual orientation or any other subject position. Although image-makers usually offer their audience a preferred view, we viewers often refuse to take their lead and sometimes we intentionally transgress. Echoing the multiple and fragmented nature of selfhood, actual viewing can be multilayered. Thus, to the five pleasures mentioned so far, the pleasure of transgression needs to be added, that is, gazing from a socially taboo position. In Chapter 4 examples were offered of how homosexual gazes gain an added thrill from being transgressive in homophobic societies. Consider the possibilities with the numerous nude or semi-nude figures, male and female, in both the history of fine art and popular culture (Figures 2.10, 6.2, 6.3). A transgressive gaze is a safe transgression because no one need know how one is looking, and because the transgression is a secret it can be especially enjoyed. Think too of what happens in totalitarian states where people develop resistant ways of looking. Many citizens of the Soviet Union became expert at interpreting official propaganda in their own way without anyone knowing what they were thinking.

Youth are expert transgressors, both secretly and socially. They commonly try out personae that are not their own. Such role-play is part of their passage from childhood to adulthood; it is a normal part of their development to experiment with different selves to find who they are. But even among adults there remains great pleasure in transgressing, in the thrill of doing something one should not do, of knowingly breaking social norms.

The power of the gaze

The symbiotic dynamic between picture, people and place is further illustrated by considering the relationship between pictures and people in terms of power. As mentioned above, to view an image is usually considered to be inherently voyeuristic, as if the power of voyeurism is inscribed into the very nature of visual representation. The subjects of representation can never speak to us as spectators. They remain forever mute, and our power as spectators is maintained even where a figure engages us with a mutual gaze. Even here it is not the person who looks back but their representation. If we adopt an attitude of superiority to the subject of a picture, the subject can do nothing; we may not be able to avoid their eyes while looking at them, but we can relax in the certainty that the figures who look out at us cannot actually see us looking at them.

Even so, power is exercised on both sides of the canvas or camera. As spectators, we are rarely all powerful. Pictures hail us, or interpellate us; they call out to be looked at. This applies to pictures in general but it is especially true of pictures that contain figures. Figures in a picture cannot speak or be spoken to but they can grab attention and even transfix us.

In many cases, perhaps even in most cases, the people in pictures were at the time of being photographed knowingly exhibiting themselves, and, moreover, precisely because they found pleasure in exhibiting themselves. This is undoubtedly the case where someone has posed to have their portrait painted or they have taken a selfie. Thus the power entailed in voyeurism usually goes hand in hand with the power of those engaging us as viewers in their own attention getting. In such cases – and they are the most common – the power of voyeurism is modified, for as spectators we view scenes that are typically intended to be looked at.

Furthermore, figures in a picture can be masquerading, putting on a face, a show. In the past, females often chose to play a submissive role but only as a mask, performing through mimicry what they had learnt was required of their role in a patriarchal society (Figure 1.5). As viewers, we may feel all powerful, but we may actually see nothing more than a decorative layer that conceals the fact that the figure has offered a false, or at best limited, view of who they are. The same can be said of numerous portraits of men who pose with the attributes of their professions and authority, or the official portraits of leaders. Equally, children learn from an early age what kind of expression is required whenever a parent seeks to take a photograph of them; they are to smile, to look happy, and if they do not, parents will coax them (Figure 6.4). Does a teacher looking at their seemingly obliging class, ever know what is really going on?

In some cases, we may feel that power is shared. In these cases, instead of possessing what we gaze upon we enter into a partnership. Figures gaze directly out at us as spectators, engaging us in a mutual or returned gaze, and the power of the figures and our power as spectators are more properly considered equal. This is especially true where the figure appears to be confrontational

Figure 6.4 Anonymous, *Happy Family Photography* (anytime).

(Figure 2.3). Also consider wedding photographs of a blissfully happy couple that seem to invite us to celebrate with them. Think of formal family photographs that welcome our spectator's gaze and seem to ask for our acknowledgment. In these cases, we spectators are like invisible guests, invited to share in the figures' happiness.

A further example of where power over the subject is limited is offered by pictures of loved ones. Consider paintings by Rembrandt of his wife bathing (Figure 6.5).

Berger argues that she is naked rather than nude, a woman simply without clothes rather than offered to the viewer as an object of desire. She embodies the specific intimacy between the artist and his wife that makes no allowance for us as spectators. Rembrandt painted her with an interior life of her own that has everything to do with her relationship with her husband, and we as spectators are left to witness their relationship. We recognize ourselves as the outsiders we are.

Perhaps only in cases where figures have been unwittingly photographed, or photographed against their will, are we as spectators fully in control. Where privacy is violated voyeurism equates to peering through a keyhole with its negative association of the Peeping Tom (Figure 6.1).

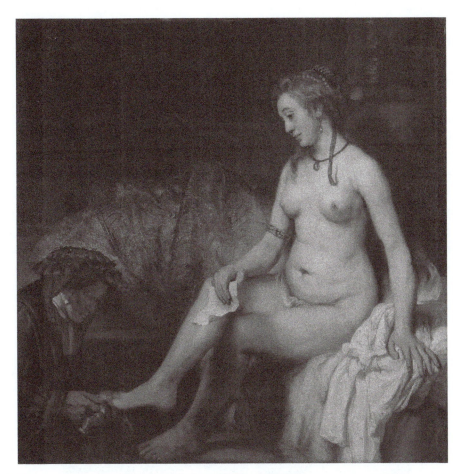

Figure 6.5 Rembrandt van Rijn, *Bathsheba with David* (1654).

Certainly, it is in such cases that the questions arise most strikingly: Is our gaze welcome? Should we be looking at all? What right do we have to look? Is our spectator's gaze violating? These are ethical issues that are at the heart of the spectator's gaze as a concept.

An ethical agenda

Studies of the gaze have usually been conducted with an ethical agenda in mind, usually to draw the spectator's attention to their socially offensive position. The agenda has been to unmask the gaze as disreputable; for example, destroying the pleasure attendant upon the male gaze by making males aware of their patriarchal assumptions about women as decorative and a distraction, but not as rational, or worthy of sharing power.

To counter these retrograde gazes, revisionist gazes have been proposed. Today, both women and some men are likely to employ a feminist gaze. This is to look critically at pictures created with a patriarchal world view as well as a willing acknowledgement that the women pictured were only playing their gender assigned role and that the pictures do not represent all that they were.

Similarly, looking at pictures created with a colonial gaze in mind, with the assumption of racial superiority (Figure 6.6), we are likely today to employ a postcolonial gaze that is not only critical of the colonial assumptions, but also able to reinterpret the pictures in light of contemporary pluralist values. A postcolonial gaze assumes that despite technological differences we share a common humanity. Thus, we can view the same pictures from very different perspectives.

The dynamic of these revisionist gazes applies equally to reinterpreting a moralistic middle-class gaze employed with pictures of poor people in terms of classism, to reinterpret such images as priggish, being more concerned with our own limited sensibilities than poor peoples' ways of life. The same is true of pictures created to appeal to an ageist gaze, an able-bodied gaze and so on.

Thus does the concept of the gaze involve much more than how we see others; the real value of the concept is that it requires of us to see ourselves seeing others. The gaze is not simply a theory about the visual; rather, it deals with the complexities and ambiguities of human relationships in which we as spectators are intimately implicated. These gazes are critical of the assumptions under

Figure 6.6 Douglas Kilburn, *South-East Australian Aboriginal Man and Two Young Companions*, daguerrotype (1847).

which sexist, classist and colonial pictures were created and they extend towards their subjects an ethics of empathy and care.

The ethics of gazing are particularly acute when voyeurism extends to sadism. Drawing attention to the dark side of our spectator's gaze has clear implications for examining ourselves more generally. It is how we look at things, literally, that forms the basis of our moral judgments with oftentimes far-reaching consequences. Becoming aware of how we are caught by our gaze means that the possibility exists for us to challenge ourselves, to reflect upon our gaze and when it is deemed necessary to move beyond it. To reconfigure our subjectivity is to take one step towards social transformation.

The above revisionist gazes each require us to look with assumptions different from those of the original image-makers, but today many pictures are created with the intent of satisfying revisionist gazes. Feminists long ago began creating images of men posed in the positions and with expressions and attributes usually associated with representations of women. Posed in this way the men are clearly shown as trivialized, as sexualized objects, and just plain silly. They pose with their heads askew, smiling demurely, and instead of holding peaches they hold bananas. They look ridiculous and so reveal how trivializing and objectified are patriarchal pictures. Similarly, many photographers have represented previously colonized countries with pictures that represent their country with its own agency that greatly complicates traditional stereotypes.

There is a second kind of social transformative aspect to the gaze. This involves the mutual or returned gaze. Figures who return our gaze often silently welcome us into partnership with them in addressing their needs. Of course, we may refuse to participate, by neglect, indifference or even by approval of their oppression. In such cases it is not the recognition of our own gaze but the returned gaze that can shame us. Consider how true this is of the returned gaze of hungry third-world children. We may feel, perhaps rightly, that our gaze is violating, an intrusion into their privacy.

In summary, the concept of the gaze has the potential to transform viewing in the direction of a kinder, more inclusive society.

Reflexivity and responsibility

The above discussion has several consequences for education. First, we should never assume that when we are examining a picture its meaning is located only within the picture itself; we must honestly interrogate our own subject positions to better understand how they help determine our viewing. This can only be done consciously of course; much may remain buried in our unconscious, but even conscious reflection, especially if made habitual, may yield insights that would otherwise be overlooked. Teachers and students alike should ask themselves: What pleasures does my own viewing arouse? And what relations of power are established between the image and myself? In what ways am I implicated in my own viewing?

Secondly, teachers and students should consider how others interpret pictures. We should not take other peoples' reports at face value. Rather, we should carefully consider their subject viewing positions, asking how their gender, sexual orientation, class, ethnicity, age, experience and so on, help to determine their viewing habits. Just as we should ask ourselves, what lenses are we using, we should ask what lenses are they using? This is another way of asking about the nature and credibility of the source, as discussed in Chapter 3 on rhetoric.

Third, we must also consider the physical circumstances under which we are viewing. The classroom is a very specific context that may render interpretations different from those of other contexts; the classroom may not be ecologically valid. In addition to looking and reflecting upon looking in the classroom, we need to consider everyday looking.

Fourth, since the concept of the gaze has ethical consequences we need to consider the consequences of our gaze. Sometimes the gaze implies social condemnation; sometimes it holds the possibility of social transformation. It follows that we must ask ourselves: What consequences follow from my use of the concept of the gaze? What is my social responsibility?

Questions

1 What is the difference between the two meanings of the word gaze used in this chapter?
2 Glancing and the tourist gaze were mentioned as typical ways in which we now look. Why is this?
3 What kinds of subjectivity help to determine our gaze?
4 What are the six pleasures of the gaze?
5 In what ways does the chapter later modify its view of the power of voyeurism?
6 How is it that the concept of the gaze can have an ethical agenda?
7 Describe an educator's responsibility in using the concept of the gaze.

Activities

1 Choose an image you come across in your ordinary daily living. For example, it could be a family photograph, something from the internet found while searching for something else, or a religious icon. Reflect on how you are looking at it. With what kind of interest and under what physical circumstances are you looking? Is there anything socially taboo about the picture or the context? What pleasures are you deriving from the image? Where does power lie between you and the image? What does your gaze tell you about yourself?
2 Write a story as if you were a figure in a picture looking out at you looking at yourself.
3 Make a list of gazes. Many were mentioned in this chapter but there are others you could consider by thinking about how you look at things under certain circumstances.
4 Consider counter gazes like the post-colonial gaze, a feminist gaze or some other gaze that is resistant to othering people as inferior. Take photographs that you intend to be read by such resistant gazes.

5 Which of the gazes above would most likely be used to look at pictures and which would more likely be used to look at real life? For example, an actuarial gaze is likely to be used in real life to assess risk, but not so much in looking at a picture. But are there exceptions? Are some gazes typically employed in looking at both pictures and real life?

6 Consider the three lists above and match them up as appropriate by asking when as viewers we are most likely to use them in combination. For example, we may take a peep when we are curious about at a taboo subject. Similarly, we may gape when scrutinizing something shocking. We might use a disciplinary gaze when looking daggers.

7 Have the females in a class find pictures on the internet of women as, for example, girlfriends, mothers and policewomen. Have them consider how males might view these pictures. Reverse the order by having males find pictures of men in pictures as boyfriends, fathers and policemen, and have them discuss how females might view the pictures.

8 Hold a discussion asking the following kinds of questions:
What are the most common ways in which you look at pictures?
Are we all sadists at heart? Do the movies merely indulge our dark natures?
If you were about to board an airplane, and think that someone who was also boarding was behaving suspiciously, what gaze would you be using?
If you were walking down the street and saw a very obese person sitting eating ice-cream what gaze would you use: a sympathetic gaze, a disciplinary gaze or something else?

9 Discuss: Do you ever exhibit yourself for someone in a picture?

10 Discuss: Do you ever have an imaginary conversation with someone in a picture?

See Chapter 8 for specific questions on the gaze: Who is looking? Where is it viewed? When would audiences typically look at it? Why do people look at it? How do you look?

7

Intertextuality

What is a text?

Typically, we think of a text as something written. However, in the field of semiotics anything can be regarded, potentially, as a text. Semiotics is the study of signs. Semiotics assumes that anything can be made to act as a sign: our clothes, our hairstyle, the car we drive and so on. As discussed in Chapter 1, in defining visual culture, even things ordinarily used as utilitarian can have a sign value; for example, while our clothes serve a practical purpose, they also tell a lot about who we are – what role we play, how wealthy we are, where we are on a spectrum from conformist to non-conformist and so on.

Just as pictures come with in-built significance as signs of values and beliefs and so are inherently considered texts, so music scores, novels, song lyrics, literature come already loaded with non-utilitarian meaning. However, all things, utilitarian and non- utilitarian alike, exist within a network of ideas, beliefs and values. As an example, consider vacuum cleaners. Ordinarily we think of vacuum cleaners in a purely utilitarian way – their job is to clean the house. But they also signify. They have use value but as participants in a whole social system they also have sign value. When we purchase a vacuum cleaner we take on the social order. Purchasing a vacuum cleaner involves consuming assumptions about gender (who is going to use the vacuum cleaner?), households (a clean house is a good house), the promise of labour saving (a broom was once sufficient to clean house), and economic progress and social standing (now we can afford a vacuum cleaner). With vacuum cleaners ranging in price from less than a hundred dollars to nearly two thousand dollars, which particular machine to purchase is as much about socioeconomic status as it is about a clean home. In short, a solitary item, be it a picture or an ostensibly utilitarian object, is part of a network of ideas, values and beliefs. It is intertextual.

What is intertextuality?

Intertextuality refers to the fact that a text always refers to other texts. No text is like an isolated island, utterly unconnected to other texts. Texts are always embedded in a network of other texts.

As noted in Chapter 1, connections can be self-referential where, for example, an advertisement might refer to a television programme that is based on a film that is based on a book. Texts are always influenced by preceding texts and many of them influence subsequent texts. The entire story of art has been written as a succession of styles, one influencing the next.

However, any picture is more than part of a linear history. It is not only the preceding style that is influential. Any picture is also influenced by many contemporary factors such as what new technologies are available, what poetry and prose is being written, what new social developments are emerging. Studying the history of art makes this point clear.

Art history is not only a story of successive styles but also an appreciation for the networks of contemporary practices. For example, the French Impressionist painting of the 1870s is a development from the French Realist painters of the preceding two decades, but also much more. The French Realists like Edward Manet of the 1850s and 1860s represented then contemporary life in a straightforward way, and the French Impressionists like Claude Monet built upon their efforts, but Realist painting was only one of many influences. French Impressionism was part of several intersecting, contemporary developments emerging in 1870s France. With its fascination with the fleeting effects of light on coloured surfaces, French Impressionist painting was part of a broad concern with what was then felt to be the speed and fragmentation of modern urban life. Former certainties of social life appeared to have disappeared with the Industrial Revolution and the emergence of open class warfare, and the Impressionists painted physical reality as if it too had lost the appearance of permanence and was instead in constant flux. Similarly, the beauty of Impressionism cannot be divorced from the then new desire for rural life as a retreat from the ugliness of the new, overnight cities with their smog and lack of sanitation. New scientific explorations in optics and the new technology of photography also played a role. Photography captured life in black and white and as if frozen in time. In response, the Impressionists sought to capture fleeting moments in a festival of glorious colour. Where one was mechanical, the other celebrated the artist's unique interpretation. In short, however much French Impressionism owed to the art movement immediately before it, it existed as part of a series of social, scientific and technological developments. It cannot be understood without appreciating its links to these other contemporary texts, and what is true of Impressionist paintings is true of all pictures.

Social semiotics

Pictures are intertextual, but so is our viewing. It is often the case that every time we view a picture we find something different in it, and, further, that we make different connections between it and other texts. One day a soft drink advertisement might evoke the desire to buy the drink; on another day it could evoke a happy memory of watching a movie when you last drank the soft drink; on a third day it could arouse anger that the advertisement depicts an offensive stereotype.

The previous chapter discussed this phenomenon as 'the picture, people, place dynamic', in which people's subject positions help determine meaning. Making meaning cannot be divorced from who we are as members of a particular gender, social class, age and so on, as well as the particular contexts of our viewing.

Another way to understand the importance of subject position is to draw upon post-structural, social semiotics. While an earlier form of semiotics, often known as structural semiotics, held that meaning lay within texts, within their internal structure, social semiotics willingly acknowledges that meaning is made as much by viewers as by the text itself. As texts, pictures are only part of the picture, people, place relationship. Instead of studying just the text, social semiotics understands that different people read pictures differently. Furthermore, even a single individual may view a picture differently at different times because, in a sense, over time they become a different person. Social semiotics studies what people make of pictures.

Consider a picture of a McDonald's hamburger (Figure 7.1). Everyone with normal life experience sees a hamburger and recognizers it as a McDonalds. Using the language of semiotics,

Figure 7.1 Author, *A McDonald's Hamburger* (2019).

this level of interpretation is called a *denotation*, a straightforward identification of the content of the picture. But this tells us nothing about what people think about the McDonald's hamburger, what meaning or associations different people make. Do people associate it with cheap food and associate that with bad food? Or do they associate it with convenience, and, in regarding convenience as a virtue, consider McDonalds a good thing? Would they associate McDonalds with its origins in the United States, and if so, how does this affect their attitude to McDonalds? Do they associate the United States with freedom, or excessive waste or imperialism? And so on. If people associate McDonalds with the United States, whatever they feel about the United States will no doubt colour their view of McDonalds. And people's views differ; people make different associations, different connections. Again, using the language of semiotics, these associations are called *connotations*.

To further explore the dynamic between texts and other texts, as well as texts and ourselves as viewers, the concept of rhizomic structures is helpful. Both intertextuality among pictures and our intertextual viewing of pictures are rhizomic.

Intertextuality and rhizomic structures

Intertextuality relates directly to rhizomic structures. The word *rhizome* is Greek in origin, where it referred to a mass of roots, usually underground, that typically sends out shoots from its nodes. Grass and ginger are common examples, though many other examples exist such as animal burrows and animals that operate in packs likes rats and ants. What each has in common are structures characterized by multiple connections that together make up a complex network.

In 1987 the French philosophers Gilles Deleuze and Félix Guattari extended this biological structure to thinking about the world in general. They were highly prescient. Today, the largest electronic rhizome is the internet (Figure 7.2). Yet as important a rhizome as the internet has become, it is only part of other phenomena with a rhizomic structure. As discussed below, these include visual culture, the way humans think, the way we think about visual culture, and the way youth are already creating. Each is rhizomic. And as explored in Chapter 9, rhizomic structures also have profound implications for organizing a visual culture curriculum.

Web 7.1
Intertextuality

While thinking in terms of rhizomes does not necessarily make us see more clearly, it does make us think differently. We forgo any sense of omnipotence, any notion that we have an overall view or final answer. Instead, thinking in terms of rhizomes forces us to embrace the disorder of the world with all its variety, connectivity, and teeming contradictions.

Trees, grass and the internet

With rhizomes, mapping in any conventional sense is impossible. There is no simple helicopter view. Figure 7.2 captures a sense of the complex interactivity of the internet, but only a small part of the internet and only as a snapshot on a particular day. With rhizomes there is no hierarchy, and

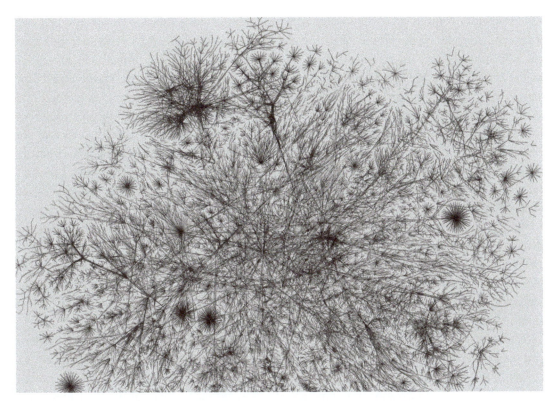

Figure 7.2 The Apte Project, *A Partial Map of the Internet* (5 January 2015).

although they must originally start from somewhere, once they begin to grow they appear to be without a discernible centre. Rather, they continually expand outwards from all their edges. In the case of grass, nodes connect to other nodes, which connect to still others; with the internet one hyperlink links to another, which connects to another and so on. There is no way to keep your finger on the pulse of it all. It is like weeding a garden where the weeds you see and pull up are only a fraction of what remains. In a continual state of depletion and creation, the disappearance of one part holds no real consequences because rhizomes are constantly rejuvenated by the addition of other parts. This means that rhizomes are highly resilient. They contain a great deal of redundancy, that is, one small part of a rhizome is more or less identical to other parts. Consider grass. A patch of grass may die off because of bad weather or because it is poisoned, but it takes a lot of poison or a lot of bad weather to completely kill off a large area of grass. Some patch of grass, however small, is likely to survive, so that normally the grass will be able to grow back and, moreover, to keep growing.

Unlike trees, which are susceptible to easy destruction, a rhizome is exceptionally difficult to destroy. Deleuze and Guattari (1987) write:

A rhizome can be broken, shattered at a given spot, but it will start up again on one of its old lines or a new line. You can never get rid of ants because they form an animal rhizome that can rebound time and again after most of it has been destroyed (9).

The resilience of rhizomes is well illustrated by the human-made rhizome of the internet, and it is worth considering the origins of the internet to demonstrate this, for its rhizomic structure was not accidental. The internet began in the early 1980s when a number of research universities in the United States began to communicate through an electronic network. The principal aim was to effect greater communication efficiency by sharing knowledge among all participants at the same time. This operation was then seized upon by the United States military as a solution to a serious problem posed during the time of the Cold War between the United States and the Soviet Union in which peace was maintained by the doctrine of mutual destruction. If one or other side of the Cold War used its nuclear arsenal against the other, the other would then strike back and thus ensure massive damage to both sides. While the United States military intelligence was centralized in one place, or at best a few different places, the Soviet Union could easily render useless both its defensive and strike capability. What the United States needed to do was to diversify its operations by placing military intelligence in many sites that were interconnected and build a lot of redundancy into the network. In the event of an attack, enough sites would likely survive and the system as a whole would not only continue to operate, it would be able to regenerate what had been lost. A complex electronic network of communications was the perfect solution.

This network was quickly adopted by commercial enterprises and it was not long before you could find information so quickly and purchase goods and services over the internet so efficiently that the internet was often referred to as an information highway. This metaphor captured the speed at which information was now able to flow, although it was also meant to suggest that information flowed in two directions, from governments and commercial enterprises to citizens and customers, but also from citizens to governments and customers back to commercial entities.

Then, in the early decades of the twenty-first century, Web.2.0 enabled not only much faster two-way communication between institutions and ordinary users but a much greater degree of interactivity. Today, we relate to government agencies, news outlets and all manner of commercial interests, as well as family and friends, in a highly interactive way.

We speak now of surfing the internet, meaning that we shift from one screen to another more or less randomly, from one link to another, which then leads on to yet other links quite unrelated to where we started. To illustrate a PowerPoint on hygiene we might start by searching a picture-sharing site to find an image of a smiling face showing gleaming white teeth. But looking up the picture might lead to pictures advertising lipstick that is hyperlinked to an article on recent fashion that is hyperlinked to an illustrated newspaper article on the jewellery worn by an indigenous tribe in Africa; and so on and on. As Deleuze and Guattari write, 'Unlike trees or their roots, the rhizome connects any point to any other point and its traits are not necessarily linked to the traits of the same nature: it brings into play different regimes of signs' (21). Any point of a rhizome can be connected to any other point. With rhizomes, there is no unity to serve as a pivot, no universal defining reference point. Always there is more, a hallmark of rhizomes being multiplicity and heterogeneity. Whereas 'the tree imposes the verb "to be" the fabric of the rhizome is the conjunction "and ... and ... and ..."' (25).

Human cognition as rhizomic

Our human ways of thinking, especially when thinking creatively, are also rhizomic. It is no exaggeration to claim that our brains are the most complex rhizome of the known universe. We are able to easily associate one idea with another, one image with another, an idea with an image, an image with a song, a song with a memory, a memory with a movie, a movie with a poem and so on and on

Rhizomes have multiple entry and exit points, and each time one enters a journey of associations the journey is likely to be different. 'A rhizome has no beginning or end; it is always in the middle, between things …' (25). With their multiple entry and exit points, we travel though rhizomes by coming and going rather than beginning and ending, for there are no ends to rhizomes. The journey is open ended. We navigate a rhizome as a nomad, wandering without a predetermined destination or goal. There are always so many possible routes available to us, and with each step the routes multiply like rabbits. Taking a journey involves adventure: backtracking, sidestepping and getting lost. It is the journey that counts, not the end state, for every apparent end state leads on to other possibilities and still others. We roam about from place to place for as long as we choose.

Let us undertake a free association thought experiment to see what possible further associations might be generated. Let us start with partnerships. What is a partnership? How does it differ from friendship or from marriage? How do pictures of national leaders shaking hands at a conference differ from pictures of you with your friends? How are friends represented in movies? A very long running television sit com in the United States was called *Friends*, which explored many different kinds of friendship.

Let us now turn to iconic national buildings. The Great Wall of China might suggest an ancient society whereas the Sydney Opera House, Australia might suggest a new one. But then neither is wholly true. Australia is the oldest landmass on earth and Aborigines have lived there for at least 60,000 years. Australia is not only ancient but also prehistoric. And China, though it too has a prehistoric past and was an empire of great antiquity, today has re-emerged as a major new force in the world. To represent Australia one might equally employ a picture of a traditional Aboriginal dance, and to represent the new China one might choose a photograph of the Shanghai skyline. Then we might consider these icons as stand-ins for national pride and then go on to consider why some national icons are based on human achievement and others on longevity, others on uniqueness, others on great suffering. And the more we keep associating, the more complex and interconnected the associations become. National icons today cannot be divorced from globalization and the need for international partnerships. This might remind us of an earlier association of national leaders shaking hands at conferences. Associations run on and on but they can also fold back on themselves. Associations flow one to another, as in internet surfing, but they also turn back to make new connections. Human cognition functions by making connections between things both like and unlike, by associating one thing with another.

Visual culture as rhizomic

Visual culture is rhizomic in structure; like grass, it spreads laterally, connected by multiple, layered references. And this operates in two ways, both in terms of visual representation and interpretation.

Any picture is the outcome of many influences, past and present, and, in turn, every individual act of viewing may conjure up any number of associations. Thus, does visual culture possess no core, no basic principles from which one must begin before proceeding further. It operates without any kind of central control, but rather by ceaselessly evolving connections between chains of references. As a rhizome, visual culture spreads like oil on the surface of a body of water, potentially spreading everywhere and connecting to everything. Contemporary visual culture draws upon the fine art of the past, but equally it engages with politics, economics and social formations, including struggles over gender, race, class, nationalism, war, the environment, poverty, consumerism – all the isms and ideologies of which social life is composed.

Web 7.2
Teaching as
Rhizomic

Collective cognition and distributed creativity

Intertextuality is described above in terms of the multiple references pictures draw upon and what associations audiences make by bringing their own experiences into play in the reading of a text. It is equally apparent in the creation of pictures. No better example could be found today than how youth are now operating on the internet to create their own forms of cultural production outside the classroom. The intertextual, rhizomic nature of online youth culture represents a microcosm of visual culture, and it has significant implications for the curriculum as discussed in Chapters 9 and 10.

In collectively creating their own online culture, youth are employing what is variously called *collective cognition* or *collective intelligence,* and *distributed creativity* or *participatory creativity.* Many of today's youth are drawn together through shared passions to belong to informal, online affinity-based learning communities. These communities are pervasive, complex, ever changing and are among the best examples of operating according to the principles of rhizomic structures. They represent what are variously called *peer-to-peer cultures* or *participatory cultures.* Instead of merely consuming media, many youth now participate in cultural exchanges as producers. While consuming professionally produced mass media, equally, they bounce off the productions of like-minded, similarly motivated amateur peers. Instead of a 'read only' culture in which a small group of professionals produce culture for everyone else, theirs is a 'read/write culture.' Their participatory culture shifts the focus of creation from individuals to community engagement, to collaboration and networking. It calls upon collective, distributed cognition, which means not only a facility with technology but also the social skills to draw upon the knowledge of others. With collective cognition, knowledge resides not in any one person, text, or technology, but is distributed across people, texts and technologies that are geographically separated yet networked. Knowledge resides within networks, and often youth networks are global.

Participatory youth cultures take many forms. They include picture blogs of conventional art media, picture blogs of fan art, and videos on any number of topics. They often involve remixes or mashups of popular cultural forms, be it movies, television programmes, toys, or music videos. This is a remix culture, forms of creative production that allow and encourage derivative works. Remix culture consists of combining or editing existing material to produce something new. On line, the growth of remix culture is exponential.

Among the numerous new cultural forms from which youth of all ages are now able to draw, Batman and Robin continue to fascinate. Some youth are highly prolific, regularly posting photographs and videos. Years before the professionally produced Lego motion, there existed amateur youth productions using Lego motion. These were usually a parody of the superheroes, sometimes mixing up heroes and villains from Marvel Comics with DC Comics, its rival.

On video sharing sites there are also many mashups of different movies. Many involve *Harry Potter* films spliced in with *Star Wars* or *Lord of the Rings*, or all three, where the heroes of one film do battle with the villains of another film. Synchronized to totally unrelated music, the effect is often hilarious. Music video mashups are also common. In the simplest example, music from one video is spliced with the visuals of another. In more complicated examples multiple visuals are remixed with a song.

So complicated is the morphing from one cultural model to the next that no simple map could ever be devised to describe their relation to one another. The connections between the numerous genres, subgenres and hybrid genres are truly rhizomic. Videos link with one another in numerous, non-linear fashions. For example, a movie mashup of original footage from films like *Twilight* or *Star Wars* inspires a Lego motion version, which inspires a version involving puppets, which then

Figure 7.3 FK Films, *Lego Batman Parody 2* (2017).

morphs into versions involving real-life actors but also spin-offs involving any number of other popular films in which the films that initiated all these productions are forgotten. Alternatively, other youths start from other movies and through various iterations of subsequent productions they may cross over at some stage to reference the *Twilight* and *Star Wars* videos produced by youth online. Influences are deeply interwoven.

Reflecting the remix, mashup nature of this online culture, it is often described by use of portmanteaus. Youth videos are called *produsage*, a contraction of *produce* and *usage* in which youth operate collectively by using the productions of others to produce their own creations. The youth producing these videos are called *prosumers*, a portmanteau of the words *producer* and *consumer* – youth who are producing their own imagery drawn from their consumption of popular mass media.

The words *produsage* and *prosumer* describe what has become a pervasive socio-cultural phenomenon among the connected generation, or 'generation C', the generation of digital natives. With the availably of low-cost networked technology, the roles of producers and consumers have imploded. Today, instead of merely consuming mass media, youth are participating in cultural exchanges as producers in an unprecedented way. Since youth have proven able to take to the new technologies like fish to water, it is not surprising that they are among the most active of prosumers in a networked culture.

Online youth culture as smart swarms

An even more startling way to consider how many youth are creating their own cultural productions is to apply the concept of smart swarms (Miller, 2010). Wisdom drawn from bee, ant and termite colonies, bird flocks and fish schools may initially seem utterly unrelated to human behaviour intersecting with new technologies. Yet they do indeed offer powerful metaphors to appreciate just how powerful and pervasive a social contagion collective cognition and distributed creativity has become among youth.

The theory of smart swarms pulls together into a consistent set of principles how youth are operating online. It also underpins the resilience of the principles of networking, and, by implication, that what young people are now doing on social networking and sharing sites represents a major shift of behaviour and consciousness rather than a passing fad. Specific social networking and sharing sites will undoubtedly pass, but the general principles on which their success is founded are unlikely to pass anytime soon; in the wild, they are millions of years old.

Smart swarm theory leverages many scientific studies on bee, ant and termite colonies, bird flocks and fish schools to demonstrate that these creatures act better in concert than when acting alone. Moreover, when we humans follow the principles on which these creatures operate as swarms, we too frequently operate far better than when acting individually. Bees, ants and so on do not need to be smart because as a swarm they are smart. Humans who follow the same basic principles of group behaviour are similarly enabled to act in ways that are flexible, adaptable and reliable. In each case the wisdom of crowds trumps the expert knowledge of the few in making good choices.

Four basic principles of smart swarms have been identified, each of which is characteristic of youth operating on the internet using distributed creativity as part of a participatory, read/write culture.

Decentralized control

Working independently, with no one in overall control, individual youth and small groups of youth are uploading their visual posts by simply following the lead of others. Consider, for example, how videos employing just one particular children's toy – Barbie dolls – have sparked many others. As part of the ritual of leaving childhood behind, youth destroying Barbie dolls was a phenomenon long before the internet, but now it is enacted in numerous videos and shared with millions. Videos include titles like *Barbie Torture*, *Barbie Lego*, *Gay Barbie* and *Gossip Girl Barbie*. In turn, these videos cross over to videos with titles such as *Gossip Girl Parody*, *Gossip Girl Lego*, *Gossip Girl Finger Puppets* and so on.

This illustrates the smart swarm principle of self-organization that consists of decentralized control, distributed problem solving and multiple interactions. By such means members of a group are able to transform simple rules into meaningful patterns, and this is possible even when members of a group have no idea about the form their individual contributions take. Termites, for example, are able to build huge mounds many times larger than themselves by following the rule of dropping a grain of soil where another termite has already done so.

A further connection between self-organizing animals and social networking and sharing sites relates to sustainability over the long haul. Some species of birds fly for lengthy periods of time over vast distances, and this is enabled by two processes: following the lead of others and regularly changing who leads. Most birds in a flock fly in the slip-steam created by birds in front of them, and the birds in the lead, who must work harder against the resistance of the air, are replaced by other birds when the lead birds tire. Similarly, most visual posts on social networking and sharing sites appear inspired by others. As illustrated above with the Barbie videos, most producers appear to model their posts on the posts of others and only a relatively few lead the way, but who leads the way is forever changing. Through self-regulation, both flocks of birds and youth's visual posts are self-sustaining.

Diversity of knowledge

Secondly, smart swarms employ diversity of knowledge, which is achieved through the encouragement of friendly competition, and a broad sampling of options, followed by an effective mechanism to narrow down choices. Together, these processes help ensure that the best choice is the one most likely to be made. For example, honeybees select a site for a new home through representative bees sampling several potential sites, communicating their findings to the whole hive, and then the whole hive deciding through what is effectively a voting system. Apparently, the bees communicate by how they 'dance'.

By comparison, not all comments on social networking and sharing sites are friendly. For example, of one video called *Barbie Torture* by torturebarbie, comments were mostly negative. They included, 'Where is the point of this. Get a life'; 'You should have done that with a live human . . . then maybe we'd be interested'. But more commonly, comments are positive. *Barbie Torture Device* by mommarina, in which a child demonstrates how an Erector set mechanism is set to torture Barbie, received comments like, 'Ur mad and twisted, like me'; 'Twisted evil kid. Awesome!' Yet whether reception is positive or negative, all producers are in fierce competition for viewers and so it behoves producers to make their videos as good as they can, and feedback offers guidance for what works in the marketplace of popular appeal as well as how to improve.

Furthermore, the interfaces of social networking and sharing sites operate as a very effective mechanism by which users narrow down choices for each other to the videos found by their peers likely to be the most interesting to would-be producers. YouTube provides an excellent example. Apart from the video itself, the interface includes the video's name, the name of its producer(s), a tag line briefly describing the video, the date the video was uploaded, the number of visits, the number of visitors who have commented and the tally of the comments classified as 'likes' and 'dislikes'. All the comments are available to be viewed, and these oftentimes include interaction between the creators and their commentators. All of this information acts as a guide to popularity and by extension whether it is worth spending a few minutes watching. And would-be producers have readily available a range of opinion on what works and what does not. Additionally, the platform offers thumbnails of videos selected on the basis of a viewer's previous viewing habits. Anyone interested in one genre will immediately have available other, previous efforts to view and build upon. And for anyone interested in the oeuvre of a particular producer there is a hyperlink to all their other videos.

Indirect collaboration

Indirect collaboration involves individuals making small changes to an existing, shared system that inspires others to make further changes so that the system itself appears to be a participant. It is as though self-organizing systems actually have a life of their own, operating independently of any one member or group. No one directs a termite to drop a grain of soil where another has, yet it is by acting on this shared impulse that termites build their huge mounds; in a sense, the mounds are an active player in the creative process. Youth on social networking and sharing sites are similarly self-motivated and work independently, but together they too constantly add to the previous efforts of others in a way that has made social networking and sharing sites major social spaces in their own right. Two decades ago, who could have foreseen what a complex, socially significant operation they would so quickly become?

Adaptive mimicking

Adaptive mimicking involves coordination, communication and copying. It refers to how individuals in a group pay close attention to one another, picking up signals about where they are going and what they know. Adaptive mimicking is capable of unleashing powerful waves of energy that race from one individual to another. In the wild, flocks of birds appear to act as if they were of one mind as seemingly all at once they turn, bank, dive and scatter. We now know that they actually communicate from bird to bird, but so quickly it eludes the human eye. Similarly, the internet generally facilitates rapid, many-to-many, viral communications. On the internet as in the wild, adaptive mimicking is characterized by the efficiency of astonishing speed. The feedback loop is almost immediate.

Moreover, it is now known that individual birds in a flock or individual fish in a school do not communicate with everyone but only about seven other creatures with which they are in close proximity. This too is analogous to the way users on social networking and sharing sites operate. Playing close attention to others becomes a powerful form of collective intelligence. Instead of communicating with the entire population of a social networking or sharing sites – an impossible task – individual users limit themselves to a far smaller number. For a visual post to become viral and be seen by millions within days, to become a meme, initially the post only needs to be viewed by a limited number of people: for example, seven people know forty-nine, who know 349, who know 2,401, who know 16, 807, who know 117,649, who know just over a million, and so on. In practice, youth on social networking sites are typically connected to many more than seven people so that a video can become a meme, literally, overnight. Additionally, it only needs a few people to turn a visual post into numerous mutations as one parody inspires another, which, in turn, inspires parodies of the parodies, and so on.

In the wild, copying is mostly exact replication. By contrast, copying on social networking and sharing sites is more akin to modelling or translation than replication. Thus, the analogy of youth on the internet to smart swarms is only partial, not complete. Producers invariably replicate only some features of another video, leaving out others and introducing their own. Continuing to employ the biological metaphor, copying equates to mutation or variation. As self-organized groups, we humans are far more complex than bees, ants, termites, birds and fish, which means that we do not act entirely like these creatures as swarms. Human systems are far less predictable, and self-organizing, non-linear systems raise as many questions as they settle. We do not know why we actively sort and screen information in the way we do, or how we choose what to ignore and what to be influenced by. That youth on the internet are unpredictable can be taken as axiomatic. Before becoming memes, some visual posts lie dormant for a year or more after being posted. Who can say at any one time what will take off and what will not, let alone why? Who can say what connections youth will make?

In creating and downloading pictures onto networked sites, youth are operating according to principles that have evolved over millions of years to deal with uncertainty, complexity and change. The principles are here to stay. Many cultural observers go further predicting that current social networking and sharing sites are merely a harbinger of things to come.

Summary and implications

This chapter has described how pictures as texts are always intertextual, situated within complex, rhizomic connections to numerous other texts. Pictures draw from many sources, and we as viewers make many of our own associations. Moreover, both as audience members and creators, youth today are using forms of collective, distributed intelligence that aligns them with the intelligence of smart swarms.

Youth are already operating intertextually, both in what they view and how they create, and both have implications for curriculum that are taken up in Chapters 9 and 10. Chapter 9 specifically addresses intertextuality. It explores how educators can connect student interest in current cultural sites to the big and perennial preoccupations of human societies. Chapter 10 builds upon the idea of students acting as smart swarms. While operating as smart swarms is highly beneficial, it also has a downside. Smart swarms are not always smart, and educational intervention is necessary.

Questions

1 What is the difference between a text and intertextuality?
2 What is a rhizome and why is it a useful way of considering visual culture?
3 What do the terms *produsage* and *prosumer* refer to?
4 In semiotics, what is the difference between a denotation and a connotation?
5 What are the four principles on which smart swarms are based?
6 In what ways can youth culture be considered as operating as a smart smarm?
7 Youth culture was described in several ways apart from a smart swarm; what were they?

Activities

See Chapter 9 for an extended discussion of examples.

See Chapter 8 for specific questions on intertextuality: What were the influences on the making of the picture? What interpretive connections can you make?

8

Picture Appraisal

What is appraisal?

The term *appraisal* is used here as a neutral term. It is intended to imply neither praise nor negative criticism. Appraisal means to estimate the nature and value of something, to subject something to careful consideration. Appraisal is used because it is important to address pictures without preconceived views as to their value. We may assess a particular picture as exceptionally significant, worthy, profound, insightful and so on, but equally we may consider it remarkably trite, lacking insight and just plain poor. We may also find that a picture falls somewhere between these polar opposites, or we may find some aspects of a picture to be positive and other aspects to be negative.

Appraisal is not appreciation. Appreciation assumes from the outset that the object for consideration is something to be highly valued. Appreciation is similar to *esteem,* which is to feel respect combined with a warm kindly feeling. Appreciation is also close to *prize*, which means not only to value highly but to cherish.

By contrast, criticism often implies fault-finding. Although criticism may denote neutral intentions, it is often associated with severe, negative critique. Thus, appraisal is to be preferred to signify neither praise nor fault-finding.

Another reason to prefer appraisal is that often the point of considering a picture is not even to evaluate it at all, but merely to estimate its character, to understand it rather than to pass judgment upon it. The important thing is not to jump to judgment without due consideration. For each of these reasons, appraisal is used here as a neutral term.

A linear sequence

In art education, the following five-part strategy has been often employed when looking at paintings and other fine art objects. It is an inductive approach that moves from factual details to a holistic assessment.

Initial reaction
Description
Formal analysis
Interpretation
Evaluation

Offering students the opportunity to express an initial reaction can be very important. Often students want to express their like or dislike of a picture, and if they are able to express their first, subjective response teachers can then more easily take them through a careful consideration of the picture. Teachers invariably have an objective in leading a conversation in a particular direction and so fulfil curriculum objectives. To do so, it is best to allow students time to get their first impressions out of their system. Sometimes students will have no particular response, neither negative nor positive. But if they have a strongly felt reaction, giving it voice is important. Otherwise, students will be thinking things like, 'I hate this picture', or 'I love this picture because it reminds me of (something)', and they will not be paying attention. A strong emotional reaction, either positive or negative, is a good place to start. Even 'Yuck' is a good place to begin because it indicates involvement.

Where possible it is equally important to distinguish between a description and an interpretation. Imagine a picture of a boy smirking. Is the boy being naughty or is the boy simply smirking in a way that suggests he is being naughty? The fact that the boy is smirking is a description. In the language of semiotics, it is a denotation. Without further evidence, the idea that the boy is up to no good simply because he is smirking is an interpretation. He could just be pleased with himself.

In the past, formal analysis has usually meant a modernist focus on elements like lines, tones, colours and compositional considerations such as balance, contrast and unity. As such, the approach is especially helpful in addressing abstract and non-representational pictures though it is also useful to consider how these elements and principles are used to support representational content. However, there is no reason that formal analysis could not as easily draw on the elements of realistic-style imagery discussed in Chapter 2 to address realistic style pictures. Both the modernist elements and principles and the grammar of realistic-style pictures are concerned with the construction of pictures and are therefore essential tools for interpreting the meaning of pictures.

To understand what a picture is about, that is, to interpret the meaning of a picture, it is often necessary to ask leading questions. Asking a broad question like 'What is this picture about?' will often result in blank stares, so it is helpful to lead up to this question by asking questions like: 'Can you tell what time of the day or season is represented? Who are these people? What are they doing? Why is a particular person given prominence? What do you look at first and why?'

At the end of this chapter there is an appendix of exercises to help students, especially younger students, describe pictures. Additionally, many of the issues discussed below in introducing the following visual culture appraisal compass approach can be used with this linear approach. Interpretive questions could include the following: What time of the day or season of the year is represented? Where is the picture set? Does it tell a story? Does it show how something looked? Each of these questions, and the many like them noted below, can be used to lead up to the principle interpretive task of asking what a picture is about. Evaluation is also addressed in what follows below by asking, for example, is the picture an accurate depiction of real life? Is it expressive? Is it attractive? Does it appear to fulfil its function? How original or skilful is it?

Affordance

The great benefit of this sequence is that it slows down the process of appraisal. It takes time to go through a step-by-step process and so notice items and make connections not otherwise made. As described in Chapter 6 on the gaze, we are all habituated today to quickly glance at pictures rather than carefully studying them. Paintings in the past were typically made with the expectation that viewers would subject them to careful scrutiny; they were made in such a way as to sustain lengthy and even repeated study. But today's magazine advertisements or moving pictures can equally support a prolonged examination. This is precisely because they are carefully designed for a quick grab, so understanding how they are so carefully constructed is important. To fully appreciate the complexity of any picture, taking time is essential.

Limitations

However, this lock-step approach has some practical limitations. First, when looking at pictures we usually do not operate in such a linear, logical fashion. We often begin by making a holistic judgment and then work to justify our first impressions by finding facts that support our initial assessment. In short, we often start with an evaluation and work backwards. This is a deductive approach.

A second difficulty relates to the first; strict divisions between each step are somewhat artificial. It is often difficult to distinguish between a description and a formal analysis or even between a description and an interpretation.

A third problem is that the approach has usually been used to examine pictures without recourse to research. The assumption has been that the meaning of a picture lies in the picture itself, and as discussed in previous chapters, the meaning of any picture lies in the relationship that is formed between the picture, the viewer and the context of viewing. Additionally, it is usually the case that to be better informed it is necessary to undertake some digging. Understanding something of the original context of a picture and the possible intentions of its maker always enriches our own understanding.

A fourth difficulty with the lock-step nature of this linear sequence is that students, no matter their age, frequently upset any predetermined sequence.

The Visual Culture Appraisal Compass

Instead of thinking in terms of a linear sequence, either inductive or deductive, it is often best to think more flexibly, to be prepared to jump in unexpected directions. For this reason, the metaphor of a compass is useful. With the different points of a compass, different aspects of a picture can be explored. And to extend the metaphor of the compass, if one is feeling all at sea with picture appraisal, there are many points on the compass towards which one can navigate.

The compass below consists of eight points in terms of eight questions: What? Who? Why? How? When? Where? Connections? Evaluation? Some of the questions ask for similar material, merely asking about the same topic from a different perspective; for example, asking about who made a picture can be to ask why the picture was made, or to ask what connections can be made between one picture and another is to ask when and where other similar pictures were made.

The following are only examples of questions that can be asked; they should be tailored to the knowledge base of particular students. Some of the questions can be asked of very young children

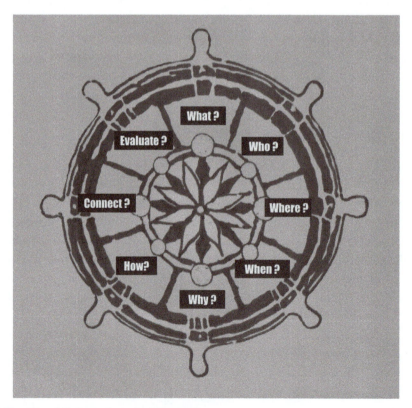

Figure 8.1 The Visual Culture Appraisal Compass.

while other questions could only be used with older students. Many of the questions need to be followed up by others that ferret out significance. For example, questions about genre are intended to spark conversations about a particular genre's identifying characteristics. The point of the question about the length of a time-based moving picture is to enquire further about how length helps to determine the nature of the form, its affordances and limitations.

What?

'What' questions describe basic facts about a picture. They address the medium, the genre and, drawing upon Chapter 2 on representation, what is represented. The following are some example questions.

What is the medium?

Is the picture a painting, a photograph, a limited-edition print, a movie, a television programme or a video game?
Is it two or three dimensions, or is it a relief?
Is it the real thing or a reproduction?
Is it time based?
What size or length is it?
Is it digital or analogue?

What is the genre?

Among paintings, is the genre historical, landscape, everyday life, portraiture or still life?
Among movies and television programmes, is the genre action, adventure, animation, comedy, crime, drama, fantasy, historical, horror, magical realism, musical, mystery, romance, saga, science fiction, thriller, western or war?
Among video games, is the genre action, action adventure, role-play, simulation, strategy or sports?
Does it belong to a subcategory of genre or is it a hybrid of genres?

What is represented?

In Chapter 2 on representation, questions were raised about what is represented, what is not represented, and misleading and false representations. Questions that can be asked include:

What can you see? Name as many things as you can see, even what might seem unimportant.
Is a stereotype represented?
Is the stereotype based on gender, race, ethnicity, age, class, ableness or something else?
Does the stereotype appear positive, negative or benign?
Does the picture seem to represent something real or a fantasy?
Is there anything that appears to be missing?

Is the representation false? If so, is the falsification of people, situations or historical events? Is the representation an idealization of the truth or a complete fabrication?

Who?

'Who' questions locate a picture in terms of the various people involved: the makers, the patrons and the viewers. They ask: who made the picture, who was it for and, drawing upon Chapter 6 on the gaze, who is viewing.

Who made it?

An individual?
An amateur or amateurs?
A team of in-house professionals?
A team of outsourced professionals?
An international team?

Who is the picture intended for?

The artist?
A mass audience?
A particular demographic like children, adolescents, men, women or another demographic?
An international audience?

Who is looking?

As describe in Chapter 6 on the gaze, how we look is practically equivalent to who we are, at least at the moment of looking. The following questions embrace our multi-faceted selves as well as the six pleasures of the gaze discussed in Chapter 6.

Does your gender, sexual identity, ethnicity, class, age or ableness help determine your looking?
Are you looking, for example, with curiosity, empathy, lovingly or reverentially?
Are you looking in a moralizing or patronizing way?
Are you condemning or disciplining what you see?
Are you comfortable or uncomfortable looking?
Are you simply looking because you love the subject?
Are you enjoying the sense of power that is inherent in voyeurism?
Are you prepared to admit that you get some kind of sadistic pleasure in looking?
Do you feel any sense that you are violating the subject by looking?
Do you identify with any of the figures?
Do you feel that the figures are exhibiting themselves for you?
Would you ever imagine that you are exhibiting yourself for a figure in the picture?
Do you sense that you should not be looking?

If you are transgressing, what kind of transgressive looking are you using?

If you are transgressing, is there a special thrill in looking in this way?

Where?

'Where' questions locate a picture in terms of place. They address where a picture was made, where it represents and, drawing on Chapter 6 on the gaze, where it is viewed.

Where was it made?

In your own country?

In a particular town or city?

Another country?

Does it look similar to things made in the same place?

Was it made inside a building or outside?

How can you tell where it was made?

Where does it show?

Is it a real place or an imaginary one?

Is there anything in the picture to indicate where it was made, such as a particular landscape or landmark, dress, customs or technology?

Where is it viewed?

As described in Chapter 6 on the gaze, how we look is partly determined by the environmental, institutional or social contexts of our looking. The following are examples of different settings.

Of environmental contexts, would you typically view this picture driving past a billboard, in a crowded train, in a movie theatre, in your own bedroom, in your living room, surfing the net, in the dentist's waiting room or in some other physical environment?

Of institutional contexts, would you typically view this picture in an art museum, in a natural history museum, a science museum, at a police station, in a classroom or some other institution?

In an institutional context, would people typically look at the picture with a categorizing, disciplinary, managerial, regulating or normalizing gaze?

Of social contexts, would you typically view this picture when you are alone, with family or with friends?

How do different contexts change how you look?

When?

'When' questions locate a picture in time. They provide context as to when a picture was made, the time a picture represents and when it is viewed. When questions are often closely tied to environmental contexts, to where questions.

When was it made?

How can you tell when it was made?

Does it have indications of aging?

Was it made to last a long time or was it made to last only a short time?

Does it look recent or old fashioned, new or dated?

When does it show?

Is it possible to say what time of day is represented?

Is it possible to say what season of the year is represented?

Does the picture represent a contemporary scene, one from the past, or from the future?

When would audiences typically look at it?

Only on special occasions?

Every day?

Constantly throughout the day?

Only in strict privacy?

As part of other activities?

Travelling to and from school or work?

When you have a moment to yourself?

When you should be doing something else?

Only when bored?

Only in class?

Why?

'Why' questions identify the reason or reasons for a picture's being. They address intention, both why pictures are made and why viewers look at them. Drawing on Chapter 3 on rhetoric, why questions ask what arguments are made. Drawing on Chapter 4 on ideology, why questions ask about what ideologies are embedded. Asking about arguments or ideology is asking the same kind of questions. Below, the questions are framed in terms of arguments but they can equally be asked in terms of ideology. For example, to ask what argument does a picture make about the environment is also to ask what ideology about the environment does the picture offer.

In general terms, why was the picture made?

To show what something looks like?

To sell a product?

To tell a story?

To arouse emotion?

For an artist to express him or herself?

To serve a patron such as the church, a king, an emperor or someone wealthy?

To make money?

In terms of rhetoric, why was the picture made?

To make an argument about gender, race, sexual identity, class, ableness, religion or politics?

To argue about the value of work, progress or technology?

Was the picture made to promote a progressive, conservative or reactionary viewpoint?

Is the argument made directly or indirectly, explicitly or implicitly?

Was it made in support of the status quo?

Was it made to challenge or to protest against the status quo?

Was it made to argue for an alternative to the status quo?

Was it made to argue that what is shown *should not* be the case?

Was it made to argue that what is shown *should* be the case?

Do you agree or disagree with the argument or agree in part and disagree in part?

To what extent do you think the maker was conscious or unconscious of making their argument?

Was it made to make either a direct or an indirect argument, an explicit or an implicit argument?

Was it made to make more than one argument?

If more than one argument is made, are the arguments consistent, inconsistent or complementary?

Why do people look at it?

To be delighted?

To learn about something?

To be entertained?

To satisfy curiosity?

To relieve boredom?

To be seen by others to be viewing?

Some other reason?

How?

There are several kinds of 'how' questions. How questions relate to the process of making a picture and, drawing on Chapter 6 on the gaze, how we look. However, most how questions relate to how a picture is able to captivate an audience. They relate to what Aristotle called the 'available means of persuasion.' These questions variously draw upon Chapter 2 on the elements of representation, on Chapter 3 on rhetoric and emotion and Chapter 4 on seductive aesthetic pleasures.

How was the picture made?

Did the picture take a long or a short time to make?

Did the picture require a lot of thought and planning?

What technical steps were required to make the picture?

Did it require more than one person to make the picture?

Did it require a lot of money to make the picture?

Did the maker have to raise funds to make it, and if so, from whom?

If the maker was dependent upon others to make the picture, how do you think this influenced the picture?

How does the picture represent its subject?

How does the framing of the picture affect what you can see and your relationship to the subject of the picture?

How does the angle-of-view help determine your relationship to the subject of the picture?

If the picture is a photograph, what effect did the lens used have on how the subject is represented?

How does the lighting of the subject affect how the subject is represented?

How does the tonal key or contrast affect how the subject is represented?

How is the meaning of the picture anchored?

How is body language employed to convey meaning?

Of moving images, how are subjective and/or objective viewpoints used to develop the narrative?

Of moving images, how is a fixed or a handheld camera employed to help create meaning?

Of moving images, how are camera movements used to convey meaning?

Of moving images, how are transitions used to develop meaning?

How do you look?

Do you feast your eyes or look daggers?

Do you gaze, glance, gape, glare or glimpse?

Do you peek or peer?

Do you scrutinize, stare or survey?

Do you look in some other way?

How does the picture attempt to seduce?

Chapter 3 on rhetoric discussed how pictures rely upon both emotions and eloquence to persuade viewers to accept an argument. Chapter 4 discussed many ways in which aesthetics acts as a sensory and emotional lure.

What use is made of emotions?

The concepts of rhetoric and aesthetics agree that both showing and arousing emotions are an important function of pictures. In Chapter 3 on rhetoric, a long list of emotions was offered. You may wish to use the list to answer the following questions.

Can you identify the emotions expressed by people in the picture?

Do the emotions expressed appear feigned or simulated, or do they appear deeply or acutely felt?

Are the emotions highly excited, charged or passionate, inflamed or excited?

To what purpose are the emotions aroused?

Are the emotions intended to address you as an individual or as part of a community?

Can you identify which emotions are aroused in you?

Do you think the emotions aroused are the same as the maker intended to arouse in you?

Are the emotions positive or negative?

Does the picture appeal because of an emotional attachment to the subject?

What use is made of sensory qualities?

Chapter 4 discussed many kinds of sensory pleasures. They include the following, though in each case there are many different kinds.

Does the picture appeal because it is bright and busy, spectacular, sentimental, exotic, violent, horrific, destructive or humorous?

Does the picture appeal because of formal elements like colour, tone and texture?

Does the picture appeal because it is well composed?

Is the picture's appeal due to its realistic style or because it is formulaic?

Is the appeal more specific to a particular cultural form; for example, animation, carnival, manga, shopping malls or video games?

It the appeal to the grotesque, or the cute, or whatever appears cool?

Does the picture have special appeal because you are a fan of the subject?

Connections?

Questions about connections locate a picture within an extensive web of other texts, from both the past and the present. As discussed in Chapter in 7 on intertextuality, questions about connections relate to both influences on the making of the picture and the wide variety of potential associations made by viewers.

What were the influences on the making of the picture?

Was the picture influenced by the maker's background story?

Were other cultural forms drawn upon to make the picture such as novels, memoirs, poetry, news stories or song lyrics?

Was the picture influenced by certain arguments or ideologies, social issues, technology, the economy or legal requirements?

Do you think the picture was influenced by the maker's perception of their intended audience?

What interpretive connections can you make?

Can you make connections of your own to different categories of pictures like popular, fine and/ or indigenous pictures?

Can you make connections of your own to other cultural forms such as novels, memoirs, poetry, news stories and/or song lyrics?

Are the connections you make based on similar media, subject matter and/or genre?

Can you make connections to pictures with similar ideologies or arguments?

Are your connections based on similar seductive pleasures, either to emotional or sensory qualities?

Can you make satiric, ironic or witty connections?

Are the connections you make directly related to the picture or are they tangential?

Are your connections based on fact or are they fanciful?

Are your connections specific or general?

Can you make historical, cross-cultural, or contemporary connections?

Do the connections you make cast the picture in a morally good, neutral or a bad light?

Evaluation?

Questions about evaluation address value. Evaluation means making judgments about worthiness. There are many criteria on which to evaluate pictures. Previous chapters have not dealt directly with evaluation, although Chapter 5 raised many moral issues regarding the pleasures pictures offer, and they are used below to complicate evaluation, to simultaneously praise and find fault.

Fine art theories

First, questions about value can be based on criteria derived from different traditional theories of fine art. Although these theories are not adequate as theories of all art, each draws attention to characteristic aspects of some pictures, and these can be applied wherever they appear appropriate to a picture. The theory or idea about fine art is named in brackets below.

Does the picture look like the real thing? (Imitation)

Does the picture move you or leave you cold? Does the emotion expressed appear to be genuine or feigned, real or manufactured? (Expression)

Do the various elements like lines, shapes and colours appear unified yet varied enough to be interesting? (Formalism)

Does the picture look attractive or arresting or is it visually dull and uninteresting? (Aesthetic)

Can you imagine that the picture could help to work out or clarify people's personal problems? (Therapy)

Is the symbolism subtle, powerful or clever, or is it too obvious and clichéd? (Symbolism)

Is the message clear or confused, deliberately ambiguous or multilayered? (Communication)

Does the picture function well or it is clumsy? Does it serve its purpose or appear to be an inept solution? (Instrumental)

Is the picture well executed or does it appear amateurish? (Skill)

Is the picture surprising or innovative in some way or is it clichéd? (Originality)

Does the picture fulfil, fail to fulfil or exceed the maker's apparent intentions? (Intention)

Using different criteria

Some pictures are strong in various ways, but also weak in others. For example, some blockbuster movies are very spectacular and thus a delight to look at, yet lacking in ideas and bereft of emotional interest. Some pictures lack skill but are nevertheless very effective in arousing emotion.

Moral criteria

None of the above criteria address moral questions, but as demonstrated in Chapter 5 on problems with pleasure, pictures are deeply embedded in moral issues. As such, pictures are not immune to being evaluated in moral terms. One especially striking example, discussed in Chapter 5, is the 1935 documentary *Triumph of the Will* directed by Leni Riefenstahl. While an extraordinary, awe-inspiring technical achievement even by today's standards, the film was used by the Nazis to spread their evil ideology. Critics have typically been torn between admiring and condemning it, praising it for its daring use of new technologies in stirring strong emotions, and, on the other hand, condemning it for its idealization of Nazi fascism. In considering Riefenstahl's achievement, it is necessary to hold both evaluations simultaneously because her achievement is equal to the horrible purpose to which it was placed. Mostly we are pleased at how effective something is, but also sometimes we can be appalled at how good something is.

Similar to the above example, the following questions, derived from Chapter 5, may complicate our evaluation of pictures that otherwise we would praise. For example, many pictures may appeal because they are exceptionally realistic but insidious because their realistic style masks the fact that they are fabrications. The quality that appeals, and we praise, can be the very same quality that works to secure questionable ends.

Bright and busy

If the picture is bright and busy, does it simply delight, or is it also so attractive that it might make people vulnerable to manipulation?

Do you feel you are able to resist such temptation?

Spectacular

If the picture is spectacular, does it overwhelm in such a way as to render people unable to employ reason?

Do you feel able to employ reason in the face of such spectacular imagery?

Sentimentality

If the subjects of the picture arouse the tender emotions of sentimentality, does the picture help create identification and so bind people together?

If the subject of the picture is stereotyped as sweet and innocent, is the subject stripped of their actual, complex reality?

If people are represented in a sentimental way, could the picture encourage patronizing public policies that treat people like infants lacking agency?

Does the sentimentality of the picture encourage viewers to ignore unpleasant realities that should be faced?

Is there a danger that the sentimentality of the picture could substitute emotional indulgence for action on behalf of social equality?

Could the sentimentality breed its opposite in brutish behaviour?

The exotic

Is the exotic nature of the picture used to spice up one's own culture or life without any negative connotations?

If an exotic stereotype is used, however positive, does it deny the complexity of the subject?

If an exotic stereotype is used, does it cast others as inferior rather than merely different?

If the picture implies fault in another society, does the picture help to ignore one's own social problems?

Violence

If the picture represents violence, is the violence gratuitous or legitimized by serious intent?

If the picture represents violence, is the violence benign or could it help create a fearful and anxious society?

If violent imagery helps create a fearful and anxious society, could it lead to allowing others to use real violence on our behalf?

Do pictures of violence reinforce the status quo by repressing dissent?

Horror and destruction

If the picture represents horror, does it encourage a perception of other people in terms of good versus bad without shades of grey?

Do pictures of destruction help liberate us from mundane reality and/or do they also engender fear and anxiety?

Humour

If a picture is humorous, is the humour uplifting or does it denigrate other people?

Is the humour liberatory or reactionary, facilitating open-heartedness or reinforcing reactionary views of other people?

Does the humour help bring people together or divide them?

Is the humour complex, creating a sense of community while also denigrating others?

A realistic style

If a realistic style is used, does the picture show a situation as it really happened or is it in some way deceptive?

Does the picture idealize its subject and thus avoid representing unpleasant realities?

Does the realistic style of the picture confuse fact with fiction, lies with truth?

Formulaic

If the picture is formulaic, does the formula offer comfort or does it appear clichéd?

Summary

The visual culture appraisal compass questions should be used flexibly. They are not set in stone. You should devise your own, and in asking one kind of question it is often important to follow up with another kind, such as a what question with a why or a how question. Bounce around from one kind of question to another.

9

Postmodern Curriculum 1:
Intertextual Connections

Recapping intertextuality

As described in Chapter 7, visual culture is made up of any number of interconnections. Contemporary popular visual culture draws upon numerous previous pictures, but it also links to other communication modes like poetry, song lyrics and novels, and in doing so it also connects to many ideas, beliefs and values related to religion, politics and numerous social issues. Additionally, we viewers make our own connections. We each have the ability to make associations that spark other associations that lead to still others. Moreover, these connections, both pictorial references and what we viewers freely associate, are typically numerous and highly complex. In a word, the structure of visual culture is rhizomic.

An intertextual, rhizomic curriculum conceptualized

The approach to a visual culture curriculum developed below both reflects and explores the rhizomic structure of visual culture. To help conceptualize such a curriculum it is helpful to address the difference between a conventional curriculum and one offered in this chapter that is based on intertextual connections. The former is modernist; the latter is postmodern. The distinction is based on another distinction described in Chapter 7 between rhizomes and trees. The analogy to different kinds of fauna offers a way to understand how to conceptualize the difference between the two kinds of curriculum.

Modernist curricula tend to be like a tree with a trunk, roots and branches, where the common factor between the roots and branches is the trunk. The trunk represents foundational knowledge, the core of the curriculum, what students need to know before moving on to anything else. This kind of curriculum is based on the assumption that students need to be led from simple to complex knowledge in a step-by-step linear sequence.

The modernist art curriculum

The typical, modernist art curriculum perfectly illustrates a core-based curriculum. It is like a tree (Figure 9.1). Not only has art education traditionally addressed only fine art, it has long used only a very limited, formalist approach to fine art. Art education has long considered fine art to possess a distinctive core, one that sets it apart from all other subject areas. According to modernist art education, the unique, distinguishing core of the art curriculum consisted of three basic things: the formal elements of line, shape, colour and so on; the principles of composition such as harmony and contrast; and the particular qualities of materials such as pencils, crayons, and paint. A major concern was what materials were best suited to produce certain forms. For example, pencils and

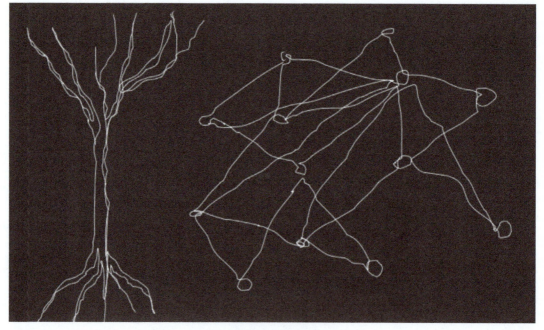

Figure 9.1 *The Flora Analogy of a Tree-like Curriculum versus a Rhizomic Curriculum.*

pens best create lines; collage is a medium with which to explore shape; colour is best explored with paint, and so on. Because this approach stresses form, it is known as formalism. The trunk of the modernist art curriculum is formalist.

Imagine now that the roots of the tree represent the histories of art. Long and thick roots can be taken to represent the art of whole continents and general geographic areas, whereas thinner roots would represent individual countries. The history of art in the West would be represented with a major root, as would the history of art in Africa, Asia and South America. China would have a very long root though thinner than Asia as a whole. New World countries like Australia and the United States would have relatively short roots.

At the other end of the trunk the branches of the tree can be used to represent all the issues with which art deals; for example, religion, national identity, gender relations, race, sexuality, patriotism, heroism, natural beauty, violence, horror and human passions. Many of these themes are age-old and would have long and thick branches with smaller branches representing many subthemes.

Trees can last a long time, and the modernist art curriculum, first developed in the West in the early years of the twentieth century, remains influential in many parts of the world. But there are several crucial problems with this curriculum, both theoretical and practical.

First, in practice, teachers who operate with little time and opportunity in school are often unable to teach much beyond what this modernist model of curriculum considers core knowledge. Especially in the lower classes, teachers often never move beyond what they consider the basics, and students are condemned to produce line exercises and colour wheels grade after grade. Students never get to study fine art history let alone the ideas and issues with which fine art deals.

Second, if teachers find the time to study art history, it is studied in terms of form and materials. Examining a painting, teachers ask questions like what colours are used, what shapes? Is the picture balanced? Is there sufficient contrast? Note the dynamism. Examine the brushstrokes. And so on. Art historical pictures are thereby considered primarily, or even exclusively, in terms of form.

With a formalist approach to art history, the many reasons for creating art in the first place are ignored. This is a third difficulty with this approach. Again, strapped for time, teachers are frequently unable to consider the values and beliefs that not only typically motivate the making of art, but are often viewers' primary interest in looking at fine art. Focused on form, students never get to consider the questions, controversies, and power struggles that both motivate artists and interest viewers.

A fourth difficulty, following from those above, is that the formalist model of art curriculum is no more the core of art than many other considerations. Postmodern art theory and practice as well as a visual culture curriculum claims that both fine art and popular visual culture exist as a series of interactions with many other human practices and concerns. Formalism equates art with form, but this is false. While a knowledge of visual form is undoubtedly unique to visual art, equating it with core knowledge ignores both intention and function. Pictures spring from the intention to contribute to the issues of the day and they function by contributing. Their value lies in contributing. Form acts as the means of making a contribution; that is all. Pictures are inspired by a desire to either confirm, challenge, dissent or offer alternatives to all the big and small issues of the time.

Postmodern theory and practice historicizes the elements and principles, that is, it considers formalism as specific to a particular historical moment. Formalism pertained to just one moment in the history of fine art, a very brief moment (early to mid-twentieth century), one that is now long past, and one that was particularly relevant only to Western abstract and non-representational art. Moreover, even during the heyday of formalist art theory and practice, fine artists were inspired by many considerations other than form.

A fifth difficulty with the modernist, tree-like curriculum is that it is especially susceptible to attack. As strong and as long-standing as trees can be, they are highly vulnerable to disease, axe or saw; similarly with formalism. Once form is understood as just one consideration among others, it can appear to modernists that art itself no longer exists. And further, if the elements, principles and the particular quality of materials are thought never to have constituted the core knowledge of art, and should have never anchored the art curriculum in the first place, the very basis of this curriculum falls apart. Trees are a relatively weak structure. By contrast, rhizomes are especially resilient. While a tree is easily chopped down it is very difficult to kill off a large section of grass. Unless a very large amount of poison is employed, what remains will sprout new growth in another space and/or will in time grow back where the grass had been killed. Recall from Chapter 7 that the internet was deliberately conceived as rhizomic in order to sustain attack by quickly reconstituting itself.

A visual culture curriculum rejects the idea of undisputed foundational knowledge, of a definitive core that in curriculum terms must be understood before proceeding further. Instead of conceiving the curriculum in terms of core and elective knowledge, the curriculum is conceived in terms of relationships between numerous areas of knowledge. Instead of introducing knowledge in a lock-step progression from core to peripheral, essential to elective, the curriculum is developed through making connections between different areas of knowledge. A visual culture curriculum is grounded in the idea that any one area of knowledge is not only interconnected, but only exists because of the interconnections between it and other areas of knowledge. In sum, visual culture exists in a rhizomic relationship with many other areas of human thought and activity.

Addressing teacher anxiety

A visual culture curriculum as described immediately above understandably creates anxiety among teachers. They legitimately ask: how is it possible to address visual culture in the classroom when first, there is so much of it, and, secondly, so much of it is ephemeral? How are teachers to address the ever-changing plethora of today's imagery?

Consider these two scenarios: Teacher A says to her class 'Today we are going to start a study of … And you will be using the resourses I have prepared for you'. This could be almost any conventional class. Teacher B says to her class, 'Over the next few weeks we will explore various topics of your own choosing. And let us start with what you are watching in the media. What is "hot" right now? It could be a new television programme or a recent movie. Or it might be a magazine or a recent internet craze. Let us take a vote on what we will focus on'. This is a visual culture teacher, but to many teachers this sounds unrealistic, an ideal that the realities of school prohibit. Where, teachers ask, are we to find the time to secure resources when every semester, perhaps every class, wants to study something different?

Basic points

There are solutions, ones described in detail below. But it will be helpful to begin by considering the following basic points. As described in Chapter 7, an intertext can start anywhere and with anything. Intertextual connections can start from almost any picture, poem, song, newspaper report, event and so on. In short, it will not matter which starting point students choose because any picture, or any other kind of text will connect, either directly or indirectly, to a variety of themes, issues and/or questions.

Secondly, among the variety of themes, issues and/or questions raised will be those that are both perennial and contemporary. The past will be linked to the present and the present to the past. Additionally, issues from one culture will also cross over and relate to other cultures. The links will be multicultural as well as historical. Even what may at first appear to be of only this moment in time, almost invariably has deep links to issues that have fascinated human societies for millennia. For example, today's celebrity culture is often thought to be a product of consumer culture, but celebrities are really only the heroes and heroines of the past; they serve the same function of providing role models. Consumer culture is a product of today and yet for the affluent of the past, such as kings and emperors, the acquisition of material goods has long been a primary preoccupation. Issues related to class, gender and sexuality are age-old, as is war, suffering, religion and political intrigue. Almost any visual story involves family, friendship, loyalty, alliances, heroes versus villains and good versus evil. Almost any picture will reference some of these perennial themes.

Third, many of the themes, issues and/or questions will be the same from semester to semester, irrespective of the starting point. Almost any popular picture in which students are interested is bound to deal with some of the same age-old themes.

Fourth, the perennial nature of these themes, issues and/or questions allows teachers the opportunity to prepare. Since whatever text a class chooses to begin with is likely to evoke similar themes, teachers have the time to develop the resources. Over time they would be able to develop a repertoire of resources for whatever text a class chooses to use as a springboard. For example, one class might choose an action movie that deals with heroes, violence and suffering. Their teacher could then turn to their resources on heroes, which they had already acquired from a previous class, and to deal with violence and suffering they might turn to their already prepared resourses on attitudes to war.

The world is now saturated with pictures as never before, but the stories they tell, and the truths they expose and/or conceal, are perennial. While new visual technologies are invented all the time, human preoccupations have remained remarkably similar. There are always new twists on old themes yet the numerous twists only underline the persistent nature of the themes, issues and/or questions.

A curriculum journey

The rest of this chapter is devoted to illustrating the above basic points. It describes my own journey in devising rhizomic-based curricula. I begin by describing my inspirations, and then I trace the various steps I took along the way. I describe begining with individual students, to working in groups, to working with a whole class, and from using computers to using the low technology of paper, pushpins and woollen yarn on a large pin board.

Hypertextual curriculum: StorySpace

I was not the first to use a rhizomic approach to curriculum (Tavin, 2002). An early notable example is Kevin Tavin's study of a *Diesel* jeans advertisement and the studies of his graduate students (Figure 9.2). Tavin could have started with an idea, a definition, song lyrics, a philosophical position, an issue or a controversy, but he started with a then contemporary advertisement. Although a rhizome has neither a beginning nor an end, an organized, timetabled curriculum must have both. Even a patch of grass may have begun with just one seed. We must therefore start somewhere.

Tavin's advertisement appropriated a famous photograph of the Yalta conference of 1945, which shows President Roosevelt of the United States, Prime Minister Churchill of Great Britain and Premier Stalin of the Soviet Union sitting together on the deck of a ship where they had met to discuss strategy for winning the war against Hitler. Several young female models have been digitally inserted so that they appear draped around these famous patriarchal, military leaders. The

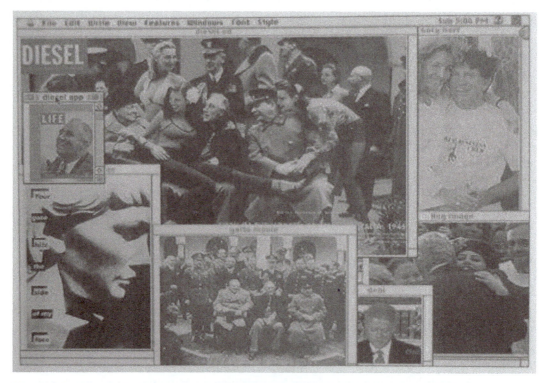

Figure 9.2 Kevin Tavin, *Diesel Jeans Advertisement StorySpace Screenshot* (2000).

advertisment used previously unrelated pictures to create a pastiche of contemporary references to consumerism with figures of great historical importance.

Tavin asked his students whether they thought the advertisement trivialized women as sexual objects. Did the picture, like so many others, help to shape an understanding of the role of women in society? Was the unequal power relationship between the men and women in the photograph replicated by us as viewers/voyeurs of the women?

The class discussion led to the creation of a hypertext using the computer programme StorySpace. A hypertext is simply an intertext enabled by computer links, as in a hyperlink. StorySpace was an especially good programme for this purpose, first because it enabled makers to create numerous links, and second, because it also enabled viewers to readily make their own connections. Each time users used it, they were likely to make different connections.

The hypertext linked different aspects of the advertisement that were then linked to other historical and contemporary references such as images of Roosevelt from *Life Magazine* and pictures of other presidents. Icons of power such as militariaism, machinery and totalitarianism were investigated that juxtaposed men and women, viewers and viewed and the complex position of viewers as simultaneously voyeurs and consumers.

Tavin's students went on to investigate other popular cultural sites. One student chose an advertisment for *Nike* and soon found more than 300 pictures related to Asian manufacturing industries as well as labour organizations fighting against exploitive conditions. He went on to construct a hypertext using eighty-five pictures and 400 connections.

Hypertextual curriculum: individual PowerPoints

Inspired by such examples, a few years ago I had my own pre-service students create a rhizomic hypertext using the hyperlink facility on PowerPoint. PowerPoint has many limitations compared to StorySpace, essentially being an old-fashioned slide show, but all computers came packaged with PowerPoint and StorySpace is expensive. Pragmatics won out. We were saved by using the hyperlink facility on PowerPoint. Though not nearly as flexible as StorySpace, students were able to make many excursions from one picture to another, to yet another, and so on. PowerPoint also allowed some choice in how viewers navigated through the hypertext and so make their own connections.

Preparation

As a warm-up exercise, I divided the class into small groups and gave each a picture. Some groups received a fine art picture; others a popular picture. I then had each group generate lists of associations and then create a rhizomic sketch with as many connections as they could establish between associations (Figure 9.3). They only had half an hour. The students drew their sketch on paper and then transferred it to a white board so that the rest of the class could see and comment. Many students then offered further connections; oftentimes back to their own rhizomic sketches.

To one group I gave a poster of the 2003 movie *The Hulk*. It shows the character with bulging muscles and an angry face lunging towards the viewer. The students immediately linked it to Hollywood and movies, and movies to monsters and superheroes. Then they became stuck. I made

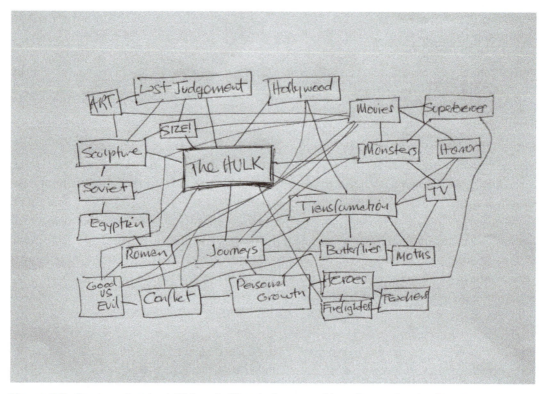

Figure 9.3 Student sketch, *A Rhizomic Sketch Generated by a Poster for the Film* The Hulk.

the suggestion to try to link the Hulk to art history and when I received blank stares I suggested examining Michelangelo's fresco of his massively muscular Christ from the *Last Judgment* as well as the monumentality of totalitarian sculpture, for by similar means they served similar functions of impressing through sheer size. Students then thought of ordinary heroes and considered many different kinds, including teachers. Since the lead character is ordinarily meek and mild and only becomes a rampaging monster when angered, I also suggested the idea of transformation or metamorphosis, which soon had students generating many other ideas, including personal journeys and the changing of grubs into moths and butterflies. Then the thought of conflict occurred to the students, and this led to conflicts of good and evil, and then they went on to think of numerous examples. I also asked students to consider what kind of pictures would accompany their associations.

Choosing a picture

I then instructed students to work individually to choose a picture and to consider it in terms of three or four themes it addressed either directly or indirectly. They could choose any kind of picture: fine art, popular art, folk art, indigenous art. The picture could be from the past or the present and from any culture. Since this was to be the major, end-of-semester project, I was concerned to ensure students chose a picture sufficiently rich in themes to sustain prolonged investigation. I therefore had them show me their picture for my approval, but I soon learned that this was unnecessary. Almost any picture could be considered to address, either explicitly or by suggestion, many different themes. With most pictures, the difficulty was not in finding enough themes; the difficulty lay in choosing which ones to investigate.

Some students chose pictures where the themes were obvious, although most chose pictures where they had to think through what issues the pictures appeared to assume as social norms. A few students appeared to have no idea why they had chosen their picture, but so long as I could see for myself that their picture had potential I left it to the student to discover this for him or herself. I believed that pictures that speak at a deeper than conscious level may have more potential than ones chosen for conscious reasons. This certainly appeared to be the case when a young, male student chose an advertisement for a product – he did not even know what the product was – which used a photograph of an adolescent male reclining in a chair with an older, somewhat predatory woman towering over him.

Evaluative criteria

I suggested that the connections they made could be of quite different kinds: confirmative, complementary, conflictual, critical, satirical, ironic. Apart from writing skills, criteria for assessment included: the validity, clarity and complexity of the connections; subtlety, invention and surprise; depth of exploration through pictures and words; communicative composition of pictures and words; and technical facility, including ease of access and movement through the hypertext.

The pictures chosen

The pictures the students chose were exceptionally varied. They included icons of fine art such as the *Mona Lisa* and *Guernica*, high art fashion photography and contemporary fine artists; other students chose movies as diverse as recent films to the 1939 classic *Gone with the Wind*; advertisements for products as diverse as clothing stores to ice cream; comics as different as Snoopy and Wonder Woman; and magazine covers as diverse as *Rolling Stone* and an early twentieth-century French magazine for fashion. Other examples have included photographs of various media celebrities such as the Olsen Twins and Marylyn Monroe, music idols like Kanye West and Bob Marley, a religious roadside billboard, John Lennon's memorial in New York, an AIDS poster, and an advertisement for breakfast cereal that used comic figures but referenced Leonardo's *The Last Supper*. As for the issues student chose to address, they included: competition, safety, transportation, private schools, heroism, cultural appropriation, drugs, war, family values and friendship.

Making connections

One student chose the trailer to the 2004 movie *The Passion of Christ*, drawing from it the themes of religion, pain and suffering and religious icons. She examined differences in Christian, Jewish and Islamic imagery as constitutive of their particular characteristics as well as pictures of religious controversies. The allegations of anti-Semitism, which the film aroused in the media, led the student to consider the Holocaust as well as racism in the United States. Under religious icons, she examined many historical and contemporary pictures of Christ that included the idea of Jesus as father, as shepherd and as judge, as well as pictures of Christ as both a white person and an African American. Paintings by, for example, Rouault and Dali led to popular, commercial images including a last supper on a lunch box, Jesus on an ash tray, a 'cool Jesus' on a T shirt and Jesus as an action figure. She concluded with a statement about her own religious faith.

Some students chose contemporary pictures and worked backwards historically. Others started with a historical image and worked forwards. Taking the latter approach one student began with the pre-historic *Venus De Willendorf* and linked her to pictures of both male and female beauty over the centuries. Of women she included figures from Ancient Mycenae; Cranach the Elder's 1528 painting *The Judgment of Paris*; paintings by Modigliani; and contemporary photographs of beauty pageants, plastic surgery and eating disorders. Of men, she included many images from Greek *Kouros*, paintings by Lucian Freud and advertisements for men's toiletries.

Most of my pre-service teachers were young women, so it was understandable that pictures of femininity were a common topic. One student chose a poster of the 2001 film *Amélie* with the issues of consumerism, remembrance and representations of women (Figure 9.4). The poster shows the central character looking up at the viewer in a conventional feminine way, which led the student

Figure 9.4 Student hypertext, *First Screen for the Movie* Amélie (2010).

to explore femininity and the various roles of women in society through their visual representation. She described why she liked being feminine and illustrated her own negotiation with femininity in terms of peer pressure and advertising with pictures of female accessories like handbags, shoes and jewellery. Elsewhere she examined how women's visual representation, past and present, constitutes certain stereotypes, including mother, housewife, delicate flower, *femme fatale* and virgin, though she also included pictures of women she called 'with personality'. She considered these stereotypes often to be masks that women wear deliberately to protect their real selves. She also examined ideals of face and body, comparing different body shapes – pear, straight and apple – as well as different ethnic facial features. She examined how over past millennia the golden section has been used to construct ideal faces, bodies, paintings and architecture. She also considered the use of pictures as a source of remembrance as employed in another French film *Amelia,* and she linked this to the functions of family heirlooms like quilts and hand-me-down wedding dresses.

Some students chose to relate their hypertext to themselves. This was especially true of a student who chose as her starting point a black and white, documentary style photograph of herself. She related the photograph to her Polish-Russian-Lithuanian-American identity, her social class, her parents' divorce, her religious faith and her love of the arts. In dealing with her ethnicity, for example, she wrote of the American notion of cultural assimilation as a melting pot, and ideas of freedom, liberty and the American Dream. The characteristics she described were related so, for example, her ethnic identity and her particular love of Polish, Russian and Lithuanian art, which she demonstrated with many examples drawn from these three countries. She described their particular qualities and unique histories. Each aspect of herself was then related to aspects of several of her friends; one friend who was also of Russian descent and another whose parents were also divorced and so on. Each friend's characteristics were described, and where they both overlapped with hers and where they were dissimilar. Taken as a whole, she described a complex network of relationships spiralling out from herself and covering many issues: how different people choose to deal with peer pressure, their education, their religious beliefs, their ethnic status and so on. Into this mix she also wove her own majority position as white and Christian compared to a friend who is of colour and Hindu. She illustrated this connection with images of Christian and Hindu art, which, in turn, led to material on white privilege and racism, accompanied by pictures of stereotypical African Americans in popular culture and orientalist paintings by Delacroix. Statistics on divorce rates were linked to statistics on working mothers and images of television families over the past few decades. In each case, she included definitions for the terms she used as well as a voice over – her own, her parents and her friends – each telling their own story.

Hypertextual curriculum: small group PowerPoints

A few semesters later I decided it would be better to have students working in small groups of three or four. Groups chose a picture and three or four themes that their picture addressed. Each member of the group investigated one of the themes and then they made connections between them. Working in groups students increased the number of links they were able to generate. It also appeared to increase the level of enjoyment.

Whole class low-technology intertexts

More recently I employed a low-technology approach and involved the whole class in the production of an intertext using paper, push pins, woollen yarn and a large pin board.

I begin with the same warm up exercise as before, but then I ask 'What is catching your attention right now? What is "hot", the newest thing?' With each class this is different, and often I have never heard of the cultural sites they mention. Because this is to be a whole class activity, I list their suggestions and they then vote. Once a site is established, I ask what are the site references, list the references the students generate and then assign individuals or pairs to research their suggested references. Some students are tasked to find definitions, others to find contemporary visual examples, and others still to find historical visual examples. Some students find relevant poems or song lyrics and some students write up their own responses.

The first time I did this I started making a list of the programmes and movies they were interested in but half way through voting one student said that since we were a visual art class we should focus on the show that was most specifically concerned with visual imagery. And so we began with the television programme *Gossip Girls* and made a list of associations that included the representation of girls, scandals, families and different economic classes both now and from the past. The students were then tasked with finding definitions, pictures, poems and any other relevant material connected to these themes.

To begin the creation of the intertext I first placed in the centre of the pin board a picture of *Gossip Girls* taken from the internet, and the students then pinned up pictures, dictionary definitions, newspaper articles and statements of their own views. The class used coloured yarn to link from the original picture to their issues and then from their issues to other related issues. By the end, the students had made so many connections that the board was crisscrossed with yarn, and the original starting point was almost buried among the connections. Students found pictures of each subject, which led to discussions about their own pre-conceptions. Two students chose pictures of girls smiling and eating ice cream, the epitome of innocent fun, which they contrasted with images of adolescent girls smoking and eating junk food. When the students labelled the two kinds of girls as good and bad, we were able to have a conversation about what it meant to grow up and the moral positions their distinction implied. When students included a picture of the Obama family posing on a picnic rug, we were able to talk about the difference between the visual strategies of informal snapshots and formal family portraits. As their teacher, and armed with more historical and cross-cultural knowledge than the students, I contributed by pinning up pictures and written texts on the representation of girls and families from the history of art, and we then compared visual strategies. We found, for example, sentimental paintings of smiling young girls from the nineteenth century used similar strategies to appeal to viewers as advertisements for hamburger chains.

In another semester, the class chose a recent picture of Britney Spears. Spears was selected because the students were talking about her at the time and because I felt that she epitomized many social conflicts both contemporary and of long standing. The class began by brainstorming what associations she evoked for them. These included celebrity culture, body image, sexuality, children and child abuse, music videos, mental illness, families and popular magazine covers.

A lengthy discussion ensued on the way in which each of the above issues had been represented, including stereotypical representations and how they connected to one another. How, for example, does the media fall back on stereotypical representations of mental illness, a subject that is not inherently visual? I made reference to the paintings of Gericault of the mentally ill. As follow up research, two students began to explore historical representations of mental illness, in which contemporary understandings of mental illness were contextualized by Gericault's paintings. Two other students searched online image banks to find contemporary fine art dealing with mental illness. A similar scenario developed with the representation of celebrity. I made some historical and cross-cultural connections to icons, noting the very different kinds of notoriety that have garnered attention in other societies, and several students began investigating this in some depth. The same thing occurred with families. Introducing the idea that historically there have been many models of the family motivated several students to research how families have had themselves represented in the past. They looked at master paintings and old photographs and made comparisons with today's informal snapshots. Other students researched the other topics mentioned above. Finally, students linked up some of their associations; for example, childhood imagery with representations of family, celebrity with childhood through famous prodigies. Students found that it was possible to link celebrity with families through *Hello Magazine*. In each case we considered the images and written material to understand how strategies of visual representation embodied the technology and social preoccupations of their makers.

A site that turned out to be an especially rich source of connections was the 2013 film *The Wolf of Wall Street*, in which the lead character is seduced by power, wealth and fame. With an insatiable need for thrills, sex and drugs, the character epitomizes excess and corruption. As a notably corrupt person, the students connected him to the anti-Christ and also to the seven deadly sins of pride, wrath, greed, sloth, lust, envy and gluttony. Pictorial material was plentiful.

By the conclusion of these exercises it becomes apparent to everyone that there is no end of further connections that could be made between the initial issues as well as to other issues. Starting from a single source and moving laterally, students are able to make connections with many forms of representation, past and present, across cultures, in a variety of media and manifesting a huge range of issues that provide alternative ways to consider current issues – issues that excite and motivate them.

Whole class using Prezi

While I was developing these projects, a colleague, Brad Olsen, developed a similar project with his class using the computer programme Prezi. Although Prezi does not allow a rhizomic interaction between ideas, I mention this project because it opened up significant opportunities that my approach did not. Unlike a rhizome, Prezi prevents crossing over from one branch line to another. However, Prezi does permit ideas to spread out laterally from a central point, branching into a potentially infinite number of lines.

Olson created a site with password access that enabled his students to post contributions whenever they chose. This allowed him to conduct the project alongside other in-class activities for

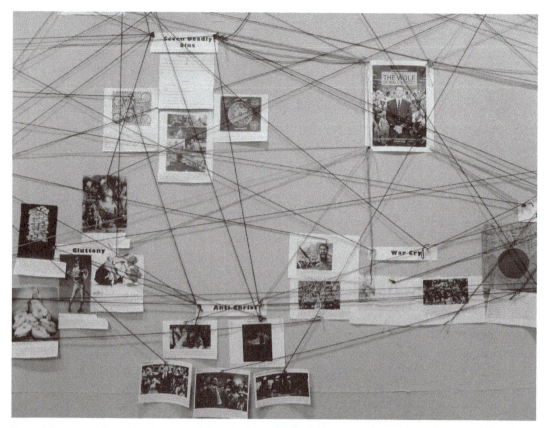

Figure 9.5 Student intertext, *The Wolf of Wall Street* (detail).

over a month. After the initial set up, in-class time was spent only for small group discussions to generate and swap ideas that were then followed up by research outside class time. Students posted day and night.

Much as I had done when working with the whole class, Olsen's class began by deciding to work on a particular cultural site. One semester they chose the television programme *Jersey Girls*; another semester they chose the popular children's animated 2010 film *Toy Story 3* from Disney. The latter class watched the movie in class and then individual class members chose various themes the class identified, again as I had done. Among the themes chosen were leadership, family, ecology, childhood, rites of passage, happy endings, technology, gender roles, imagination, good and evil and heroes and villains.

Some students posted still pictures; others inserted movie clips, and they also contributed personal reflections. Olsen kept an eye on their progress and occasionally made contributions himself that were intended to spark further student additions.

A particularly rich theme proved to be heroes and villains, with a number of students contributing; for example, an anthropological interpretation of superhero iconography, villainous masterminds turned good, and gender stereotyping with Barbie dolls. Students also found

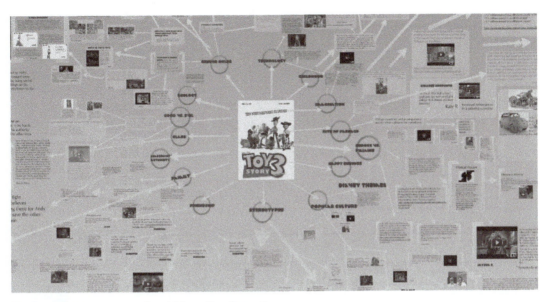

Figure 9.6 Whole-class Prezi Map, *Toy Story 3*.

connections to fine art artists like Russian/French artist Marc Chagall with his imaginative paintings of childhood, as well as to contemporary artists; the latter included Indonesian artist Agan Harahap, who inserts images of superheroes and villains into wartime photographs, and the British artist Robert Bradford who creates sculptures from recycled toys.

The benefit of this approach was that it enabled an ongoing investigation that harnessed students' out-of-class time. Students were motivated not only to investigate a cultural site in which they were emotionally invested but also by the fact that they had the time to investigate in-depth in their own time.

Summary

By developing these rhizomic activities, students were able to discuss many themes, current trends, and age-old human practices in terms of the visual rhetoric employed: how visual stereotypes are perpetuated from one site to another; how different kinds of representation support, critique or oppose a wide range of ideologies; how different kinds of aesthetics work to seduce; how contemporary visual culture is indebted to a long historical legacy; and so on. And all this proved possible by treating just one picture as an intersection of competing ideas, beliefs and values. As always at the conclusion of these rhizomic activities, whether using a computer programme or just pins, paper and yarn, students saw that the rhizome they had created could be extended to include further issues, to continue indefinitely.

Questions

1 What are the major differences between a modernist and a postmodern curriculum?
2 What are the limitations of a modernist curriculum? What are the advantages of a postmodern curriculum? What might be some of the limitations of a postmodern curriculum?
3 What are the benefits and limitations of the different computer programmes StorySpace, PowerPoint and Prezi?
4 What are the affordances of the paper, pin and yarn approach over the use of a computer programme?

Activities

1 Produce your own intertext, starting with a picture.
2 Alternatively, produce an intertext starting with a music score, a book, an event, a celebration, anything. Using your imagination, you could even start with a rock.
3 Consider if the intertext should be individual, a small group or a whole class exercise?
4 Once at least two intertexts are produced, consider how they can be linked together to form an even larger intertext.

Postmodern Curriculum 2: Movie Making

The dominance of visual narratives

A major feature of today's visual culture is that it is narrative. Pictures are harnessed to tell stories. Since narratives have always been a major part of human life, this is not surprising. First told around campfires when our ancestors still lived in caves, it has been through storytelling that human societies have always passed on their knowledge, inculcated their ideological positions and instructed the young on behavioural norms. We are a storytelling species, and one of the major ways we have told stories has been through pictures. Storytelling has been one of the traditional, principal functions of the fine arts, and today our major cultural forms are dominated by narrative genres. Nor is it any wonder that armed with a camera and a computer, youth are among the most enthusiastic to make their own movies.

As mentioned in Chapter 7, some youth produce their own videos in their own time of their own accord as part of a participatory and convergence culture. Youth feed off the popular mass media to produce their own inexpensive videos. Fans create scenarios that fill-in where producers leave storyline threads underdeveloped. Plots that are abandoned on television or left vague and obscure in movies are developed as videos, which are then posted online to one of the movie hosting sites like YouTube. Many of these posts consist of parodies and they are seemingly motivated not only by a sense of fun but the power inherent in exhibiting mastery of the rules of a given cultural form. In some cases their motivation also appears more complicated. Vampire fandom often concerns the physical pain endured by vampires as they shift back and forth between seemingly ordinary people and their vampire persona. Fans often 'talk story' with one another, creating plot structures and characters, while simultaneously talking about their own physical pain. By contrast, while science fiction fans talk story in the same way, they typically interweave discussion about their own psychological pain. In short, fans appear to recycle their preferred cultural forms according to their own preoccupations. However, most videos online exemplify the mocking, satirical fun that has long been typical of youth culture.

It would be wrong to dismiss these videos as nothing more than pastimes, because they play important developmental functions. For youth, fan communities represent spaces in which to develop identity in terms of self-efficacy; exercising curiosity; meeting challenge; attaining public recognition; and enabling social interaction and support from like-minded, similarly focused others. Youth's facility with networked technology helps to distinguish them from their parents and teachers alike. The digital divide is generational as much as economic.

Collective creativity

As discussed in Chapter 7, youth online often operate with a collective consciousness. They pool knowledge and compare notes towards a common goal. They are often part of self-organized knowledge communities, voluntary and temporary affiliations of peers brought together through common intellectual enterprises and emotional investments. They operate as self-sustaining systems out of mutual interests and a reciprocal exchange of knowledge and acknowledgement. Fans make no distinction between their intellectual and emotional commitments. They have always defined themselves though their affinities rather than locality, and today they are able to exploit the seemingly liquid flow of the many communications enabled by the internet. Their posts establish and maintain affinity, and this often operates irrespective of race, class and gender, where the social production of meaning is more than individual interpretation multiplied. Participants feel connected to others, gaining the emotional support of a community eager to see their productions. As described in Chapter 7, they interconnect like rhizomes. Their videos are often not only highly inventive, but also hilarious. The videos delight with the irrepressibility of young people to create fresh perspectives. Also, as described in Chapter 7, so prevalent are their videos, and so networked with their peers, youth operate according to the principles of smart swarms.

Stupid swarms

Alas, smart swarms are not always smart. Like swarms gone bad, youth productions on the net can be quite dumb. Swarms can be exceptionally stupid. Ants, for example, can sometimes get turned around and go the wrong way, though this is nothing compared to the damage locusts can cause when they swarm. Similarly among humans, crowds are not always wise; they can turn into irrational mobs where blindly following the herd has often proved catastrophic. Self-organized groups are not necessarily healthy, and youth on the internet are not always inventive or even clever. For all their knowledge of popular culture and 'tech smarts', youth are prone to peer pressure, vulnerable to the hedonism of commercial culture, and many of their unsolicited productions are almost entirely derivative. By any standards, many of their videos are talentless, inane and offensive. It is easy to dismiss them as narcissistic and a waste of time. It is not for nothing that schools have often limited access to picture sharing sites or banned access altogether. Furthermore, while youth's own videos often reward with their outrageous humour and insights, many lack even rudimentary skills.

Enter education

The poor quality of many videos produced by youth in their own time provides educators with important contributions to make. Teachers have a central role to play, not by providing all the answers or giving specific directions, but by offering guidance, establishing mutually agreed-upon classroom norms and providing learning objectives to accomplish.

The implication here is for teachers to embrace youth's interest-driven, friendship-driven informal ways of learning by regarding picture-sharing sites as creative platforms. If institutional education is to remain relevant it must begin by acknowledging that we have entered upon a very different world in which informal learning communities are now a major part of our students' lives. We must recognize that students now come to us with the expectation of being able to employ their own agency in exploring the world they are to inherit.

A first, small, and manageable step in this direction is for teachers to embrace time-based media. Teachers need to teach the applications of framing, points-of-view, editing, types of lens, camera movements and so on, as described in Chapter 2, and so help students better articulate their intentions.

Web 10.1
Instagram and Video Production

A second step is to create projects, inspired by internet genre, that are downloaded onto picture sharing sites and then to respond to the critique they garner from viewers with further productions. This would be to transform the typically closed classroom into a site of social networking linked to the creative energy of youth culture. It might even be possible to use the feedback by the students' youthful peers to assess their work.

A third step is to attempt to reconcile the hedonism and inanity of youth culture with the rationality expected of formal schooling. Teachers would need to draw up rules of engagement so that offensive material is either censored or becomes the focus of discussion. Either way, a pedagogy of playfulness rather than one of pre-emptive criticism needs to be embraced. Otherwise, by seeming to criticize youth culture teachers would merely reinforce the separation between youth culture and themselves as representatives of institutional schooling.

Web 10.2
Dialogic Pedagogy

Movie making in the classroom

I describe below two exercises undertaken with my undergraduate students. The first exercise involves making a film of ninety seconds according to a short scenario; the second involves retelling a full-length movie in just a few minutes. In each case I describe just one class as typical of class dynamics and the kind of solutions that students devised. In both exercises students worked in groups of between four and six. Most students had never before made a movie, so I ensured that each group contained at least one person with prior editing experience. To film, students used either their mobile phones, still cameras with a movie function, or inexpensive movie cameras. To edit, they used *I movie* or *Final Cut Pro*.

Preparation with still pictures

For both the exercises described below I prepared the students in a similar way. I introduced a series of activities designed to teach the language of movie making. I began by showing a PowerPoint of the elements of realistic-style still pictures discussed in Chapter 2 on representation. The presentation used pictures from both the fine arts and contemporary photography to emphasize that the elements apply to both. For example, it included paintings by Raphael and Van Gogh, photographs of children from Thailand, paparazzi photographs of celebrities and a photograph of football players. Students then followed up by making their own PowerPoint presentations, as suggested at the conclusion of Chapter 2. The students took photographs of each other using different framing, angles-of-view, lighting and so on, and then they compiled a PowerPoint with labels for each picture. We discussed the group presentations as a whole class and a few pictures needed to be relabelled. Throughout, we discussed how each picture places us as viewers in a specific spatial relationship to the picture, and how even a slight change in any of the elements can significantly change our relationship thereby altering a picture's range of possible meanings.

To reinforce the language of realistic-style pictures, I then introduced a second preparatory activity. Following another suggestion from Chapter 2, the students made an advertisement for a product of their own choosing. They had to select the particular elements for the photograph that contributed to the purpose of advertising their specific product. They then wrote about their experience. For example, one group created a picture of three students wearing warm winter hats in front of a fireplace, and they wrote, in part:

> We decided on a neutral angle. Using a low angle would not have shown the hats enough ... Using a high angle would not have allowed the viewer to see the facial expression of the models. We experimented with framing, but in the end we chose a half frame because a full frame did not focus on the hats. With a smaller frame we were able to show the hand gestures pulling on the hats.

Another group, who produced a photograph of a soft toy, wrote in part:

> We chose a neutral view, a full frame and high contrast with selective focus. We chose a neutral view to capitalize on the gaze of the toy. This established an approachable relationship, a necessity when

marketing to children . . . We used high contrast and selective focus to heighten the drama and direct children's attention.

An additional requirement of the advertisement was that it had to consist of both a photograph and written text. This meant that student attention was drawn to the different kinds of relationships that could exist between a picture and accompanying words. I asked the following kinds of questions: 'Do you need these particular words? Are they merely repeating what the picture shows?' I also asked questions like, 'Why not set up an ironic or satirical relationship between the photograph and the words?' In short, students were tasked with considering not only the significance of anchoring one communication mode by another, but also how one mode can anchor in different ways.

Web 10.3
Anchoring

Preparation with moving pictures

I then combined the elements of still images with those of moving pictures by introducing camera movements, transitions, and subjective versus objective shots, again as described in Chapter 2. I showed just a short ninety-second sequence from a typical narrative movie. I began with the audio on mute and the whole class counted the number of shots. In groups, students were then assigned to variously identify the elements both of still and moving pictures as well as the number of times they occurred. For example, while one group was counting the high, neutral and low-angle shots, another group counted the different camera movements. Then we considered significance. Why was a neutral shot used in one scene but not another? What was the effect of a particular panning shot? Would a handheld shot have been as effective as the fixed camera shot? And so on. This meant repeated viewing, sometimes as often as nine or ten times. Then I introduced audio, which demonstrated how sound anchors meaning. I asked questions like, 'How does the music help create mood? What does the dialogue tell us that the images alone do not? How do certain shots help us to interpret others?'

I have discovered that it is necessary to show a relatively slow-moving film. Recent action thrillers move too quickly to analyse. At the same time there need to be sufficient changes of shots, people and action to illustrate the general point that all the elements work together and in a variety of ways. Students often discover that the pictures tell us a great deal; sometimes the audio track merely confirms what they have already guessed about who the people are, their relationships and what is going on. However, it is only on repeated viewing that all the visual cues are brought to our notice. Nevertheless, the visual cues exist and when viewing just once, we process them unconsciously.

With some appreciation for all the decisions that need to be made even with a very short ninety-second sequence, students are then ready to make their own movie. Invariably, they are very keen to do so.

Web 10.4
Making Films

Filming from short scenarios

My first venture in movie making with students was to offer short scenarios that were to be exactly ninety seconds in length. I offered two alternatives:

1   A person drives a car, parks, gets out, goes to the boot, and finds a body.
2   Someone goes down in a lift, comes out, and bumps into someone.

If you imagine each of these scenarios in your mind's eye you will notice that each can be easily accomplished in less than half of ninety seconds. Students asked why I insisted it be ninety seconds, no less and no more. I told them that it would become obvious as they continued to work, though I also pointed out that they had some flexibility because they could use some of the ninety seconds with opening and closing credits. My intention was to force students to use the elements of figurative imagery, still and moving, to create interesting footage. I believed that they could only fill up ninety seconds if they deliberately explored these elements.

However, this was not all that happened. Each group developed a story in which my scenario was only part of their narrative. I came to understand that the students were too inexperienced to dissect a scenario by the elements alone. However, their solution did confirm the narrative orientation of human cognition.

Storyboarding

Each group began by drawing a storyboard. I stressed that the storyboard had to be detailed, arguing that preparation was vitally important because without it they would waste time when

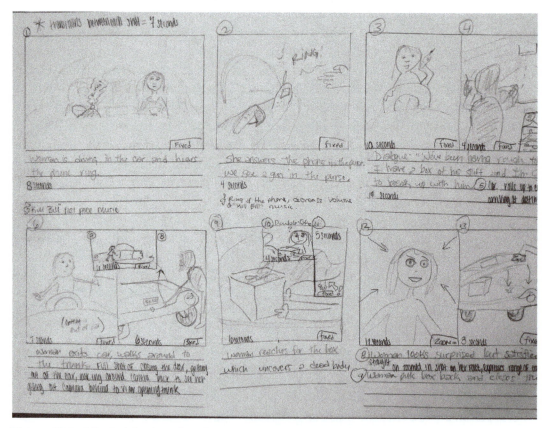

Figure 10.1 *A Typical Student Storyboard.*

filming. Not all the students were good at drawing so each group also wrote down their intentions regarding framing, angles-of-view, camera movements and so on. They also included dialogue, voice-overs, suggestions for music and an approximation of the time for each shot. Some wrote all their dialogue and instructions on the storyboard; other groups also wrote a separate script.

The groups commonly overestimated the length of their shots and I urged them to check their watches, shut their eyes, imagine the scene taking place in their mind's eye, and then check on how long it had taken. Sometimes I suggested cutting down a scene. In one of the movies that starts with the woman driving, the scene went on way too long but when it was cut down the students had less than ninety seconds. I suggested, 'When the woman exits the car she should drop her keys and then take some time fumbling to open the boot'. To do this the students needed to use close-up shots, thus introducing more variety of shots than they had initially planned. It also built tension.

Filming and editing

Once I was satisfied that the storyboards were sufficiently detailed, and that the student groups had scouted out locations and acquired props as needed, the students left the classroom to film. Since the groups spread out across the campus I was unable to follow their actual shooting. When the groups returned to edit on their laptops I hovered about and made suggestions. For example, once a group had a rough edit I made the following kinds of comments: 'See how nothing much is happening over here. Why not crop it out?' 'You've established the context with a loose full frame but now the scene is going on for too long. Why don't you use it for a few seconds and then crop to the person talking?' 'There is a second or two at the end of the shot you don't need'. I also made comments about continuity: 'How will you transition from this episode to the next? With written text or a voice over?' 'Have you thought of how to use music to tie this scene to the next?'

Web 10.5
Video
Editing

Creative solutions

Although the students did not always exploit the use of the elements as I had hoped, there was no denying the inventive solutions students devised. One group who chose the elevator scenario began with a half shot in neutral view of a young man wearing headphones inside an elevator with a voice over of instructions on how to behave 'in romantic situations'. He is apparently listening to the advice. He exits the elevator and immediately bumps into a young woman, not once but several times, each time with a loud bang, and each shot from a different viewpoint. The bottle of water she had been carrying falls to the floor and spills. He immediately jumps down and takes off his shirt to wipe up the water, and in response she smiles with appreciation at this naked chest. Alas, having behaved gallantly, he panics and runs back up a flight of stairs, failing to heed advice on how to behave in a situation pregnant with romantic possibilities.

It was delightful to find how different groups devised very different solutions. One group who chose the 'body in the boot' scenario began with a woman driving a car while chatting dismissively about her hopeless ex-boyfriend. She parks, gets out and drops her keys, retrieves them, goes to the boot and has trouble opening it, but when she does open it she quickly backs off, arms in the air, and shrieks in horror. Viewers are then offered a shot of an evidently meant-to-be-dead male body

Figure 10.2 Student video, *Screenshot from* Discovering the Body.

that pans to his forearm on which he has tattooed a heart and the words 'I love you'. Whenever I have shown this to subsequent classes this scene is met with sustained hilarity.

Another group who used the same scenario developed a story where a woman parks, gets out, and opens up the boot to find a dishevelled, unshaven male cooking eggs for breakfast, singing badly and seemingly drunk. Angry, she points to a calendar suggesting that he has been living in her boot for some time and has long outlived his welcome. The film ends with her slamming the boot in frustration.

Still another group developed a dream-like, surreal sequence in which a woman gets out of the car, opens the boot, and is immediately hit by a toaster that inexplicably falls from the sky. Knocked unconscious, she has a short dream in which someone speaks to her in nonsense rhymes about the toaster. She then wakes up and makes toast. The film ends with the car driving off with her as the body in the boot.

These films were designed to teach basic skills and knowledge of film making, as an exercise in creativity, and a way to acquire language with which to critique professional films. The second exercise goes a step further and draws upon youth's networked culture, both its possibilities and its challenges. Rather than simply an in-class activity, the following exercise opens up to embrace the world of online fandom on internet sites and thereby directly engage on the platforms on which so much of today's visual culture is played out.

Movie-in-minutes

When I first discovered movie-in-minutes its pedagogical potential was immediately obvious. Movie-in-minutes refers to a genre on movie sharing sites like YouTube in which youth, some as young as seven or eight years, collaborate to reduce a full-length commercial movie to just a few minutes. These short videos are typically achieved by eliminating all but what is needed to chronicle key episodes with only essential characters, and overcoming the use of highly expensive, high technology special effects with inexpensive low technology solutions. Some videos involve captured imagery or audio from the original movie, though more commonly the videos rework scenes with live actors, animations, puppets, dolls or soft toys.

Favourite movies include blockbusters from years ago. In the 1997 film *Titanic* the climatic sinking sequence involved a full-scale model, several large-scale models and extensive computer-generated graphics. Youth productions that rework this episode take a variety of inventive, low technology forms. One example uses a paper boat in a sink with the plug taken out so that the paper boat swirls hectically. Another shows a large plastic boat floating in a child's paddling pool with an anxious voice over predicting disaster. A third shows a plastic ship lying on a blue bedcover that is lifted up and down to create the illusion of giant waves. In one of the many movie-in-minute versions of *Harry Potter and the Philosopher's Stone* the scene where Harry flies about on a broomstick is achieved by having the actor repeatedly jump up in the air, and editing together only the second he is in the air. The effect is remarkably successful in suggesting that he is flying as he appears suspended in the air for about six seconds. In these videos, males who act as females typically wear a wig, while females who act as males typically sport a moustache or beard. In short, many of the videos exemplify the kind of inventiveness and gender bending role-play that is typical of youth culture and existed long before the internet made it visible to a wide audience.

Initially, I thought that the movie-in-minutes already on the internet offered a cohesive narrative. I later realized that most of them sacrificed a coherent storyline in favour of essential set-up scenes and a series of iconic, emotionally charged scenes that make sense only by reference to the original. Even so, I was inspired to transfer the movie–in-minutes genre to the classroom. Making these movies involves a range of skills and knowledge relevant to operating in a critical way in today's narrative-based visual culture. Like the above scenario exercise, movie-in-minutes offers students an insider's understanding of movies, requires creative problem solving, relies upon co-operative learning and they are highly motivating. Additionally, they address the nature of filmed narratives as well as being engaged with contemporary youth culture.

Preparation

I first introduced the same exercises mentioned above in relation to the short scenarios: the elements of realistic pictures, making PowerPoints and an advertisement, and analysing a short professionally produced movie sequence. We then watched a number of movie-in-minutes examples posted on one of the movie hosting sites, which we critiqued in terms of interest, originality and coherence. Students also used the criteria employed on such sites – what they liked and disliked – and considered the comments on the films already posted on the YouTube interface. It is exceptionally useful for students to critique these amateur efforts since students learn from negative models in a way they cannot by watching only well-crafted professional productions.

Again, students were divided into groups with at least one student with editing experience in each group. Their first task was to select a movie, and then to identify its primary narrative.

Web 10.6
YouTube and
Video
Production

They had to decide on which scenes and characters were necessary to retell the narrative; discard everything extraneous; choose a medium such as live actors, toys and so on; develop a storyboard; and consider how to achieve special effects with whatever they could muster. Through trial and error, I have learned it is necessary to insist that students choose movies that primarily involve more than everyday experiences. The bigger the blockbuster, the more inventive they are forced to be.

The original movies

For simplicity's sake, I am going to describe just one class as typical of other classes. The class broke into three groups of three and four students to produce three separate movies of their own choice. One group chose the first of *The Hunger Games* films from 2012. Another group chose the 2001 *Harry Potter and the Philosopher's Stone*, which, following many parodies already on YouTube, they retitled *Harriet Potter and the Sorceress's Stone*. The third group chose *Sisterhood of the Traveling Pants* from 2005, which they too retitled, again using models on YouTube, *Sisterhood of the Traveling Yoga Pants*.

The *Philosopher's Stone* film is the first in the Harry Potter series. It introduces many of the main characters and situations. The trio of young heroes, Harry, Ron and Hermione, discover their friendship, and prove themselves by doing battle with a series of dark forces. *The Hunger Games* film involves a future utopian society that has replaced war with a game in which youngsters are 'reaped' and set loose in a forest to fight to the death, all the time being watched on television by an excited mass audience. Essentially, the film combines real war with a reality TV show. The *Sisterhood* film involves four teenage friends who discover that despite their different body types they each fit into the same pair of jeans. The jeans then act to connect them as they spend their first summer vacation apart discovering themselves as individuals.

While the films are very different from one another, they share remarkably similar thematic material. The themes include friendship, self-discovery, mistakes made and mistakes corrected, bonds of loyalty, both physical and moral trails, adventures into the unknown, family dysfunction, courage, heartache and the recognition of the specialness of individual protagonists. *Harry Potter* and *Hunger Games* also emphasize heroism, demonstrations of high-level skills, and the triumph of good over evil, while *Hunger Games* and *Sisterhood* also involve budding romance.

The *Harry Potter* film was released when my students were small children, and *Hunger Games* and *Sisterhood* are quintessentially late teen/young adult films. Each film was based on best-selling books and in turn each proved not just a 'hit' but a box office phenomenon. In the life of my students the films had been seminal, and when I reviewed the films it was easy to understand their appeal. Each was exceptionally well crafted, with deep emotional resonance, especially for my students' age group.

Different methods of working

Left to their own devices each of the three groups devised different working methods. One group discussed at great length which scenes to include, storyboarding as they went; another group selected what to use from watching the original film; and the third group watched previous movies-in-minute versions to consider what they could use, what they thought they could improve upon and where they wanted to invent their own solutions. Their discussions were peppered with comments that often began, 'What if we tried ... Do you think it would work if ...?'

As before with the scenario exercise, I checked their storyboards, making suggestions and asking questions to clarify what they were thinking, a necessary step to ensure that they had at least considered the issues they would face. I was intrigued to find who had been assigned which roles; the costumes, makeup, and the disguises they intended to use; and the locations they had considered. Each group had carefully storyboarded each scene with particular framing and angles-of-view, and two groups shot their films accordingly. However, *The Hunger Games* team decided to shoot with different frames and from different angles with the intention of later choosing the best, though when editing they decided to create excitement by using snippets from most of their different frames and angles. As before, my only role at this point was to observe and suggest.

Learning the language

At the conclusion of the movie-making process each team wrote about their experiences, reflecting upon the decisions they had made, problems encountered, solutions found, happy accidents and what they thought they had learned. Among the comments students wrote that indicate they had acquired a working knowledge of basic grammar, the following excerpts are typical:

'We used a neutral angle-of-view to suggest that the viewer is seated in the train with the characters, drawing them into the conversation, but a low angle to exaggerate Hagrid's size.'

'We began with a loose full-frame of Bridget, then we zoomed into her face, then tilted the camera down to show her pregnant belly.'

'When the four girls sit in a circle symbolizing their never-ending friendship, we chose a 360 degree pan to emphasize their connection to one another.'

'We utilized panning, tracking and zooming to follow characters and add emphasis, and we found that using handheld shots worked best to create the illusion of constant movement.'

'For most of our film we used a static camera, but for action scenes we used quick panning.'

Each team stressed how they discovered the importance of anchoring.

'Without music our film seemed flat and the transitions between scenes were not very fluid. However, the moment the first song was layered over, the film became dynamic and dramatic.'

'Running up and down the corridor made no sense until we added the dog barking.'

'The creepiness of the villain's voice is essential to the scene.'

Learning the basic language of the formal grammar of movies is important because it helps focus attention on how movies are constructed and the effect they have on the viewer. Familiarity with this language equips students to better appreciate professional film making as well as better positioning them to resist manipulation. The skills and knowledge of traditional media are specific to the media, and so it is with film.

Creative solutions

However, the students' movies-in-minutes were more than an exercise in acquiring formal language. They also involved two kinds of creativity: the invention of ingenious solutions and the creativity inherent in translating from one cultural form to another.

Students had to devise a range of solutions to overcome the modest means with which they were operating. In the original *Harry Potter* film, the Quidditch game is played by flying furiously around in the air by no other means than broomsticks. In the students' adaptation Harriet and one antagonist simply run towards each other with broomsticks between their legs. The scene in the original film where the three main children are entangled by the tree roots is managed in the students' film by the three protagonists clutching low lying branches, flailing about and crying out. Instead of a giant three-headed CGI dog, their movie relies on a sound effect of a dog barking and the heroes' own terrified reactions. To recreate the scene in which characters attempt to catch keys the students stood in front of a movie screen on which they projected keys flying, which they combined with a few real keys dangling from string.

The *Sisterhood* team was faced with the problem of devising four distinctly different locations, including in Greece and underwater. I suggested that they could stand in front of projected images. In this way, they created an illusion of travel in very different locations, including underwater.

The *Hunger Games* team avoided the need to substitute big budget special effects with low budget ones by focusing almost entirely on scenes in the forest that did not require special effects. One problem they did need to solve was how to stay faithful to their storyboard, which called for hitting a squirrel with an arrow. Although they managed to film a squirrel appearing from behind a tree, killing it was of course out of the question so they created the illusion of a kill with editing and the sound of a speeding arrow.

Of course the main challenge the students faced was reimagining full-length movies taking place in just a few minutes. Each of the original films had already undergone a process of selection and recreation to condense book-length stories to a few hours of film time. Already the original

Figure 10.3 Student video, *Screenshot from* Harriet Potter and the Sorceress's Stone

films were the result of weighing up and deciding from many alternative possibilities; they were already a creative reimagining. For example, in the *Sisterhood* book, two of the main characters have siblings who are omitted in the film. One of the remaining character's adventures is markedly different from the book, and instead of taking place over four summers the film takes place over just one. Making movies-in-minutes involved making further difficult decisions about what to include and what to exclude. In particular, it involved making drastic contractions while still retaining some semblance of the original.

Although each of the original films construct a traditionally coherent narrative, like most of the YouTube examples, none of the student videos do so. They follow the chronology of their original, but consist mostly of a serious of separate scenes that are dependent for understanding upon knowledge of the original.

Emotional resonance

Considering the many possibilities available to the students, what they selected was highly instructive, for they not only indicated just why these films were chosen in the first place, but also why students showed such enthusiasm in making their own movie versions. In carefully reviewing their videos, I found that in each video the scenes students chose were either essential to help set up the action to follow or were emotionally charged. The delight students took in making their videos appeared primarily to be due to the opportunities it offered to recreate key moments of deep emotional resonance.

Like the original *Harry Potter* film, the student version begins by establishing location, but it then immediately shows numerous postal letters arriving that herald something very unusual is about to happen, and immediately afterwards Hagrid appears to declare Harriet a wizard. This eliminates most of the build up to Hagrid's declaration and all of Harriet's family members. The purchase of school requirements is similarly eliminated and instead we move directly to the three protagonists meeting on a train. The original film involves many adventures and many characters, but here the students included only a few iconic scenes of trial and triumph: testing out their broomsticks and wands, fighting with tree roots, playing Quidditch, escaping the three-headed dog and confronting the principal villain, Voldemort. The movie ends with Harriet, having vanquished Voldemort, unconscious, clutching the sorceress's stone in her hand. All the subsequent sequences of the original are jettisoned, but with the greatest danger defeated and the use of highly emotional music the film ends with its conclusion satisfyingly open.

The *Sisterhood* movie-in-minutes version begins with the mothers in a gym exercising much like the original, but unlike the original, one of the mother's waters break, which introduces a carnivalesque touch that is typical of youth parodies. Then, unlike the original, which uses a voice-over narrator, we are shown a short textual passage to bring us into the present where the girls are now late teens. Like the original, the girls are shown cheerfully walking arm in arm along a sidewalk and into a clothing store where they each try on the miraculous yoga pants. What in the original is a lengthy scene is contracted with each girl emerging one after the other from the booth, each surprised that the yoga pants fit. In the original there is a whole series of scenes involving Carmen whose father is remarrying; Carmen is initially confused and her anger is built up over many scenes. Here, Carmen's expresses confusion and anger as an initial reaction. The original film constantly shifts back and forth between the separate adventures of the four girls, whereas the contracted version shows only one or two scenes per girl. In each case one of the more dramatic scenes was chosen. Similar to the original, the movie ends with the girls reunited and swearing life-long friendship. Thus, while radically reduced, the structure of the student movie follows the original, with the four girls together, separated, and then reunited.

The original *Hunger Games* movie involves basically three locations, the poor district from which the two main protagonists come, Katniss and Peeta; the affluent city with its bizarre inhabitants; and the forest in which the youngsters fight. In the student's version the focus is almost entirely on the forest scenes and only one character from the city is employed. Almost all the action involves the protagonists fighting, supporting one another and surviving in the forest.

The student version begins with a panning shot that locates the heroine Katniss in the forest hunting wildlife and thereby establishing her expertise in the trial that is to follow. We then see Katniss comforting her younger sister, her sister being the reason Katniss volunteers for the 'reaping' of young people for the game. We see Effie, the chaperone from the city select Katniss and Peeta; the two preparing for their ordeal; the start of the contest, and hunting in the forest; Katniss befriending Rue, the twelve-year-old who saves Katniss's life; Rue's death; Katniss and Peeta's developing romance; and finally their challenge to the autocratic rule in which they risk everything. Apart from Effie, none of the bizarre characters from the city are shown; instead, the focus stays on the teens whose lives are in constant danger.

Web 10.7
Criticality versus
Critical
Discourse

Each of the movies consists of a selection of either set-up scenes or key moments of emotional connection, in which danger is faced and overcome, people die, friendship is established and tested and romance initiated. Scenes demonstrate self-sacrifice, courage and loving relationships.

Learning to appreciate and appraise movies

I believe that in making these films, students gained a glimpse into the complexity of professional movie making. They acquired a basic language with which to analyse movies. They employed a technology with which they were familiar as users but gained confidence as producers, being owners of insider knowledge. And while students were motivated by the problem-solving challenges inherent in the activity, it appeared that it was the emotional resonance of the activity that truly excited them. As the *Hunger Games* team wrote:

> On completing our film we had a new perspective on the professionalism needed to make films. This project took many hours of work and effort yet our film is less than five minutes long. The skills involved in using camera angles, lighting, audio, special effects and acting in professional films became much more apparent after this project. And as students, how often do we get to work on something we really love? Overall, it was challenging and a revelation. Considering all we learned, it was highly educational.

Evaluative feedback

Making these movies did not end there. Each video was uploaded onto YouTube, and students watched as people responded to them with clicks on 'like' and 'dislike' as well as the anonymous comments of viewers. Initially, I was ambivalent about uploading to YouTube, but the students were enthusiastic to share, and I conceded. Sharing their videos with the world had powerful motivational value. Nevertheless, I felt it was important to point out the problematic nature of such sites. Although social networking and sharing sites offer unprecedented opportunities to share and communicate, equally they are deeply problematic.

Operating online

As described earlier, for youth, social networking and sharing sites are primarily cultural spaces of community building and shared experience. Although most are advertising-driven commercial enterprises, their use by youth demonstrates how strong the desire is for an alternative to commercially produced content. They indicate a desire for alternatives for both consumption and platforms for creative self-expression.

However, neither community building nor self-expression was ever the primary intended function of picture sharing and social networking sites. From an economic perspective, these sites are nothing more than traditional marketing tools, their only major innovation being to use user-generated material to attract eyeballs to advertising. From this viewpoint, they might be considered exploitive of youth. The sites largely operate to collect data in order to make their search algorithms ever-more efficient for advertisers.

Big data

Picture sharing and social networking sites are sites of Big data, a term that refers not only to very large amounts of data, but to the ability to aggregate data from multiple sources to reveal patterns of and trends in human behaviour. Whenever we are online we leave a digital trace that can be aggregated; what we read, listen to, play, remix, share, and comment upon on can all be combined to provide a portrait of who we are, what we are susceptible to, and even where we are at any given moment. We leave our digital footprints whenever we search on line, use a GPS, email, tweet, uploaded media and indicate our likes and dislikes. We are tracked as we hover our curser over an image or written text. Face recognition technology of photographs we upload track our connections to friends and relatives. Using highly sophisticated algorithms, connections can be made about us and conclusions drawn.

Big data sites that invite picture sharing and social networking undoubtedly help build community and offer the opportunity for expression, but, from an economic perspective, they only exist to nourish data. Posing as free public services, they mask their actual function as huge trawlers, aggregators and analysts of data, with the primary goal of maximizing profits. From this perspective, they are simply a new way to attract the attention of consumers who might not otherwise be easily caught by traditional media.

Traditional media outlets produce their own means of attracting attention to advertising. From an economic perspective, television programmes – be they comedies, dramas or news – are considered the breaks; their economic purpose is to show advertising. By contrast, social networking sites do not even go to the expense of producing their own content; they rely on users to provide content free-of-charge. Thus, while exploiting the unprecedented opportunities offered free-of-charge by social networking sites to reach an audience, equally, they exploit their users. But the seduction of free services is hard to resist.

What then are we as educators to make of big data? To upload material to social networking sites is to buy into a massive marketing machine. What are we to do?

The responsible use of big data internet sites

In using big data sites it is important to acknowledge the power of commercial interests and the ambiguities this brings to the educational task of producing citizens. If we accept the benefits offered by big data sites, educators need to address at least two issues. First, should we have our students effectively working for big business by producing free content? Secondly, should we be helping business invade the personal privacy of our students?

My own uneasy view is that youth are already buying into these sites so that both points are rather beside the point. The collection of our students' personal data is already as pervasive as the use they make of social networking sites; their privacy is already compromised. Therefore, using big data picture sharing and social networking sites in the classroom is no more compromising than what is already a pervasive, established reality. I have more trouble with offering students as free labour to help business maximize profits and give higher returns to shareholders, but the bargain they offer is tempting. The fact is that social networking sites are so very popular because they do offer considerable opportunities for creative work, both vast resources to draw upon and platforms on which to create.

However, because many youth may not be aware of how they are being used by these sites, one of our responsibilities is to inform them about the role they play in relation to big business. It follows that it is our responsibility as educators not to ban these sites but when using them to inform our students as to their commercial intention and possible abuses of privacy.

There are three kinds of people dealing with big data: those who input data, those who collect data and those who are able to analyse the data. Clearly, our school students and we educators are among the first kind, and while we are numerically the largest by far, we are also by far the least powerful in determining how the data we input is used. Thus, any use by educators of social networking sites and image banks with students must begin with a full awareness of our relative power in relation to big data. How we exploit the many benefits offered by big data sites must be mediated by an acknowledgment that we are willing to allow our own exploitation and invasion of privacy. These are major issues, but they are just part of operating in today's highly pervasive, highly invasive visual culture with all its problems and its possibilities.

Finally

Whether or not educators choose to engage with the internet, it is crucial that students have the opportunity to learn to appraise the dominant kinds of pictures in contemporary society. Without such knowledge, students are rendered inarticulate. Students should be granted the opportunity to experience the pleasure of creating pictures. And, consistent with Aristotle's motivation in teaching rhetoric, students should know how to respond when the interests of the mighty appear in conflict with their own interests.

Questions

1. In what ways is making movies in the classroom today a postmodern activity?
2. How do today's movies function to socialize as storytelling has done ever since the beginning of our species?
3. What kind of stories do movies typically tell?
4. What benefits are there to students making movies in the classroom?
5. What is the appeal of movie-in-minutes to students?
6. How would you explain the nature of social networking sites to students?

Activities

Apart from the movie making exercises described above, a number of youth fan-based activities already appearing online suggest further in-class exercises.

1. *Recontextualizing.* Produce short movies that seek to fill in the gaps in mass media narratives that suggest additional explanations for particular actions. For example, does a villain act because he or she has had a troubled childhood? Is a suitor interested in money as much as love?
2. *Expanding the timeline.* Produce short movies that provide background history – a backstory – to characters not explored in their original mass media form. Alternatively, suggest future developments beyond the timeframe covered by the mass media form. What was the main protagonist's upbringing like? What does the hero go on to do afterwards?
3. *Refocusing the focus.* Produce short movies that focus attention away from the main characters to secondary ones. Offer centre stage to a character who in the original was a secondary character. For example, retell *Harry Potter* from the perspective of Hagrid or Dumbledore.
4. *Realigning the morality.* This is a version of refocusing. Produce short movies that change the moral universe of the original mass media version. Imagine the good characters as bad and the bad characters as good. Image what damage Harry Potter would do if he was a villain? Alternatively, imagine that the moral

universe stays the same but the story is told from the perspective of the bad characters. For example, imagine Harry Potter from the perspective of Lord Voldemort.

5 *Shifting genres*. Produce short movies where the characters from one genre appear in another; for example, where science fiction characters are relocated to a romantic musical comedy.

6 *Crossing over the characters*. Produce short movies where characters from one mass media form are introduced into another; for example, characters from *Star Wars* might appear in the same story as characters from *Batman*.

7 *Dislocating the characters*. Produce short movies in which characters are relocated in new narrative situations with new names and identities.

8 *Projecting yourselves*. Produce short movies where the makers of the movie insert themselves into the mass media form; for example, a student group could join Harry Potter to fight villains.

9 *Intensifying the emotion*. Produce short movies – sometimes called 'hurt-comfort' stories – where the emotional level is considerably ramped up and at least one character has an emotional crisis. Imagine Superman with a mid-life crisis. Imagine Spock from *Star Wars* having an emotional meltdown.

10 *Exploring sexuality*. Produce short movies that explore the erotic side of a character's nature; for example, explore alternative sexualities. Imagine Harry Potter discovering he is attracted to Ron Weasley.

11 *Mixing the modes*. Produce short movies that use the visuals from one mass media source with the audio from another; for example, a short sequence from *The Lord of the Rings* overlaid with the audio track of the cartoon series *The Simpsons*.

12 *Movie trailers*. Produce a movie trailer for a favourite film or an imaginary film.

Glossary

Some of the words below have long and complicated histories and consequently different meanings. The definitions below refer to how the terms are used in this book.

Aesthetics is often still equated with beauty, but today it is also widely used to refer to all kinds of visual appearances and their sensory and emotional effects upon viewers. The term is derived from the Ancient Greek word *aesthesis*, which meant sense data. Aesthesis was used to distinguish between those things that could be perceived and those things that could only be imagined. The opposite of aesthetic is anaesthetic, the absence of sensation. As used here, aesthetics refers to all kinds of sensations, pleasant and unpleasant, as well as all kinds of emotional responses. Although *modernism* contrasted aesthetics with *rhetoric*, rhetoric is equally concerned as aesthetics with sensation and emotion.

Appraisal is the act of estimating the nature and/or value of something and is similar to critique. Used here in relation to pictures, it is intended as a neutral term to avoid the overly positive associations of appreciation and the oftentimes-negative associations of criticism.

Connotation refers here to the meaning of a picture that is evoked by what is depicted or *denoted*. It is a key term of *semiotics*.

Convergence culture refers to crossovers between *vernacular culture* and *mass culture*, where mass media productions inspire vernacular productions by *prosumers* and their vernacular productions influence mass media production.

Critical theory refers to a body of theory characterized by a reflective assessment and critique of society, especially in terms of how power is established and maintained by social actors through the dissemination of *ideology*.

Culture is a complex word with quite different meanings. It is used here in three ways. Sometimes reference is made to *high culture,* or to its anthropological sense of a whole way, or whole ways, of life. But it is primarily used here, drawing on *critical theory*, to refer to whole ways of life that are in competition, sometimes conflict, with one another, that is, whole ways of struggle.

Denotation refers to the identification of a particular subject matter. It is used in combination with *connotation*.

Fine art refers to the art of art museums, and it is associated with *high culture*. It includes both the selected tradition of the allegedly finest art of the past and new art that attempts to articulate emerging social realities. Both kinds of fine art are often contrasted to *popular culture*, and both kinds tend to play an oppositional role to popular culture.

Folk art. See *vernacular art*.

Formalism refers to a major early twentieth-century belief and practice that the most significant feature of *fine art* was its form, namely elements like line, tone and colour, and the principles of organizing the elements like similarity, proximity and symmetry. It ignored subject matter or ideology. It was especially employed for abstract and non-representational *modernist* art.

Gaze refers to a prolonged examination, but it is used here primarily to refer to all the many ways of looking. It involves the nature of the viewers looking, what they are looking at, and the physical, social and institutional contexts that contribute to how they look.

High culture refers to the art of social elites and is associated with *fine art*. It assumes a hierarchy of social values and was central to *modernism*. It was often claimed to possess quasi-spiritual qualities.

Iconography is an art historical methodology that focuses on the subject matter of pictures as signs, and is related in this sense to semiotics. It is used to unearth the once conventional motifs, allegories and personifications that are no longer widely known.

Ideology refers to a characteristic way of thinking, a style of thought. It is sometimes used prejudicially to refer to ideas that are considered too narrow or doctrinaire, but here it is used descriptively to refer to any interpretive scheme employed by people to make the world intelligible to themselves. It is a key term of *critical theory*.

Intertextuality refers to one *text* referencing another text. It relates closely to networked communications and the concept of the *rhizome*.

Mass culture is typically produced by teams of highly specialized professionals working for, or outsourced by, global corporations. It tends to reproduce the mainstream beliefs and values of a society. It is sometimes called dominant culture, partly because there is so much of it and partly because it is closely tied to the dominant forms of economic arrangement in a society. Existing in a highly competitive market, it relies for its economic success on appealing to a large number of people and is often equated with *popular culture*.

Melodrama refers to works that are typically sensational and designed to elicit strong emotions, commonly from stereotypical characters and situations. They are more plot-driven than character-driven. Originally the term applied to nineteenth-century European stage plays but it is now applied to many popular forms of culture, especially to soap operas.

Modernism refers to many different phenomena. With reference to *fine art*, modernism is usually identified with the emergence in France of the avant-garde around the 1850s who self-consciously rejected the art of the past. Modernist art stressed experimentation, artistic individualism, innovation in styles and materials and reflected, and sometimes critiqued, modern society. Styles tended towards abstraction. It is typically underpinned by the eighteenth-century Enlightenment idea of inevitable progress; the idea of a singular truth only needing to be discovered, and the erection of a hierarchy of cultural categories, notably the view that fine art is inherently superior to popular culture.

Multimodality refers to the reliance for meaning upon more than one communication mode, in the case of printed material of pictures and words. In the case of time-based forms, it refers to the interaction between pictures with spoken and written words, music and ambient sounds.

Multisensory refers to the reliance upon more than one sense. While printed material includes pictures and written words – it is multimodal – it relies only on sight, while time-based forms typically combine the sense of sight with the aural sense. Pictures can also evoke the senses of touch, taste and smell.

Popular culture refers not only to *mass culture*, but also to *vernacular culture* and *convergence culture*. Mass culture is often considered to be imposed from above, vernacular culture to bubble up from below, while convergence culture mediates between them. What each has in common is that they are widely used by many people. They are often contrasted with *fine art*.

Post-modernism refers to a rejection of modernism. Especially significant for this book, it involves an implosion of the modernist hierarchy of cultural categories. Meaning and value are considered to be contextual. With reference to *fine art*, post-modernism stresses individual artists' personal narratives rather than particular styles. With regard to curriculum, it refers to an embrace of contemporary cultural forms rather than traditional fine art forms, and of the intertextual, rhizomic nature of knowledge.

Post-structuralism involves a rejection of *structuralism*. It is a major element of *post-modernism* and it aligns with the idea of different *reading positions*. It argues that the meaning of a *text* lies not in the text itself but in how a text is viewed, which is determined by who is viewing and under what circumstances. This means that a text is remade every time it is viewed; almost invariably its meaning not only differs from person to person but changes over time.

Power is used here to refer to the power of images to hail and influence viewers as well as the power of viewers to choose how to interpret images. Consistent with *post-structuralism*, power is shared between images and viewers. Power is also a key term of critical theory.

Pre-modernism refers to Western art prior to the development of the *modernist avant-garde* around the 1850s. In terms of wider social expectations, it refers to a time prior to the Enlightenment of the eighteenth century with its assumption of inevitable progress.

Preferred reading refers to the meaning of a picture that is intended by its producer or at least is perceived by viewers to be the intended meaning.

Prosumer is a combination of the words *producer* and *consumer*. Prosumers produce pictures based on their consumption of other pictures. Typically, prosumers are untrained amateurs that produce *vernacular culture* drawn from their consumption of *mass culture* to produce a form of *convergence culture*.

Reading position refers here to three basic attitudes adopted by viewers towards pictures. First, viewers may accept entirely what they perceive as the *preferred* or intended *ideology* of the picture makers. Secondly, viewers may entirely reject the ideology or, third, they may accept some aspects while rejecting others. These three basic positions are respectively called dominant, resistant and negotiated. The idea of reading positions is central to *post-structuralism*.

Representation refers here to pictures that substitute, or make present, something that is absent, yet they also embody *ideology*. Representations *denote* a subject while they also *connote* ideology. They can describe what is, or what should be, or should not be. They do not merely reflect the world as if mirroring reality, but rather are created by means of selecting aspects of reality while conforming to conventional rules.

Rhetoric is the use of all the available means of persuasion. Used here, rhetoric consists of a directly or indirectly stated argument, emotion and eloquence. The latter involves sensory qualities and an internal consistency of argument. Success is dependent upon how the source of a communication is perceived, understanding the pre-existing emotions of the audience and the eloquence of the delivery. Rhetoric relates to *aesthetics* in being concerned with both sensation and emotion and to *ideology* in arguing for ideas, values and beliefs.

Rhizome originally referred to a mass of roots that sends out shoots from its nodes, like grass and ginger, but also animal burrows and animals that operate in packs like rats and ants. Used here, these biological examples are extended to the associative nature of human cognition and the networked, *intertextual* nature of today's human communications, notably the internet.

Semiotics is the study of signs, of artefacts, in terms of what they signify, namely the values and beliefs to which they refer. Semiotics embraces all kinds of images and artefacts without assuming a hierarchy of value such as *high culture* versus *popular culture*.

Society of spectacle is a phrase intended to describe a new kind of society in which ideology is mediated through pictures more than at any previous time.

Structuralism is the practice of finding the meaning of a cultural *text* within the form itself commonly by finding binary or triadic relationships within the text.

Text is an inclusive term that refers to anything from which meaning can be made, though more commonly it refers to things that are intended to communicate meaning. Rather than referring to just written text, it includes song lyrics, music scores and all kinds of pictures.

Vernacular culture refers to the production and use of images by untrained amateurs primarily for their own pleasure. It refers to traditional forms of folk art as produced in pre-modern rural communities prior to industrialization as well as their continuing production today, though today it also refers to all the pictures produced and shared by almost everyone through networked electronic technology.

Visual culture refers to all the ways in which information, values and beliefs are pictured, distributed and used in society. In this book, the focus is on pictures that are constitutive of ideas, values and beliefs in the context of conflictual social processes.

Voyeurism refers to observing someone who is unaware of being observed and involves the power of the viewer over the viewed. It is a key to the concept of the *gaze*.

Further reading

Visual culture concepts and methods

Barnard, M. (2001), *Approaches to Understanding Visual Culture*, London: Palgrave Macmillan.

Heywood, I., and B. Sandywell, eds., *The Visual Culture Handbook*, London: Bloomsbury Academic, 2017.

Gilian, R. (2016), *Visual Methodologies; An Introduction to the Interpretation of Visual Materials*, 4th ed., London: Sage.

Sturken, M., and L. Cartwright (2017), *Practices of Looking: An Introduction to Visual Culture*, 3rd ed., Oxford, UK: Oxford University Press.

Visual culture and curriculum

Buckingham, D. (2019), *The Media Education Manifesto*, Cambridge, UK: Polity Press.

Duncum, P. (2006), *Visual Culture in the Classroom: Case Studies*, Reston: National Art Education Association.

Scheibe, C., and F. Rogow. (2011). *The Teacher's Guide to Media Literacy: Critical Thinking in a Multimedia World*, London: Corwin.

Share, J. (2015). *Media Literacy is Elementary: Teaching Youth to Critically Read and Create Media-Second Edition (Rethinking Childhood*, 2nd ed., New York: Peter Lang.

Bibliography

Aristotle (1997), *Poetics*, new edn. trans, M. Heath. London: Penguin Classics.

Aristotle (2007), *On Rhetoric: A Theory of Civic Discourse*, 2nd edn. trans, G. A. Kennedy. New York: Oxford University Press.

Baudrillard, J. (1988). *Jean Baudrillard: Selected Writing*, ed., M. Poster, London: Polity Press.

Berger, J. (1972), *Ways of Seeing*, London: BBC.

Billig, M. (2005), *Laughter and Ridicule: Towards a Social Critique of Humour*, London: Sage.

Coss, R, G. (2003), 'The role of evolved perceptual biases in art and design', in E. Voland and K. Grammer (eds.), *Evolutionary Aesthetics*, 69–130, Berlin: Springer.

Debord, G. (1995), *The Society of the Spectacle*, trans, D. Nicholson-Smith, New York: Zone.

Deleuze, G. and Guattari F. (1987), *A Thousand Plateaus*, trans, B. Massumi, Minneapolis: University of Minnesota Press.

Foucault, M. (1977), *Discipline and Punish: The Birth of the Prison*, trans, A. Sheridan, New York: Pantheon.

Goldstein, J., ed. (1998), *Why we Watch: The Attractions of Violent Entertainment*, New York: Oxford University Press.

Kant, I. (1973), *The Critique of Judgment*, trans, J. C. Meridith, Oxford: Clarendon.

Khatchadourian, H. (1965), 'The Expression Theory of Art: A Critical Examination', *Journal of Art and Art Criticism*, 23 (3): 335–52.

Lacan, J. (2001), *Écrits: A Selection*, London: Routledge Classics.

Lehmann-Haupt, H. (1954). *Art Under a Dictatorship*. New York: Oxford University Press.

Miller, P. (2010). *The Smart Swarm: How Understanding Flocks, Schools and Colonies Can Make Us Better at Communicating, Decision Making, and Getting Things Done*. New York: Avery.

Mulvey, L. (1988), 'Visual pleasure and narrative cinema', in C. Penley (ed), *Feminism and Film Theory*, 57–68, London: Routledge.

Rosenbaum, R. (1998), *Explaining Hitler: The Search for the Origins of Evil*, New York: Random House.

Tavin, K. (2002), Engaging Advertisements: Looking for Meaning in and through Art Education: *Visual Arts Research*, 28 (2): 38–47.

Vickers, B. (1988), *In Defense of Rhetoric*, Oxford: Clarendon.

Index